Hua Pang
Comparing German and Chinese Student's Social Media Use
with a Focus on Political Participation

AF209305

TUDpress

Hua Pang

Comparing German and Chinese Student's Social Media Use with a Focus on Political Participation

TUDpress

2016

Die vorliegende Arbeit wurde an der Philosophischen Fakultät der Technischen Universität Dresden als Dissertation eingereicht und am 25. September 2015 erfolgreich verteidigt.

Vorsitzender: Prof. Dr. Bruno Klein

Gutachter:
Prof. Dr. Lutz M. Hagen
Prof. Dr. Oliver Quiring

Prof. Dr. Maria Häusl, weitere Hochschullehrerin
Prof. Dr. Werner J. Patzelt, weiterer Hochschullehrer

Bibliografische Information der Deutschen Nationalbibliothek
Die Deutsche Nationalbibliothek verzeichnet diese Publikation in der Deutschen Nationalbibliografie; detaillierte bibliografische Daten sind im Internet über http://dnb.d-nb.de abrufbar.

Bibliographic information published by the Deutsche Nationalbibliothek
The Deutsche Nationalbibliothek lists this publication in the Deutsche Nationalbibliografie; detailed bibliographic data are available in the Internet at http://dnb.d-nb.de.

ISBN 978-3-95908-083-5

© 2016 w.e.b.
Universitätsverlag & Buchhandel
Eckhard Richter & Co. OHG
Bergstr. 70 | D-01069 Dresden
Tel.: 0351/47 96 97 20 | Fax: 0351/47 96 08 19
http://www.tudpress.de

TUDpress ist ein Imprint von w.e.b

Comparing German and Chinese Student's Social Media Use with a Focus on Political Participation

Dissertation

zur Erlangung des Grades eines Doktors der Philosophie

an der

Philosophischen Fakultät

der

Technischen Universität Dresden

Institut für Kommunikationswissenschaft

vorgelegt von

Hua Pang

geb. am 21.06.1984 in Henan

Betreuer: Prof. Dr. Lutz M. Hagen, Technische Universität Dresden

Gutachter:

      1. Prof. Dr. Lutz M. Hagen, Technische Universität Dresden

      2. Prof. Dr. Oliver Quiring, Universität Mainz

Promotionskommission:

Vorsitzender: Prof. Dr. Bruno Klein

Mitglieder: Prof. Dr. Lutz M. Hagen, Betreuer/Gutachter

              Prof. Dr. Oliver Quiring, Gutachter

              Prof. Dr. Maria Häusl, weite Hochschullehrerin

              Prof. Dr. Werner J. Patzelt, weiterer Hochschullehrer

Termin der Verteidigung: 25.09.2015

Acknowledgements

I am indebted to a lot of people for their long-lasting support and encouragement which was invaluable for the successful completion of this dissertation. However, I am aware of the fact that there are many more and these words cannot express my gratitude and appreciation I feel for all of those. The research was carried out in the Institute of Media and Communication at the Dresden University of Technology during the period between 2011 and 2015 under the advisory of Prof. Dr. Lutz M. Hagen. The research has been financed by the Chinese government for 4 years starting from October 10, 2011 to September 30, 2015.

First and foremost, I like to take this opportunity to express my deep sense of gratitude to my supervisor Prof. Dr. Lutz M. Hagen, who has supported me throughout my thesis with his patience, invaluable assistance and guidance whilst allowing me the room and freedom to do this research during my doctoral study at the Dresden University of Technology. I can't say thank you enough for his tremendous support and help during the past four years. I attribute the level of my doctoral degree to his greatly encouragement, effort as well as confidence in my abilities to finish the project. I am also sincerely grateful to the China Scholarship Council for supporting me make this work possible and financing all the requirements associated with studying and living in Germany for four years.

My sincere thanks go to the many members of staff of IFK for their scientific discussion, advice and continuous support throughout the course of this project. Among them, Prof. Dr. Wolfgang Donsbach gave me many valuable ideas, suggestions and help. And my colleagues Claudia Seifert and Antje Odermann who showed their kindness and assistance in translating and modifying the German version of the questionnaire that I needed for completing my thesis. I like to express further greatest thanks for help and encouragement of Elias Kukali, Yulia Lukashina, and others I had the pleasure to work with sometimes literally day by day.

Last but not the least, I am particularly indebted to my parents and sisters for their never-ending encouragement and ongoing support of my work emotionally through phone calls that have allowed me to become who I am today, and without whom I would never have enjoyed so many opportunities.

Dresden

Hua Pang, 2015

Comparing German and Chinese Student's Social Media Use with a Focus on Political Participation

Abstract

The rapid development of network technology brings about the expansion of social media on the global scale. Meanwhile, the unprecedented prosperity of the local social media applications in China has led to the liberalization of public discourse and provided the citizenry with new opportunities for political participation. However, comparing with globally social media such as Twitter and Facebook which have been well documented, the popular local social media in China such as Sina Weibo and Renren have not been well aroused the attention of academic circles. In addition, mechanism of social media use for political participation is still inconclusive although divergent views among a number of scholars. Therefore, it is necessary to reconsider the relationships between politics and individuals urgently.

In order to better understand the role of social media in political communication realm, this study offers a step forward by reporting on findings from a cross-national survey of German and Chinese university students that furthers our understanding of how social media as a resource affect their political participation in their daily lives. Rather than simply looking at how much student uses social media, the study contributes to comparative research about what are the different of young people's social media usage between a developing country and development country in terms of their political participation. Besides, the study gives insights into the interplay between social media and traditional media news use in both Germany and China.

Results show spending time on social media has no significant influence on young people's political participation in Germany and China. However, certain online activities through social media are clearly and significantly related with political participation in the two countries. There are also significant different level of political participation between Germany and the Chinese college students. Besides, the results demonstrate that the use of social media news sources is positively associated with different types of political participation. Most interestingly, the study finds that although social media emerges as an important predictor of political engagement in the online domain, it doesn't replace or substitute the role of traditional media in the political communication field. Implications of the findings for youth participation in politics in both countries are discussed.

Key words: social media, traditional media, political participation, media system, political system, political communication

Introduction

Research background

With network technology in constant development and popularization, social media platforms such as such as Facebook, Twitter, and MySpace are currently exploding worldwide. The rapid growth of social media has aroused great public concerns about its potential impact on changing people's daily online communication behaviors. The recent and obvious cases are the crucial role of social media in the "Arab Spring", which unmask the truth that social media is increasingly transforming into a platform for the masses expressing their voices, exchanging their opinions as well as engaging in politics. In response to the growing political use of social media, scholars have sought to understand how these new web application services contribute to political change across different regions in political communication landscape (Gaiser, De Rijke, & Spannring, 2010; Zhang & Lin, 2014; Martin, 2012; Esche & Thurau, 2012).

Although several social networks such as Facebook and YouTube are to be banned from being used in mainland China, the rapid spread of domestic social media in China has opened a new channel for individuals to exchange information and to participate in political processes (Zhang & Lin, 2014). In Mainland China, by the end of 2012, the total amount of Chinese people online exceeds the entire European Union population (Lu, 2012). The latest data shows there are over 307 million social media users in China in 2012 and estimates the figure of social media population will hit 488 million by 2015 (Wee, 2011). Also, in Germany, with the rapid spread of high-bandwidth Internet service, coupled with a wide array of interactive social media, the information and communications technology industry has become an important catalyst for the development of German economy. Since 2012, social media platforms became mainstream and are now heavily used by all classes and strata of the German population (Esche & Thurau, 2012).

A key issue in political communication is the relationship between various forms of media use and individual's level of political participation. Distinct from old forms of media, social media can consist of both web-based and mobile technologies. As a consequence, the dynamism that social media bring to political participation may exceed that of traditional media (Mou, Atkin, Fu, Lin, & Lau, 2013). As Hyun put it, "the decentralizing features of new media technology, represented by the Internet, have raised expectations that it may undermine elite dominance in traditional communication platforms and revitalize the public sphere for citizen deliberation and participation" (Hyun, 2012). This suggests that social media can be a useful tool for ordinary citizens in communicating with diverse people and motivating them to engage in various political activities in the digital media environment.

Innovation in the technology development and the proliferation of social media contribute to a number of changes in public communication field. By dramatically decreasing the costs of interpersonal communication, social media platforms have opened new possibilities for citizens to gather political information and to engage in political participation within their personal networks. In fact, the advent of social media brings about two key changes to how individuals communicate with others: first, it enlarges the number of information to which individuals are exposed; and second, it affects the size and diversity of personal communication networks (Barberá, 2014). In contrast to traditional broadcast pattern, social media's "mass-self broadcasting" model implies "a qualitative change in the structure of information transmission and circulation" (Anduiza, Jensen, & Jorba, 2012).

Moreover, social media is changing the nature of communication due to it is a platform that is being used to mobilize individuals in another way that has never been done before. Users are able to connect directly to politicians and campaigns and engage in different types of political activities in new ways. For example, people could use Facebook to add every politician's Facebook which they like, upload their photos, videos or political contents in their own space and comment about it, as well as participate in political groups. Meanwhile, the option for users to share, like, or retweet political information instantaneously has opened up a new avenue for politicians, political parties and institutions to reach out to citizens. A survey made by the Pew Internet Project found that 75% of SNS users say their friends post at least some content related to politics and 37% of SNS users post political material at least occasionally (Rainie & Smith, 2012).

For China, "the ever-expanding communicative space online has provided Chinese individuals with unprecedented access to an exploding base of user-generated content and has engendered innovative ways of mass collaboration and grassroots participation in the information production process" (Tai, 2015). An interesting case is that the information of Obama's re-election was far and away the top and crucial topic of public discussion, with nearly 25 million posts on "Obama wins American presidential election" in Weibo (Bandurski, 2012). The fact shows the significant impact of Weibo especially on pushing forward the freedom of the speech and civil society. Moreover, Chinese government is facilitating youth political participation via new media which means a more favorable political environment for young people. As Zhou stated that "as youth is an important political force, facilitating youth in political participation symbolizes equality and progress of a society", and "China called on the international community to respond to new features of political awareness and ways of expression among young people, providing them more channels and options, such as virtual organizations and Internet-based new media" (Zhou, 2011). In China, online social networks have become a major platform for the youth to gather information and to make friends with like-minded individuals (Guo, 2011).

For Germany, the relevance of social media based online communities for political communication is steadily increasing recently (Stieglitz & Dang-Xuan, 2013). Especially, microblogging services (e.g., Twitter) and social network sites (e.g., Facebook) are deemed to have the potential for increasing citizen's level of political participation (Stieglitz & Dang-Xuan, 2013). At present, Twitter is an ideal platform that enables users to disseminate not only information in general but also political opinions publicly through their online networks and political institutions (e.g., politicians, political parties, political foundations, etc.).

Nowadays social media platforms have become a part of daily life, particularly among young people, who have "embraced digital technology's interactive capacities and quite reasonably expect the old politics and the old media should too" (Watson, 2013). As a result, young voters in Germany spend more time online in social networking sites such as Facebook or MySpace than using traditional media such as watching television or reading newspapers (Stieglitz & Dang-Xuan, 2013). Likewise, in terms of China's top social networking sites, about 80% of users are between 20-34 years old (China, 2011).

In the academic field, the growing popularity of social media has provoked a new debate about the connection between their use and the types of political participation adopted by young people (Feldmann-Wojtachnia *et al.*, 2010; Gaiser, De Rijke, & Spannring, 2010; Loader, 2007; Martin, 2012; Sloam, 2011; Spannring, Wallace, & Datler, 2008). Fenton and Barassi deem we are in a critical juncture where "the interrogation of the nature of political participation on offer through social media practices becomes paramount if we are to fully understand and critique the broader claims made for the transformation of political participation in society" (Fenton & Barassi, 2011). Previous studies have documented the positive influence of digital media use on young people's participation in political activities (Gil de Zúñiga *et al.*, 2012; Spannring, Wallace, & Datler, 2008).

Moreover, compared with a lot of prior research done on the adaptation of influence and evolution of trends in Western online social networks, Chinese social media has not been well-studied. Chinese Internet users are actively engaging in social media—especially home-grown social media platforms which provide domestic social media channels differ in various ways from Western platforms. While some researchers suggested that the new media technology as a space for political re-engagement, particularly for young people (Carpini, 2000), this has not come to fruition in a censored and authoritarian political environment such as China. Meanwhile, In Germany, whereas the rapid development of online communication has been regularly documented by the public broadcasting corporation ARD and ZDF, there is still lack of further analysis of differentiated types of media use and how they affect citizens' political knowledge, attitudes and behaviors (Zeh & Holtz-Bacha, 2015, p. 45).

Against this background, this study reviews the previous findings and offers a perspective on how and why young people use social media participating in politics both in China and Germany. This dissertation is organized as follows: First, the research respectively reviews the histories and the recent developments of social media in China and Germany. Next, the study provides comparative studies on the media system, political system and modes of political participation in the two countries. At last, the final part draws a conclusion, pointing out the insufficiency of this research and dedicating further research directions for contrastive political communication studies between different countries.

Research significant and importance

This topic is significant and important for several reasons:

Firstly, the arrival of social media has offered new channels through which individuals are able to engage in politics. As Carpini notes, "a new communication environment, driven largely by the growth in the Internet and World Wide Web, is rapidly changing the economic, social and political landscape" (Carpini, 2000). In the context of today's socially-networked-society, social media has been lauded for its potential political value by academics, journalists and politicians, yet we know little about the citizenry's use of social media to engage in politics.

Secondly, with a concern for the scarcity of adequate cross-national investigations in political communication area, this study attempts to expand the research effort to obtain further understanding of differences and similarities in people of diverse societies by adopting a comparative examination between China and Germany. The selection of these two nations is mainly based on that very little comparative research has been conducted between China and Germany, despite the fact that social media has brought great changes in those two countries during the last decade.

Thirdly, with the increasing economic development and social progress, the possibilities of China's improvement in participatory politics and democracy become a big problem. In a way, social media such as Weibo, Renren have to get together bringing a revolution in online political communication field in China, especially when Facebook and Twitter are banned in China's special political context. As Liu said, "the emergence of new media, especially Weibo, China's nascent participatory politics has become even more dynamic and promising" (Liu, 2011). Social media has already become an important aspect for Chinese people's everyday life, and in some features and terms of use are different from other countries (Baumann, 2012, p. 1), which are well worth studying and attention.

Finally, in recent years, the issue of a decline in traditional forms of engagement in youth adults in particular has spurred both public and academic interest all over the world. "Impatience with politics in Germany, disenchantment with political commitment and individualization are labels frequently attached to the political involvement of young people" (Gaiser, *et al.*, 2010). Nevertheless, for youth adults, that phenomenon seems to be changed in recent years, because the rapid development of new technology as a key ingredient in encouraging young people to engage in politics, especially those in this age are obviously more likely to use this new technology (Cheuvront, 2009). The political participation via social media among young adults still remains a scarcity research area for communication scholars.

Dissertation structure

Chapter 1 focuses on the histories and latest developments of social media in Germany and China in order to better understand the rapidly evolving field of social media in the different context. Finally, after reviewing the recent literature on social media use in

Germany and China, and its effect on political participation, the chapter proposes the research questions and hypotheses.

Chapter 2 places research focus on the political and media systems in Germany and China by explanation and comparison of the party systems and electoral systems in China and Germany. Then, this chapter comparatively analyses of the media landscape (newspaper industry, TV and radio industry, Internet and other media outlets) between China and Germany. Finally, the author discusses the difference in political and media systems between China and Germany, intending to insight into the modern political communication field.

Chapter 3 starts with providing the definition and theories of political participation, placing special emphasis on how to measure it. Later, the section discusses about the development of political participation in Germany and China and makes a conclusion about the cause of different political behaviors in the two countries. After that, the study pays close attention to young people's political participation based on theories of media use and political participation. In the end, this section points out the existing undeveloped areas in the field of political communication.

Chapter 4 focuses on some important social media such as Facebook, Blogging and Twitter, by investigating how those different types of social media affect political participation among citizens. The subsequent section presents the main changes for political communication in established communication patterns which try to explore the continuing influence of social media on political communication field in both Germany and China. Ultimately, on the basis of above study, the chapter generalizes a conclusion and puts forward other research questions and hypotheses.

Chapter 5 begins with clarifying methodological basis and study sample. In addition, statistical data is conducted in different two universities in Germany and China so as to obtain the representative sample for the research. Moreover, the questionnaire surveys are conduct in German and Chinese which is essential to for young people to better understand all the questions. Then, the study explains data analytical strategy used in the dissertation. At last, the study tests the validity and reliability of independent and dependent variables.

Chapter 6 presents the obtained results of comparing China and Germany university student's social media use, traditional media use and political participation. After that, the section investigates several hypotheses and research questions using SPSS based on the data above. Next, this study explains and discusses the results on the hypothesis, including the association between specific social media use and political participation, the interplay between traditional media and social media use, and the correlations between three political variables (political efficacy, political knowledge and political trust) and political participation among university students.

Chapter 7 sums up the main findings of the thesis in terms of young people's political participation via social media in Germany and China. Later, the author points out limitations and barriers of the research in this section. Finally, the thesis gives a prospect and some suggestions on the further research in both democratic societies and nondemocratic or transitional societies (see Figure1.1).

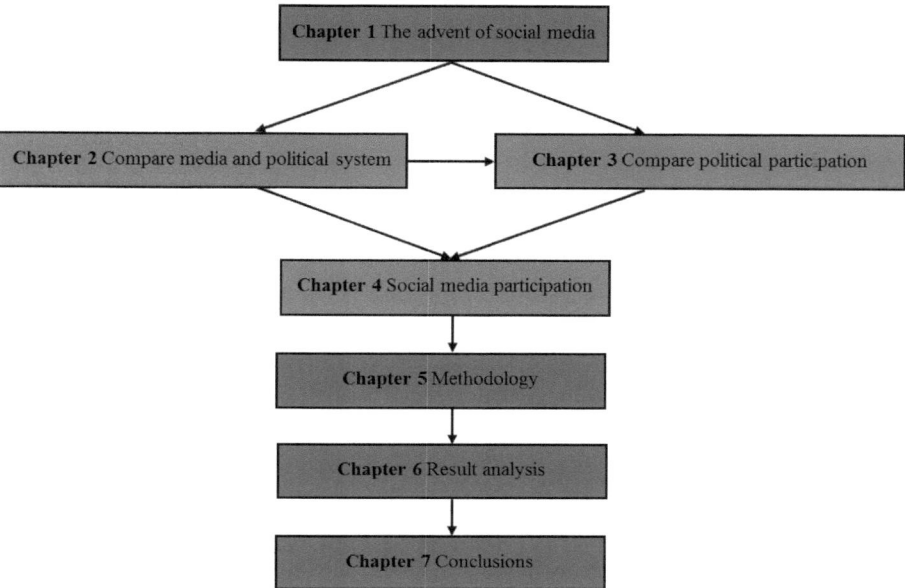

Figure 1.1 Outline of the dissertation

Chapter 1 The advent of social media

1.1 Introduction to social media

During the past few years, the growing popularity of social media has provided new platforms for individuals to access political information and engage in political activities. As some researchers claimed, "the Internet is evolved into one the most significant enables of political innovation since the emergence of mass democracy. However, few areas of social and political life have escaped its influence" (Anduiza, Jensen, & Jorba, 2012, p. 39). Social media has been constantly transforming since their inception, its potential forces have challenged traditional communication theory frames (Anduiza, *et al.*, 2012, p. 16) and influenced the social relations of power (Loader & Mercea, 2012, p. 3). Despite the tremendous growth of social media platforms, there is limited empirical research on the effects of using these services on citizens' political attitudes and political behaviors.

In this chapter, the author begins by defining what constitutes a social media and then briefly introduces the development history of it. In the next step, the study relies on related theories of social media in attempting to better understand the how the novel capabilities of social media platforms might affect the political communication field. Finally, the section proposes the research questions and hypotheses on the basis of the literature review.

1.1.1 Social media's short history and development

As Baskin noted "we simply cannot understand social media without delving into the histories of social experiences" (Baskin, 2011, p. 10). Surely, a careful study and interpretation of media history will help to comprehend technological progress and social environment behind media. The development of computer networks technology exploits a variety of new social media tools catering to different segments of the masses' current needs, and with it engenders the term 'social media'. It was in the second half of the nineties, when the Internet penetrated into everyday life and changed the fabric of communication, people just began to speak of the term 'social media'. As Smith argued, no matter which term of social media is used, obviously when the use of computers is not restricted to elites and was widely used by the public, those terms attempted to label the computer technology and emphasized the role and impact of Internet (Smith, 1999, p. 3).

The term social media is defined as "a group of Internet-based applications that build on the ideological and technological foundations of Web 2.0, and that allow the creation and exchange of User Generated Content" (Kaplan & Haenlein, 2010). Howard and Parks proposed further the concept of social media, including "(a) the information infrastructure and tools used to produce and distribute content; (b) the content that takes the digital form of personal messages, news, ideas, and cultural products; and (c) the people, organizations, and industries that produce and consume digital content" (Howard & Parks, 2012). This definition lacks the interactive characteristic of social media and the virtual space where information communication happens between people with common interests. Thus, two points shall be added to the definition of social media (d) the tools of interactions among different people in which they communicate with each other having same interests and hobbies, (e) provides people with a virtual space for users to create and share information more freely (Shirky, 2011).

Social media can be thought of as being hybrid, "in that it springs from mixed technology and media origins that enable instantaneous, real-time communication, and utilizes multi-media formats (audio and visual presentations) and numerous delivery platforms (Facebook, YouTube, Blogs, to name a few), with global reach capabilities" (Mangold & Faulds, 2009). Bay proposed three aspects of characteristics of social media including: technical-structural, psychological and social, economic and political (Bay, 2012). The technical-structural characteristic mainly relates at a many-to-many communication model for web users. Psychological and social characteristic refers to the value and the power of social media sites coming from users. Economic and political characteristic means social media is able to expand the scale of communication, improve communication speed and reduce cost of coordination of activities (Bay, 2012).

Based on social media's definition combined with the author's own understanding and interpretation, the recognized prototype of the social media in the world was named SixDegrees.com, which generated in around 1997. It was originated from a concept-six degrees of separation which means anyone can be connected to any other person in the world through a chain of acquaintances that has no more than five intermediaries (Riordan, 2003). Though millions of people were welcomed during the first two years, the platform failed for economic reasons in 2000. Meanwhile, from 1997 to 2001 some new sites appeared such as Asian Avenue, MiGente, and BlackPlanet after the emergence of SixDegrees.com. Those early social networks at that time were popular amongst the public, according to some data indicates that BlackPlanet.com had already fascinated more than three million unique visitors every month as early as 2008 (Goble, 2012).

If the timespan from 1997 to 2001 can be regarded as a social media preliminary development period, then, from 2002 to 2006 should be deemed as social media rapid growth period. Along with the Internet continuous to innovation and diffusion, a great number of new social media patterns emerged within just a few years. As depicted in the social media timeline (Figure 1.2), we can see between 2002 and 2006, ten kinds of social media appeared, with almost there appeared at least three new forms of social media emerging every year. In 2002, Friendster was founded, which is a dating and making friend website in the nature. It accumulated nearly 3000000 users during just the first three months because of the doubled 'Circle of Friends'. One year later, MySpace launched and quickly became the main competitors for Friendster.

In the same year of 2003, LinkedIn emerging as a business networks used in professional manner (Önder & Gümüşkaya, 2011), its unique business-oriented trait enable people maintain their pre-existing relationships by using a list of contact details named 'connections' (Önder & Gümüşkaya, 2011; Papacharissi, 2009). Then two Harvard university students created Facebook in 2004, it quickly spread to the global and became the most popular social networking site surpassing MySpace after opening its doors for everyone in 2006 (Chapman, 2009). Until now, with more than one billion active users (Fellow, 2012), Facebook have made great success on global scale expansion. Following on the heels of Facebook's prosperity and successful, YouTube and Twitter launched in 2005 and 2006 respectively. At present, YouTube has the same success with Facebook and becomes one of the most popular social networks among users. Twitter as the global real-time communication tool which offers users a limited 140 characters to share and exchange their current status with friends (Java, Song, Finin, & Tseng, 2007), now this site has over 500 million users (Dugan, 2012). From 2011 until now, there are still some new patterns of social media emerging, such as Google+ and getlunched.com.

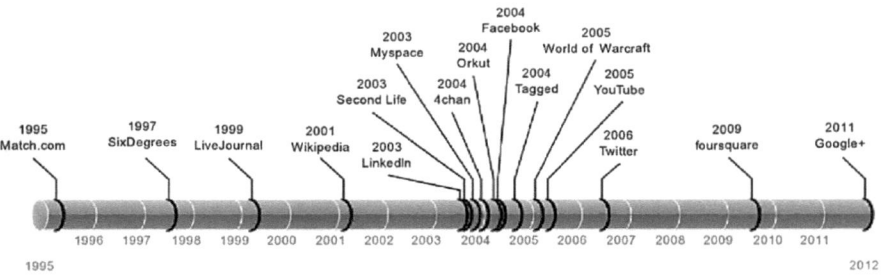

Figure 1.2 Social media timeline (Brunty & Helenek, 2012)

1.1.2 The rise of social media globally

Along with Internet technology development, the emergence of Internet-based social media provides ordinary citizens with the capabilities that allow them to connect, communicate and interact with one another in new ways that are difficult or impossible to do in earlier online or offline settings. For example, Facebook users are able to monitor their friends with regular updates on what they are doing by following news feed. And not only that, these services allow users to create and join communities of like-minded individuals. Hence, the organizers and participants of social and political movements can access to useful political information that may be difficult to obtain otherwise, such as finding new opportunities to become engaged in politics.

According to eMarketer forecasts there will be up to 2.13 billion social network users in 2016, indicating a 1.16 billion increase from 2010. Figure 1.3 shows continuously growth of social media users from 2010 to 2018 worldwide. In the last decade, social media has expand quickly throughout world and has grown not just in terms of number of users on popular platforms, but also in terms of new nationally leading platforms tailored for specific Internet populations (Alexa, 2015). Facebook, with nearly 1,317 billion monthly active users, has easily become the largest social media website in 130 out of 137 countries (Alexa, 2015). Asia as the largest continent of Facebook user with 410 million users followed by Europe (292million) and North America (204 million) (Alexa, 2015).

Number of social network users worldwide from 2010 to 2018 (in billions)

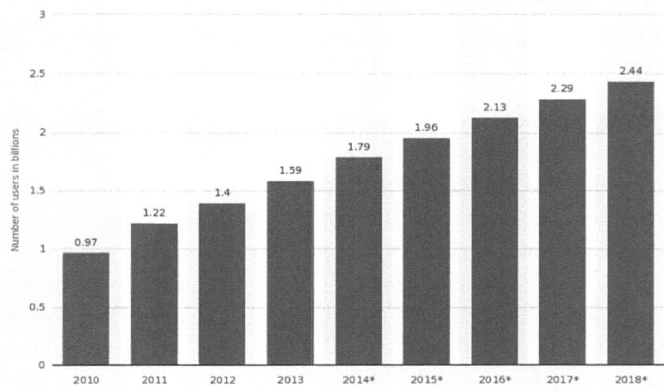

Figure 1.3 Number of social network user worldwide from 2010-218 (eMarketer, 2015b)

In the field of political communication, social media services are becoming increasingly populated platforms in which voters interact with politicians and express their viewpoints about the recent public affairs. A new study displays that nearly 66 percent of social media users have used social media platforms to discuss about political candidates and attend civic political activities (Evangelista, 2012). Unlike the mass media, which is a one-way channel of communication, social media allow individuals to both publish and read political information in a networked environment. In this way, the social media technologies have accelerated speed the flow of political information on a global scale, people now are able to use social media to share political messages more quickly and conveniently.

In October 2007, Twitter was introduced to China, then two years later Sina Weibo launched. In just five years, China experienced a rapidly growth of Internet population jumping from 170 million to over 500 million today, and social media platforms play a huge part in everyday Chinese life with Internet's booming (Olesen, 2012). Similarly, social media began to surge in Germany, eMarketer anticipates Germany has far more social media users than any other country in Western Europe, with the total number expected to close to 37.3 million in 2017 (eMarketer, 2015a).

In addition, with social media platforms have begun playing irreplaceable roles in the society, more and more governments and politicians have quickly adapted to these Internet technologies by adopting a variety of responses and measures to cultivate a popular image. For example, Chinese government agencies made use of vast number of government microblog accounts to promote information disclosure, public service and citizen participation. According to the Chinese Government Microblogs Assessment Report of 2011, the total numbers of Chinese government microblog accounts outnumber 50,000 by the end of 2011 (Olesen, 2012). At the same time, German government officials are more likely to reply to public opinions using tools such as Blog, Facebook and YouTube, not only such kinds of social media have large quantity of users, but they can also enhance the interactive activities among media, politicians and the public timely and rapidly.

1.1.3 Theories of social media

In this section, the author tries to use Uses-and-Gratifications and Diffusion/Adoption theories to give an explanation for the advent of social media. The basic premise of uses and gratifications theory is to rather ask what people do with the media than how the media impact on the individual (Katz *et al.*, 1974). In other words, the focus of the theory is on viewing the audience as actively choosing and using media to meet and to find ultimate gratification (Lariscy, Tinkham, & Sweetser, 2011). With the widespread adoption of social media, U&G has been used in recent research on social media such as Twitter, Facebook, and MySpace (Chen, 2011; Raacke & Bonds-Raacke, 2008). Those studies on social networking sites highlight that gratifications such as entertainment, information searching and seeking, socializing, and establishing status and reputation are important in the usage of social media to facilitate social interaction and group discussion (Dunne, Lawlor, & Rowley, 2010; Park, Kee, & Valenzuela, 2009).

In addition, some studies suggested that specific gratifications and uses of social media may mediate civic and participation political involvement. One study of the relationship between users' needs and civic and political participation indicated that information motivations of social media were more associated with civic and political action than to entertainment purposes (Park, *et al.*, 2009). Moreover, the social needs of these online groups strengthen social contacts, community engagement, and attachment by connecting the whole community through networks (Cheung, Chiu, & Lee, 2011). It's worth mentioning that a key distinguishing characteristic of social media is interactivity, which means the ability of users to provide content in response to a source or communication partner. And the main factor that made social media such a popular place is its simple and user-friendly nature (Koçak, Kaya, & Erol, 2013).

Diffusion of innovation (DOI) is a theory that helps to explain the adoption process of an innovation by modeling its entire life cycle according to the aspects of communications and human information interactions. The diffusion of innovations is defined as the process by which an innovation is adopted and gains acceptance by members of a certain community over time (Folorunso, Vincent, Adekoya, & Ogunde, 2010). Rogers noted that four major elements influence the diffusion process is the innovation itself, how information about the innovation is communicated, time, and the communication channels of the social system into which the innovation is being introduced (Rogers, 2010). Meanwhile, the theory proposed five beliefs or constructs that impact on the adoption of any innovation, these are relative advantage, complexity, compatibility, trialability, and observability (Rogers, 1995).

According to decision-making process of innovation, it contained five basic stages like knowledge, persuasion, decision, implementation and confirmation (Rogers, 1995, p. 163). When applied the process model to social media, the fast-evolving social media make people surprise about it. As a result, individuals feel the need of using social media to communication and begin to obtain knowledge about it. At the second step named persuasion, citizens become more psychologically involved with the social media and decide about whether to use it or not. In this step, characteristics like compatibility, complexity, trialability, observability and the relative benefit are significant factors for persuasion. Under the decision process, individuals can provide adaptation or rejection decision after a pre-application meeting period. Individuals can prefer to use social media for its communication, socialization, self-expression benefits, entertainment and economic profitability reason for individuals to use social media. It is clear that social media boosts this diffusion with its dynamic, interactive, user-centered, user-friendly characteristics and with its opportunities that offers individuals more control over the contents and that enables users to turn into producers as well (Koçak, Kaya, & Erol, 2013).

1.2 State of social media in China and Germany

1.2.1 Social media boom in China

Recently, the "Ningbo citizens against PX project" incident in China has received immediate attention all over the world. On October 2012, thousands of local protesters took part in the procession against the government setting up a petrochemical factory in Ningbo City, Zhejiang Province. Because of PX project may release toxic chemicals which stoked up local residents' discontent and angry. This case spread quickly through the Internet and numbers of people discussion about "what do you think of the PX project" in Microblogs platform. Facing pressure from Internet public opinion and citizens' protest, Ningbo Municipal Government promised to firmly stop the construction of the PX project in the end. In the case, social media played a significant role, which not only provided a channel of related information create and exchange, but also helped organize and plan the demonstration.

With the transformation of Chinese society, the breeding and creeping of environmental pollution, political corruption and a series of social problems made Chinese Internet users more tend to freely express their opinions and discuss about major social issues through social media. When social media has changed or is changing Chinese society, they refer to both related trends "increasing dynamism in China and increasing demand for individual collective rights" (Anduiza, et al., 2012, p. 221). Meanwhile, mass media are still controlled by the government today in China (Scotton & Hachten, 2010), local social media such as Sina Weibo and Renren provide Chinese people with an alternative channel via which they can more safely and effectively express opinions and discontent than conventional media. As Pan et al. stated, the Internet is also an alternative conduit for information of plural sources, a window to the world beyond the representational confine of the state-controlled mass media, and a platform for horizontal communication among Chinese citizens (Pan, Jing, Liu, Yan, & Zheng, 2012).

The latest data demonstrates that China's social media users are the most active population, with 91 percent of interviewee declaring they visited a social media site in the previous 6 months, compared with just 30 percent in Japan and 67 percent in the United States (Lu, 2012). These figures above may confirm that although the prohibition of the use of some western social media such as Facebook, YouTube and Twitter, Chinese Internet users are remains enthusiastic about engaging in social media—especially local alternatives platforms that differ in various ways from Western. In fact, many of the factors that have fostered Chinese citizens involving in social media than people in other countries, including the rural population immigrant to the city leave their own families, the one-child generation feel of spiritual loneliness, ordinary people distrust of news from official media (Crampton, 2012b).

The beginning of social media in China could be traced back to the early 2000s when BBS was launched, until 2006 when Blog debuted in China opening the genuine prelude of development of home-growth social media. One year later 'Chinese Facebook' Renren launched and its functions are similar to Facebook. In 2009, Sina Weibo was launched by SINA Corporation, 'Weibo' in the Chinese language refers to the word 'microblog'. Then the other kinds of social media appeared, which are rapidly gaining China Internet market share such as QQ, Kaixin and so on. Wee stated "China has the most complex, fragmented, and developed social media landscape in the world with a unique online culture that requires its own specialized understanding" (Wee, 2011).

Today, China's several popular social media are Sina Weibo, Renren and Tencent Weibo, QQ and Qzone (Schroeder, 2012), not just because of their possession of huge user groups, but also because their unique functions could meet users' demands. For example, Sina Weibo with nearly 368 million Chinese users in 2012 (Millward, 2012), which could be considered as the Twitter of China, its unique capabilities and leadership position in the Chinese social media landscape can be attributed to the ability of permitting users to insert their own favorite image, video files and music (Mei, 2012). Figure 1.4 shows so far, there are more than 40 different kinds of domestic social media sites in China which reflect the very fierce competition of local social media sites (Crampton, 2012a).

As domestic social media landscape becomes more diverse and participatory, Chinese Internet users have more opportunities in such digital age to access to information and participate in the discussion of public events than ever before. Such uses have attracted more scholars paying close attention to the online behaviors. Anduiza and co-workers deem online behavior is the biggest difference between China and the rest of the worlds (Anduiza, et al., 2012). The distinct online habit between China users is the tendency of preferring getting and receiving political information from social media. The data from Nielsen confirms: getting and sharing news are the one of most important reason for social media usage (74 percent and 69 percent respectively), just after connecting socially (e.g., communication with friends, share photo), entertainment (Nielsen, 2012).

Actually, in China, social media in the initial period of development was linked close with political and democracy. As early as 2005, Zheng and Wu explored the democratic function of the Internet and summarized the Internet as a tool for communication, public space, and a way for collective action (Zheng & Wu, 2005). However, MacKinnon argued the Internet will not bring about democracy for China society, the role of social media in China is "more likely to involve political evolution—not revolution" (MacKinnon, 2008). Because social media just promotes long-term political change not actually results in political or regime change in consideration of Chinese government Internet censorship (MacKinnon, 2008). Esarey and Qiang draw a conclusion by content analysis of newspapers and blogs that blogs have more freedom to offer political information compare with newspapers (Esarey & Qiang, 2011). Harp Bachmann and Guo explored the encouragement and mobilization function of social media for activists in different countries and pointed out activists exploit greater potential of social media to facilitate discussion (Harp, Bachmann, & Guo, 2012). The latest research indicates the role of social media in amplifying the information and stimulating heated public debate about corruption in government and financial transparency behaviors (Zhang & Chan, 2013).

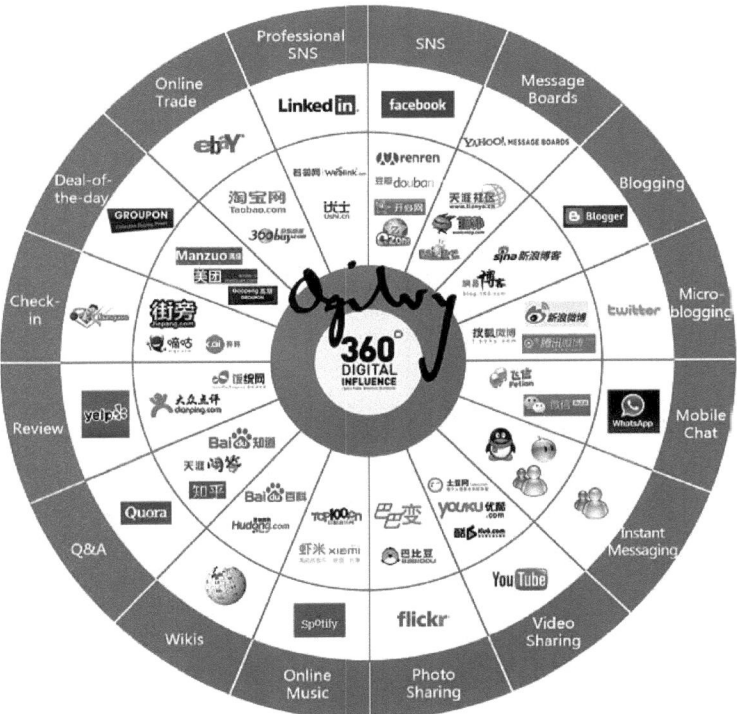

Figure 1.4 China local platforms landscape and major international equivalents (Crampton, 2012a)

These studies above have two significant meanings, first, they confirm social media has provided and enlarged information communication space for Chinese citizens, which may led to a certain extent to improve the degree of democracy and politics in China. Second, although the flow of information online is still strictly controlled (MacKinnon, 2008), the prosperity of local home growth social media sites has great influence in Chinese society.

1.2.2 Social media environment in China

As Baumann noted, "the use of social media cannot be taken for granted considering the strong governmental control over citizens personal life a couple of decades ago, and in some aspect its characteristics and terms of use differ from the rest of world" (Baumann, 2012, p. 1). Although western social media such as Twitter, YouTube and Facebook is banned, the rapid development of homegrown social media equivalents such as Weibo, Renren and Youku seems to be supported and encouraged at the same time by Chinese government. In fact, after the Chinese economic reform in 1978, the field of communication landscape has become more "pluralized, commercialized and liberalized" (Zang, 2011, p. 156), and the government adjusted and regulated policy which ensure the healthy growth of Internet in China's complicated political and economic environment.

The basic reason for the very difference of China's social media environment from the west can be attributed to the Chinese Communist Party not merely keeping the power of one-party regime, but also maintain social stability (Li, 2011). With the policy of opening and reform, Chinese government have enacted a series of regulatory and policy measures about every aspects of society in order to secure a more dominant role, particularly aimed at various kinds of Internet media sites and increasing numbers of the netizens. Since 2003, the Ministry of Public Security of China has implemented 'the Great firewall' and employed computerized filters monitoring, screening out certain information or erasing sensitive information (Esarey & Qiang, 2011; Li, 2011), so as to guide the correct orientation of public opinion online.

Indeed, on the one hand, social media has gradually become a significant platform for the governments and statesmen to hear the public voices and generate ties with the masses, which in turn has promoted and improved the process of democratization. Compared to traditional media, social media sites have greater freedom from restrictions. The relative flexibility of today's media environment also makes the number of social media mobile phone users continue to raise in China, with over 100 million mobile social users in 2010, the number of users is expected to grow by about 30 percent per year (McKinsey, 2012). Not insignificant, however, is that the tool of social media platforms in China has been transforming the way of communication by young adult. As Zang argues "the numerous netizens, the urban youth in particular, prefer to express opinions, exchange ideas and share information with their peers on the Internet" (Zang, 2011, p. 159).

But on the other hand, Chinese government attempts to establish a series of Internet censorship measures aiming at social network security and public opinion guidance. For example, Microbloggers are required to use real-names registration in five cities by government lately, which enable services providers to monitor speech and identify persons who post online efficiently (Wines, 2012). China is now under ever-changing and complex media environment, as Hu *et al.* notes "a vibrant online civil society and a sophisticated party-state propaganda and control system actually coexist" (Hu *et al.,* 2012). This raises the paradox of increased that public opinion expression and increasing control of authorities, e.g. barring western websites and social networks such as YouTube and Twitter. As a recent report summarizes "there are two opposing forces in fierce contention: the drive for control, and the drive that seeks open expression" (Hu *et al.,* 2012).

In addition, China's domestic social-media sector of today is quite fragmented (Chiu, *et al.*, 2012), and highly competitive among different types of social media that already exists. Nearly every kind of social media platform has two or more major players, but they have different advantages, audience segments and geographic priorities (Chiu, et al., 2012). For China's netizens, various types of social media spaces meet their requirements on different levels of society. For government, this fragmentation and competition media landscape heightens the difficulties of Internet restrictions and control. Therefore, the social media environment in China offers opportunities but is also filled with challenge. As China's Internet population continues to increase, social media landscape is rapidly evolving and growing to become the platform for ordinary people exchanging viewpoints and communications. Besides, the ever-increasing number of online platforms and communication patterns will transform the landscape of the media and the structure of social communication (Esarey & Qiang, 2011).

1.2.3 Social media state in Germany

As social media continues to embrace around the globe, Germany is no exception. With both domestic and foreign social media coexisting in one county, at present the layout of the social media landscape presents diverse, vitality and complex picture. "The Internet is deeply embed in the everyday life of a large part of population of Western Europe society and has transformed many aspects of social and economic relations" (Anduiza, *et al.*, 2012). According to a new survey by eMarketer the number of social media users in Germany is larger compared to other Western Europe countries, the total population is expected to hit 29.9 million in late 2012 and the number will reach 34.4 million in 2015 (eMarketer, 2015b), which means that over half of Germany's cyber citizens will access social networks (McNaughton, 2012).

However, because of the loyalty of the Germans to their local social network, international social media was no match for domestic social network platforms in the initial early phase of diffusion. But later, after Facebook had experienced a rough establishing and developing period since 2008 (Pavie, 2011), until October 2011 it has become the most popular social network in Germany, German local social media platform StudiVZ sites and Wer-Kennt-Wen.de to the verge of insignificance (Eimeren, 2015). In addition, it is interesting to note that the nation's young crowd has become the mainstream of social media use, the data shows 18-to-34 age group makes up 53 percent of total social media population, with men accounting for 52 percent and women 48 percent, and they have begun to use Facebook instead of StudiVZ, which led to the growth of German local social media were unable to remained strong (eMarketer, 2012).

In Germany, social media as a popular media is infiltrating into the economic, political and cultural areas, not only changing people's way of communication and lives, but also providing ordinary people with obtaining wealth of information more easily and quickly today. This also pertains to political information: 67 percent of German online users at the age of 14 to 29 regularly get their general news from social networks with search engines being the only more frequently used news source (Eimeren, 2015). Still, comparing with social media political use in the USA, Germany lags behind concerning in the political context (Stieglitz, Brockmann, & Xuan, 2012). Social media's potential concerning political communication e.g. in blogs is still hardly used (Lardinois, 2009) and has little effects on the German local politics (Lardinois, 2009). However, with Obama's dazzling and partly Internet driven election victory in 2012, the political power of the social media has been recognized by lots of German politicians and governments when they want to be liked by younger voter groups and expand influencers in the country.

	Year	CDU	SPD	FDP	Grüne	Linke	Average
Activity							
# tweets posted	2012	1.562	3.933	1.318	3.159	5.502	3.095
	2011	857	1.948	1.186	2.454	2.851	1.859
	2010	461	889	611	1.813	1.421	1.039
# pictures posted on Flickr	2012	0	3.804	3.067	632	1.952	1.891
	2011	0	3.585	2.263	972	2.022	1.768
	2012	0	2.121	1.379	712	1.260	1.094
# YouTube videos posted	2012	449	482	909	1.058	1.524	884
	2011	321	341	614	827	920	605
	2010	235	186	364	627	113	305
Popularity							
# followers on Twitter	2012	18.673	23.419	19.292	41.963	3.781	21.426
	2011	10.202	11.952	10.351	20.156	1.908	10.914
	2010	5.315	5.448	5.494	9.225	1.211	5.339
# Facebook fans	2012	17.706	25.357	15.927	29.768	14.375	20.627
	2011	9.100	15.916	9.285	15.913	6.596	11.362
	2010	1.787	5.418	5.428	5.039	2.652	4.065
# followers on YouTube	2012	2.645	3.132	2.554	3.653	6.474	3.692
	2011	2.220	2.558	2.519	2.991	4.871	3.032
	2010	1.727	1.950	2.208	1.932	1.260	1.815

Table 1.1 Statistics on political social media landscape in Germany from 2010 to 2012 (Stieglitz, *et al.*, 2012)

As Detsch wrote "In the meantime there is hardly a campaign being run without the help of Web 2.0 communication technology, hardly a politician who does not have a Facebook or Twitter account" (Detsch, 2012). In the following table, Stieglitz and his colleagues provide an overview and analysis of the German recent social media landscape (including Facebook, Twitter, Flickr and YouTube) in political background. And they keep tracking data from 2010 to 2012 about the activity and popularity of social media usage in five big political parties (CDU, SPD, FDP, Linke, Grüne) in Germany (Stieglitz, *et al.*, 2012).

Overall, these statistics demonstrate the continuation of the upward trend of social media use from the angles of politicians and ordinary citizens. It is notable, that the total population of fans for Facebook rises the most (407% more fans) among all parties from 2010 (4.065) to 2012 (20.627), comparing with Twitter (301%) and YouTube (103%) respectively (Stieglitz, *et al.*, 2012). In addition, the activity of social media use in five parties has been improved greatly during the past three years, with average number increasing 2056 tweets posting, 797 pictures posting on Flickr and 597

YouTube videos posting.

Meanwhile, with the revolution of social media in the increasingly global scale, the case of "Stuttgart 21" has pushed forward social media to the center civil protests in Germany. In the context of this demonstration against the large-scale railway station project known as "Stuttgart 21", social media such as Facebook and YouTube made protesters and community action groups maintain close communication and keep timely contact. More than 100,000 people joined the Facebook community against the "Stuttgart 21" railway station project (Detsch, 2012), and numerous Internet users saw the parade from different kinds of social media sites.

The wide spread adoption and ever-increasing political impact of social media in Germany has attracted numbers of experts and scholars both at home and abroad from the communication and political field to explore political influences of these new communication technologies (Detsch, 2012). Until now, related research about potential political power of social media in Germany concentrate on these aspects: the role of social media in the election campaign (Tumasjan, Sprenger, Sandner, & Welpe, 2010), people's political participation via social media sites (Vissers & Stolle, 2014), political communication change (Emmer, Wolling, & Vowe, 2012), the relationship of social media and traditional media for political use (Gerhards & Schäfer, 2010).

In 2009, it was the first time social media platforms such as Facebook, Twitter and other social networking sites been used for political reasons in 2009 Europe parliamentary elections and been employed by the parliamentary parties in their campaigns (Lilleker & Jackson, 2011, p. 99). Tumasjan and his cooperators deemed Twitter is indeed used widely for political deliberation during German federal election (Tumasjan, et al., 2010). Albrecht and Verboord examined the political use of Facebook and Twitter by German political youth organizations in the background of the 2010 state election, and concluded that social networks strengthen the relation between user and political actors which in turn leads to positive effects on political trust (Albrecht & Verboord, 2010). In addition, a recent study explores politicians' use of Twitter during selected federal state election campaigns in 2011, and finds that statesmen make use of Twitter in either a "personal-interactive" or "topic-informative" style (Thimm, Einspänner, & Dang-Anh, 2012).

With Internet playing an increasingly important part in the field of political communication, some researchers in Germany begin to focus on relationship of the traditional media and social media in the communication field. Gerhards and Schäfer compared the Internet and mass media communication, and then draw a conclusion that this is not very different between the offline debate and Internet communication (Gerhards & Schäfer, 2010). However, a panel survey from Germany pointed out that "new forms of political communication are mainly a complement to existing forms with few substitution effects", and underlined the important role of citizens participation habits in the area of political information seeking (Emmer, Wolling, & Vowe, 2012). Otto revealed that party web pages on social networks are primarily populated by party followers, party preference occupies a large share of success and the interactivity and authenticity significantly of the pages anticipate success on SNS (Otto, 2012).

In sum, based on these researches and explorations above, the study demonstrates that social media in Germany plays an important role in the political area. First, social media platforms create a new arena for political use, which break the traditional political communication mode. Second, different forms of social media continue to be popular by that governments and politicians, political organization which put up further questions on the political communication.

1.3 Review of related literature

The present results in literature display us that the decline of participation for young people in politics in prior Internet tools making people put their hopes in social media that this new media could bring a new turning point for improving young people's political participation. Much recent research has explored the role of different media use plays in political participation and how digital media use for informational purposes contributes to foster political democratic process. Nevertheless, in the context of today's socially-networked-society and the rise of social media applications (i.e., Facebook), new perspectives need to be considered.

Social media use and political participation

In recent years, the advent of social media has stimulated discussion about the possibilities of the new technology reinvigorating for political participation. There have been seen a decline in political participation among young people since in the late 20th century. With the rapid spread of social network sites, social media has become one of the most popular media among young people. The turbulent evolution of Internet environment, there are more opportunities to involve and empower youth in campaigns and work of representatives and government. It was thought as a major challenge and made definition of this trend as "Crowdsourcing" (Effing, van Hillegersberg, & Huibers, 2011). There has been a gap between the growing popularity of choosing social media as a new platform for political communication and declination in the number of political participation, which impels scholars to explore.

More scholars tried to research about social media's effect on political participation, there are both optimistic and pessimistic viewpoints about the relationship between social media and political participation. Social media revolution in political field shows alterations for people's political participation and its effect have already attracted by a number of scholars since around 2007. As early as 2002, the positive effect of media use on political participation has been realized by lots of scholars in communication field. Some scholars argued that social media fosters participation and increases the freedoms, enables new ways to think and act, provides a new online sphere and enables awareness of new political communication and new factors for participation, contributes to make an informed decision depending on regular and alternative source of information (Dutton, 2008; Fenton & Barassi, 2011; Kweon & Kim, 2010; Shirky, 2011). While other researchers held pessimistic viewpoints and suggested that social media platforms are not effective tools for participation in politics, even produce harm about unequal access, privacy, increase alienation from society and public life, create colonization, might result in fragment of citizen's opinions and frustration (Barnes, 2006; Best & Krueger, 2005; Grossklags, *et al.*, 2011; Gurevitch, Coleman, & Blumler, 2009; Valenzuela, Park, & Kee, 2009).

The outcomes of the previous empirical research on the effect of social media for political participation have been mixed. Refuting dystopian views of newer technologies, many studies have found a relationship between informational uses of the Internet and political participation and civic engagement. Moy and Xenos found a positive relation between exposure to online political information and civic political engagement (Xenos & Moy, 2007). Bakker and de Vreese tested the relationship about Internet use and different patterns of political participation among young people. Their study confirmed Internet use has positive relation with different forms of political participation comparing with weak relationship between uses of traditional media and participation (Bakker & de Vreese, 2011). Gil de Zúñiga made further study about seeking information through social network sites is a positive and important predictor of people's political participatory behaviors, online and offline which supported Bakker's study (Gil de Zúñiga, 2012). Himelboim and his co-workers examined relationships about interpersonal informational trust and openness with social media political activities and attitudes. They found that both interpersonal political openness and trust are positive association with political participation (Himelboim, Lariscy, Tinkham, & Sweetser, 2012). Meanwhile, they proposed the categorization of online spaces and activities into consumption or interaction types, which makes research about online media use more specific.

Ward and his colleagues explored the relationship between political consumerism and more traditional strains of political participation, they found a positive relationship between political consumption and online participation as well as offline civic participation, however, this relationship would disappear with offline political participation (Ward & de Vreese, 2011). Recently, drawing on an original survey of a representative sample of Italians who talked about the 2013 election on Twitter, Vaccari *et al.* provided evidence that the more respondents access political information via social media and express themselves politically on these platforms, the more they are likely to take participate in certain political actions such as contact politicians through e-mail, campaign for parties or candidates via social media and attend offline events to which they were invited online (Vaccari *et al.*, 2015).

While some worry about that news in the online environment may cause societal fragmentation and displacement of community, others deem the online environment as a space for specific groups of young people's political participation along with social media becoming the focus of the heated disputation in academic circle recently (Bakker & de Vreese, 2011; Bennett, Wells, & Freelon, 2011; Grossklags, *et al.*, 2011; Kushin & Yamamoto, 2010; Theocharis, 2011). And scholars still concern on in-depth studies of the political participation mechanism on young people and tried to realize the "dynamics of these complex socio-political youth participation issues" (Auškalnienė, 2012). In fact, online information seeking through social media has been linked to enhances online interactive political messaging that consequently result in higher levels of political participation (Gil de Zúñiga, Molyneux, & Zheng, 2014; Vaccari, *et al.*, 2015). Overall, previous studies provide evidence that informational social media use does matters for young people's level of political participation, but they did not make study about how young people use social media engaging in politics across an array of online activities.

The relationship between social media and traditional media

"The weakening of traditional institution of socialization, the ongoing process of individual, and the growth of social network modes of social relations" has promoted the political participation environment change (Dahlgren, 2009), which makes traditional media lost less appealing attractive for political participation. Meanwhile, social media can bring about a relatively new option for news consumption and political participation (Hyun & Kim, 2015). Whether the potential advantages of the expand in practice of social media's political participation only complement the benefits of the traditional media, or whether they are empower in get enough replace them? As the popularity of the Internet using, more research began to discuss about the relationship of the new media and the traditional media and the trend of media development.

As for the research about relationship between new media and traditional media, Johnsson-Smaragdi and his colleagues studied how young people combine Internet with old traditional media in Flanders, Germany and Sweden. They found that television still hold a dominant position in young people's activities (Johnsson-Smaragdi, d'Haenens, Krotz, & Hasebrink, 1998). Althaus and Tewksbury chose 520 undergraduates as samples to do research about whether Internet would like to supplement or substitute traditional media. They found that use of Internet unlikely to diminish substantially use of traditional media (Althaus & Tewksbury, 2000). The importance of social media in contemporary society has sparked a wide array of research on the news access via social media recently. In particular, Nielsen and Schrøder conducted a comparative analysis of social media news consumption in eight developed countries and found that television remains both the most widely used and most important source of news in all those states, and that even newspapers are still more widely used and more significant sources of news than social media (Nielsen & Schrøder, 2014).

When used for political purposes, social media platforms contribute to various patterns of participatory behaviors such as traditional and non-traditional political participation. Although social media could offer various functions that potentially increase the level of political participation, previous studies have not fully addressed the relationship between social media use and traditional media use in terms of individuals' participatory behaviors since social media has become a hot topic since 2002 in communication area.

Findings from previous research regarding the relationship of social media, traditional media and political engagement are quite mixed. Some studies discovered compared with other media, social media use as a better channel for political connection and had a stronger relationship with individuals' level of political participation (Hyun & Kim, 2015). For example, recent research has suggested that young people may be abandoning conventional types of 'dutiful' citizen participation such as voting and being a party membership, in favour of engaging with politics in a much more individualized way through digital media or consumer activism (Amnå & Ekman, 2014). In addition, activists in China assigned greater importance to the role of social networking sites than traditional media in motivating people to participate in political and social debates (Harp, Bachmann, & Guo, 2012). More recently, based on panel data in Swedish national election campaign, Holt *et al.* found that the youngest group is more often use social media such as Facebook and Twitter for political purposes than any of the older age groups (Holt, Shehata, Strömbäck, & Ljungberg, 2013).

On the contrary, still few others found news consumption in traditional media is a more significant predictor of both conventional and online political participation (Skoric & Poor, 2013) and that social networking use is not correlated with increased political participation (Baumgartner & Morris, 2009). On the one hand, these inconsistent conclusions may arise from distinct definitions and methods of measurement of the political use of social media. Social media political use has been gauged in different ways, such as use social media for news sharing (Lee & Ma, 2012), social media use for political purposes on participation (Holt, *et al.*, 2013) and receiving political messages from SNS use (Baek, 2015). On the other hand, different types of social media usage serve for distinct political functions and involve varying levels of citizens' involvement, which should result in different political outcomes (Klinger & Svensson, 2014).

In fact, unlike the mass media, which is a one-way model of communication, social media platforms offer various opportunities for individuals to create, publish and exchange a great deal of political messages in a networked environment. New media technologies represent a distinct pathway from through which young people get involved, resulting in enhancing, supporting, and even motivating their levels of political participation. Together these studies demonstrate support for social media news use may more associate with young people's political behaviors than traditional media news use in the political communication field. In short, although these studies above point to a growing trend of social media use for young people, they do not provide a consistent account of whether that political use are more related with political engagement than traditional media. And few literatures have offered a theoretical framework to map the youth civic media use from the perspective of comparative study.

1.4 Research questions and hypotheses

Based on the empirical findings summarized in the preceding studies, the impact of social media on political participation indicated an overall positive effect. Although still a number of studies have failed to demonstrate that social media does not have apparent effect on political participation. For instance, Bichard *et al.* found that depend on social networking sites had no effect on political participation although it was significantly related to civic participation (Zhang, Johnson, Seltzer, & Bichard, 2010). Dimitrova and his colleagues found no significant impact of social media use on vote intention in the 2008 U.S. presidential election (Dimitrova, Shehata, Strömbäck, & Nord, 2011).

As demonstrated shows that the number of studies that found positive effects significantly outnumbered those with negative effects. Our hypotheses and research questions support the optimists about the use of social media platforms have positive effect on political participation. Besides, young people are also more likely to engage in politics through social media platforms due to its technological features cultivating more social interactions and networks. To capture the nuanced capacity of social media use for political participation, this study considers and tests how traditional media, social media influence college students' political behaviors. Specifically, author gives two questions and relevant hypotheses are as followed. In addition, as research continues, other research questions and hypotheses will be presented in Chapter 4.

RQ1. Why and how do college students engage politically via social media in Germany and China?

Based on the discourse analysis above, the study also proposes the following assumptions:

Hypothesis 1: The frequency of social media use will correlate positively with their political participation.

Hypothesis 2: Social media use for political news will correlate positively with their political participation.

RQ2. To what extent do college students use social media to engage in political participation, comparing to traditional media?

Hypotheses 3: Use of social media for political news correlates more strongly with political participation than traditional media.

Chapter 2 Compare media system in the political context between Germany and China

2.1 Introduction

As a matter of fact, the main challenge now is to face the developments and consequences derived of modernization and globalization of political process (Pfetsch & Esser, 2004, p. 4). Moreover, the Internet has created and started more channels for new expressions, new ways of interaction and engagement and for redefinition of what makes up politics (Esser & Hanitzsch, 2012, p. 26). All of these changes have triggered comparative study and are necessary for an understanding of contemporary political communication field. In the current study, despite some research on comparative media study produced research accumulated during the past decades, comparative political communication research are still far less explored (Strömbäck & Dimitrova, 2006).

Thus, this comparative study mirrors the process of media and political system change that is going on in China and Germany, which also offers a point of entry for a better understanding of the potential influences of social media on the functioning of political communication sphere today. The research firstly places focus on the political systems between China and Germany, by concretely analyzing the primary characteristic of party systems, electoral systems in both countries. Secondly, the layout of the section is around summing up the most important forms of media system in such dimensions as: newspaper industry, TV and radio industry, Internet and other media outlets in both countries. At the same time, it places more emphasis on the analysis of the Internet industry in the digital media context.

2.2 Dimension of comparing political system between Germany and China

With modern political communication processes highly mediated (Strömbäck & Dimitrova, 2006), the Internet not just as a main source of political information for people but has provided "an almost unprecedented level of transparency, rule of law, and official accountability" (Elizabeth, 2011). Against this background, the current research of comparative political system has been placed in the context of a very focused and popular area, with numbers of publication and achievements are gradually increasing during the last decades (Esser & Hanitzsch, 2012; Freeden & Vincent, 2013; Ishiyama, 2011; Vergeer, Hermans, & Cunha, 2013). Those current studies range from researching the comparison of party systems, governmental systems, constitutions and political campaign to election systems.

There is a need to make the concept of political system clear first, which is the basis of the comparative study. Almond gave a comprehensive definition that "the political system is one important set of social institutions concerned with formulating and implementing the collective goals of a society, or groups within it" (Almond, 1974, p. 4). This comparative political system focuses on the profiles of political parties in both China and Germany, stressing differences in fragmentation and stability of the political scene which arose mainly due to historical background. Differing political systems in a country are a result of many reasons including economic, legal, geographical and cultural factors. Cross-national comparison reveals Germany and China have very different political system. The key elements of political system are determined by the form of government: Germany's government being a representative democracy and China's being a relative totalitarian regime.

2.2.1 Political system in China

China's political system here refers to the political structure, basic laws, regulations and some important implementations of the practice in the mainland of China with regulating the state and government power, as well as the relation between the state and society since the founding of the People's Republic. The main characteristics and superiorities of China's political party system can be understood from the party system and electoral system. This system involves a special political landscape, which basic and essential characteristics are multi-party cooperation, political consultation, governance by the CPC, and participation by multiple parties under the leadership of the communist party of China.

Party system in China

As Stockton noted that institutionalized parties and party systems have long been thought as essential prerequisite for democracies to implement and maintain effectively (Stockton, 2001). Thus it can be seen that the party system for nation is key skeleton of the modern democratic society. The greatest difference between a western-style democratic system and China's political system is in the party system (Cai, 2011). According to the Chinese government documents says "The political party system China has adopted is multi-party cooperation and political consultation under the leadership of the Communist Party of China (CPC), which is different from both the two-party or multi-party competition systems of Western countries and the one-party system practiced in some other countries" (China.org.cn, 2007).

Needs to mention specially, the 'multi-party cooperation' means mainly the Communist Party of China has won continuously cooperation and support from eight other parties: they are Revolutionary Committee of the Chinese Kuomintang, China Democratic League, China National Democratic Construction Association, China Association for Promoting Democracy, Chinese Peasants and Workers Democratic Party, China Zhi Gong Dang, Jiu San Society and Taiwan Democratic Self-Government League (China.org.cn, 2007). It may be said those democratic parties are close companions of the CPC and they participate in state affairs, the exercise of state power, the consultation in fundamental state policies and the choice of state leaders, the administration of state affairs, and the formulation and implementation of state policies, laws and regulations. As Cai has put it, "the multi-party cooperation system replaces antagonism and struggle among parties with cooperation and consultation" (Cai, 2011).

In addition, political consultation as the most significant political and organization form (take the form of Chinese People's Political Consultative Conference). It serves a social and political function as followed "under the leadership of the CPC, all parties, mass organizations and representatives from all walks of life take part in consultations of the country's basic policies and important issues in political, economic, cultural and social affairs before a decision is adopted and in the discussion of major issues in the implementation of the decisions" (China.org.cn, 2005). Thus, the peculiar features of party system in China contain two points: firstly, the CPC's leadership must be upheld; Secondly, under the reign of the CPC, other eight democratic parties participate in and deliberate on state affairs. At the same, the CPC and other minor parties supervise each other, which check on the abuse of political power and serious corruptions in adherence to the rule of "long-term coexistence, mutual supervision, treating each other with sincerity and sharing each other's weal and woe (Mohanty, 1993)".

By tracking the history development of the Communist Party in China, we can see its development passing through several basic political phases. The Communist Party of China was founded in 1921 and today it has become the largest political party around the globe with more than 80m-strong memberships (News, 2012). On October 1, 1949, The Communist Party has undergone a serial of proactive reforms and development since its establishment, all these effort make Chinese political system "more competitive, transparent, and participatory" (Lawrence & Martin, 2012). The reform and development initiated by the Communist Party, at the same time, expand the number of party members making the party's solid foundation. During the nearly-90-year development, as Lye and Hofmeister put it, the number and composition of CPC's membership has transformed from groups of farmers and factory workers to a more broad social strata and professions (Lye & Hofmeister, 2010, p. 24). With the enlargement of the universities' enrollment scale in China, the number of the Party member of student increases year by year. As Lye and Hofmeister noted, joing the CPC is more attractive to college students, the percentage of newly recruited members of students is account for 38 percent of the total numbers (Lye & Hofmeister, 2010, p. 26).

In former and recent literatures written about the party system in China generally seems to prove important fact: China's political system has confronted with new challenges and opportunities since the reform and opening-up (Schoenhals, 1999), as well as the process of the political modernization. To constantly keep the Communist Party of China development and promote democracy-oriented reform, the Chinese leadership has a range of measures designed to maintain its dominant position with Chinese characteristics (Yu, 2002). In a word, the political party in China as the core of modern democratic politics, and also the investigator of modern democratic politics now with party reform become an increasingly important agenda in China (Zheng, 2009, p. 3). Nevertheless, the function of the CPC and China's party system differ from that of western parties because of the difference among party, state and society. As Zheng noted, political revolution, the importation of Leninist state as its guide, the role of party founding the new China, and boost social-economic reform and development, all these elements make China's political parties in China other than those west countries (Zheng, 2009, p. 67).

Electoral system in China

Since China led by the Communist Party, and especially since 1978 China has come into operation direct elections at village level, China's elections system has been a topic of mass intrigue and controversy as to its unique characteristics and profound influence. On the one hand, China's voting system achieved encouraging advances by breaking through the yoke of various conceptual restraints under the guidance of socialist democracy during the past 20 years. On the other hand, anecdotal evidence and empirical analysis confirmed people's democratic awareness and skills have improved which needs to expand the scope of direct election (Guo, 2003, p. 200). These two aspects also appear prominently in the mass media coverage of Chinese politics. Considering either or both of these two aspects show that the choice of an electoral system inevitably involves questions to do with political parties.

At present, China's electoral system is composed of three elements: the electoral system of grassroots autonomous organizations such as village residents' committees; the electoral system of the people's congresses at all levels; and the electoral system of officials of governmental organs at all level (Feng, 2013). Unlike western electoral system, China's electoral system may be divided into two types: direct election and indirect election. Deputies to the county and township level People's Congresses are directly elected by their local constituencies, while delegates to the National People's Congress, China's parliament and to the people's congress of provinces, autonomous regions, municipalities are indirectly elected by the respective local People's Congress at the next lower level. As Chiu notes Chinese election procedures for its highest leaders are essentially based on a series of representative elections that begin with a direct vote of the people for local and village elections performed by local election committees (Chiu, 2013). "China's electoral system can be characteristic of hybrid of between so called the nomenklatura system and popular election" (Wong & Li, 1998, p. 6). In other words, the most evident feature of current China's electoral system is a hierarchical structure, different type of elections occurs depending on different subordinate levels for deputies.

In addition, the people's congresses in China is composed of five levels from low to high what includes the National People's Congress, the people's congresses of provinces, autonomous regions and municipalities directly under the Central under the leadership of central government, the people's congresses of cities divided into districts, and autonomous prefectures, the people's congresses of cities not divided into districts, municipal districts, counties and autonomous counties, and the people's congresses of townships (Figure 2.1). These regulation and law about the various levels for people's congresses were determined by the Chinese Communist Party under the leadership of Deng Xiaoping in the late 1970s and the early 1980s (Chen & Zhong, 2002). Although implementation of the democratic elections in all the levels of the people's congresses, it is worth noting that the NPC represents the highest layer of state authority of People's Congresses and only the National People's Congress is entitled to vote and remove

28

"China's President, Premier, Vice President and Chair of the Central Military Commission as well as the President of the Supreme People's Court and the Procurator-General of the Supreme People's Procuratorate" (Chiu, 2013). Meanwhile, as Wang noted, "how to select and design an electoral system for China is a question about how the CCP will position itself in a national direct selection" (Wang, 2003, p. 270), in reality, the CCP has somehow the command of these democratic elections, which firmly carry out the principles of the one-party rule and related regulations.

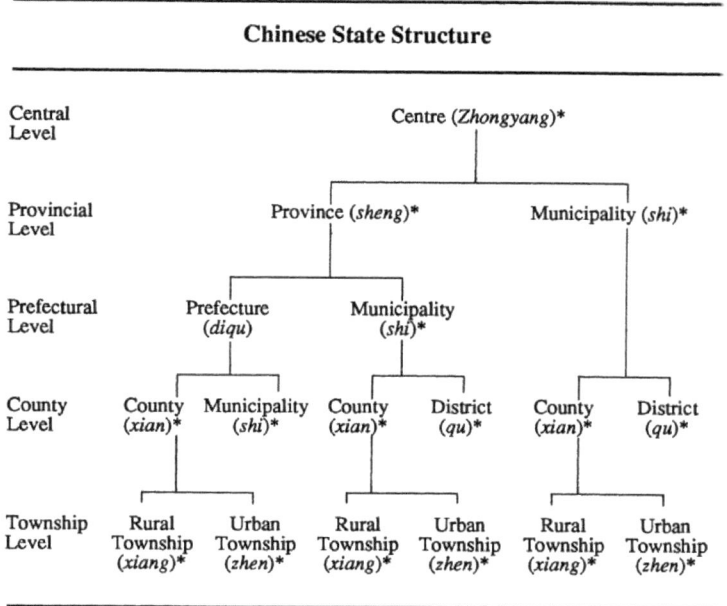

Chinese State Structure

* Unit has a People's Congress

Figure 2.1 China state figure (Jacobs, 1991, p. 172)

Besides that, if viewed from the historical context, it's not uncommon to find the practice of China's voting system experienced a constantly improvement and progress course in the past decades. Since China's reform in the late 1970s, the NPC has been considered as "barometer of China's political reform and democratization" (Wong & Li, 1998, p. 6). Thereby, electoral reform in China is centered around strengthen the political power of NPC and enlarge of democratic elections, and also the other emerging changes. Actually, the election system in China had been built up by the first Election Law introduced in February 1953. However, this first official electoral law had not been good since the promulgation of implementation, due to a range of factors such as the ten year of Cultural Revolution from 1966 to 1976 (Feng, 2013). The second election law was enacted in 1979, along with the introduction of direct elections for grassroots on the township and county level people's congresses. Afterwards, the election bill and organic law have been modified five times (Delisle, 2010) aiming to institutional reform of the current electoral system and promotion of the democratic election system.

After three decades of change unleashed by reformist policies, a series of achievement had been continuously acquired in electoral system reformation, which established a stability basis for democratization of politics in the future. The expansion of direct ballot from levels of township or village to country; the improved of electoral competitiveness transforming from one-candidate elections to multi-candidate elections; further enhancement of the universality and equality for in the right for voters to the people's congresses. Moreover, various electoral reforms have been carried by the Communist Party of China by taking Marxism-Leninism theory as fundamental principle for Chinese voting system. Under the guidance of the Marxism-Leninism theory, the CPC plays its leading role, and from 1997 electoral reform of CPC organ in villages has been tested in different localities in China (Cheng, Zheng, & Chan, 2012, p. 68). As pointed out, so far electoral system in China cannot meet the increasing demand of building political civilization and the expectations of the general public yet (Chen, 2004). Nowadays, there are two main insufficient aspects in the system of elections in China. One is the lack of assessment system and regulation mechanism, people's supervision and feedback is not timely been solved during the election campaign. The other is excessive intervention of the local organization and government which makes the electoral process lack of competition thereby removing the enthusiasm of the voters.

2.2.2 Political system in Germany

As Allen noted "for much of the post-1945 period, the German electorate was one of most predicable and the German party system one of the most stable of advanced West European democracies" (Allen, 1999, p. 30). A significant feature of political parties and party systems in Germany is stability, because of the central role played by German political parties in political arena over the past century, and Germany is deemed as a "party state" (Solsten, 1999, p. 371). Unlike the two-party system found in democracies such as the United States which essentially has been largely established for centuries, the current vitality of Germany's democratic political system is a much more recent construct since 1949 when Germany was divided into the Federal Republic and Democratic Republic.

Party system in Germany

Now Germany has a multi-party system, which generally considered as a system where more than two parties exert influence on the political life of the nation. As primary power owner and political organization, parties were also proposed as integral element of the political organization of German democracy. However, parties in Germany did not derive from the parliament and parliamentary groups or cliques but from social and political campaign (Glaessner, 2005, p. 101). As early as 1850s, a variety of parties which represent different class interests emerged after the failure of the liberal revolution. During World War I, it had already existed a party system that developed and challenged the country's parliaments. In the Weimar republic from 1918 to 1993, the party system had been highly fragmented (Glaessner, 2005, p. 103), because of the fierce competition between parties and the shifty political and institutional structures. During that period, both the Central party and the Social Democrats party threw out challenges towards the democratic republic system.

From 1949 to 1990, Germany experienced the establishment of the Federal Republic of German and unification of state, over almost a half century, the landscape of German party system virtually has been under the control of two major parties: the Christian Democratic Union (CDU/SCU) on the right and the Social Democratic Party (SPD) on the left, add some smaller parties such as the Liberal Democrats (FDP). In those fifty years, German party system was generally considered to maintain steady and solid development. In addition, a series of small parties appeared in the Western German political landscape but fade like a flash in the pan, quantities of party reduced obviously in the Bundestag from ten (1949) to three (1961). Because of lack of competence, the fates of these smaller parties could not escape from being gobbled up by big parties or exceeding the 5% threshold (Detterbeck & Renzsch, 2003). From 1962 to 1982, the Bundestag consisted of representatives only from three parties: the Christian Democrats (CDU/ CSU), the Social Democrats (SPD) and the Liberals (FDP). The FDP played a pivotal role in the party system, between 1969 and 1982, the center-left alliances were forming among the Social Democrats and the Free Democrats which dominated Germany. After that, the Free Democrats aligned with the Christian Democrats forming a new alliance which governed Germany from 1982 to 1998. Before 1990, political system of German was actually a two-and-a-half party structure—mainly as a result of the FDP coalition with two different parties, which played a decisive role for the German government structure.

When the Greens entranced into the political arena in the Bundestag in the 1980s, accompanying with the unification of East Germany and West Germany in 1990, a former models of two-and-a-half party system has now be replaced by a stable five-party system. Thus, we may say that Germany achieved a real sense of multiparty system because of five relevant parties' influence in the parliament. The Greens won its parliamentary seats in 1983, five years later, firstly participated in the federal government in the form of political alliance with the Social Democrats. From 1980 to 2005, four parties made in to the Bundestag: CDU/CSU, SPD, FDP and the Green party. However, several other minor parties have won more than a few elections in particular polls without existing for a long time and develop continuously. Unification radically transformed the German political spectrum, the party system had evolved into the two camps' confrontation in the bipolar structure, with Centre–Right bloc of Christian Democrats and the Liberals on the one side, and on the other side, the anew alliance between Social Democrat and Greens on the other side of the political landscape. And the party system of the former Federal Republic after unification seems toward de-concentration. Meanwhile, the traditional people's party experienced a decreasing public support decline after 1990 and the appearance of parties on the regional level lead to political changes.

Beyond that, though the East and West Germany were existence as one political body after unification, political diversity on the regional level further exacerbated because of the uneven socio-economic and culture circumstances. As Glaeßner noted that "a new party system has now emerged which is less coherent, more complex and regional diverse" (Glaeßner, 2011, p. 203). As a whole, the original party system was quite different from the former, two of Germany's CDU and CSU from east and west merged respectively and the SED reestablished as the Party of Democratic Socialism. However, unification has also affected the pattern of party competition at the federal level and two small parties (FDR and Greens) had not been changed much by this unification. Thus, a new party system composed of CDU/CSU, the SPD and, with the PDS as a new type of mainstream left party, followed by the competition gradually shifting from national level to the regionally.

Recently, the division of German party system has changed only very often, in 2007 the eastern German PDS merged with the WASG to become a new party die Linke, the left. The left party become the third-largest political power in the Bundestag which challenges the Social democrats as leading party in German politics from the left. During the Bundestag election in 2009, the Left Party earned 8.3% votes from the west, 28.5 % from the east and 11.9 % overall. By May 2010, it even had seven of ten western regional parliaments' seats of western German (Patton, 2013). By contrast, the election unsuccessfully for the SPD in the general election of 2009, it broke the traditional the party system landscape.

In addition, now there is a large body of literatures published about German party system, the stability has been approved by many scholars. Those previous studies have, for example, focused on description and explanation of transformation of party system (Allen, 1999; Saalfeld, 2002), on comparative party system (Barbara Pfetsch, 2001; Picot, 2013), German politics and the political campaign (Gibson, Römmele, & Ward, 2003). Those related studies and articles examining the German party system generally wove around three points: the big parties in power, the survival of the smaller ones and the coalition between different parties. A connection between these points seems that the alliance becomes the key factor to decide whether parties will government the country. However, political parties are important parts of political system and indispensable actor in the each political campaign in Germany, "there has only been minor interest in studying their domestic response to but none capture the all the intricate connections and multiple dimensions of political process in Germany" (Roberts, 2006, p. 1).

In conclusion, German party system has kept characters of the stable and consolidated, however, in recent years this view is shattered by increased volatility because of issue voting and personalization of politics (Klingemann & Wessels, 1999). Meanwhile, the evolution of German political parties from the mode of 'two and a half' to the current five-party system, which can generally be attributed to changes on the fierce competition between parties and the ever-improving social legislative and institutional framework.

Electoral system in Germany

Germany has a mixed-member proportional voting system under which constituents cast two ballots: one directly for a candidate in their constituency and the second for their preferred party. This second vote determines the distribution of seats in the parliament. As Bartl notes, the electoral as one of the important characters of a democracy society and a representative government (Bartl, 2003, p. 4). As a democratic federal parliamentary nation, the significant feature of German electoral system is the combination a personal vote in single-member districts with the core principle of proportional representation. This voting system not only guarantees a close relationship between voters and preferred representatives but also prevents any one party form holding power alone.

This electoral system was designed by the Parliamentary Council in 1949. In each of 16 German states, the proportion of ballot tickets determined distribution of seats for parties per state. Beyond that, only political parties obtained at least 5% of the valid second votes at the national level can access to the parliament. Currently, there are total 656 seats in the German parliament, and the Bundestag, since its creation, has displayed a continual increase with the addition of a further expansion and the unification in the nation. Meanwhile, the Parliament of the Federal Republic of Germany is comprised of a lower house, the Bundestag, whose member is elected by direct popular adult voters, and an upper house, the Bundesrat, consisting of representatives appointed by the Länder (Simon & Gueorguieva, 2008, p. 49). These bodies are not possessing of equal rights, by contrast, the Bundestag is the more powerful chamber. Furthermore, German Basic Law regulates that Bundestag elections are to happen every four years and people reach 18 years old can participate in the elections.

Moreover, in the German political system, the member of the Bundestag are elected for every four years by ballot. The method adapted in the election is named the Mixed Member Proportional Representation (MMPR), it is this very complex electoral method ensures the accuracy of the results. From 1985 until 2008, Bundestag seats were apportioned among qualifying parties by means of the Niemeyer variation of the largest remainder method of PR. In Germany, it is interesting that vote-splitting is pretty common phenomenon during the election. Some small party supporters usually give their second vote to their preferred small party, due to leaders from smaller parties had almost few opportunities to win votes during direct elections. Meanwhile, supporters of bigger parties frequently vote one small party within the coalition to guarantee that it will legally pass the 5% threshold. Therefore, vote-splitting is actually an election strategy, which used by voters to back up their favorite party coalition.

To date, the MMP system has not shown any great drawbacks in Germany. It has enough to have a high level of institutionalized legitimacy; the basic principles single-member districts and list PR representation have been left unaltered since 1949. However, some minor changes of the electoral system have taken place. Chief among these was the switch to two separate votes in 1953, before then the voter had only a single vote to apply to both district and national PR allocation. Nevertheless, several attempts to reform the electoral system substantially have been made since 1949, and most intensely in the 1960s, when opponents of the PR system demanded the introduction of a FPTP system. More recently, the electoral system has been criticized for producing too many surplus seats without compensating the disadvantaged parties in Parliament.

How can electoral system make difference, there are at least three important aspects of electoral system can affect the structure of the part system and the power of parties within electoral politics: these are the ease with small parties can obtain seats, the exaggeration effects of the electoral system on the majority of governing party or coalition, and the extent to which party hierarchies can control the composition of its parliament party group (Roberts, 2006, p. 12). Some of the features that are most characteristic of the current German arrangements—including giving citizens two ballots and the legal threshold set at 5% of the national vote—were absent in West Germany's first electoral law. These points were incorporated into the German law as the result of partisan struggles, contests whose outcomes were shaped by the shifting contours of West Germany's evolving party system. In other words, although the circumstances of total regime collapse and temporary occupation created rare opportunities to develop a political consensus for principled experimentation with new institutional designs, the German 'model' was as much an ad hoc creation as it was the product of theoretically inspired engineering.

2.3 Conclusion

China as one of the world's few remaining communist states. And over the past few decades, with the market economy developing, China's political system manifested slightly more participatory. However, Germany is a federal parliamentary republic state with a multi-party system since 1949. Distinct differences between political systems in two countries including as follow:

That first difference is the very important difference between the parties systems. And there are five mainly parties in Germany though just one in China. In Germany people can vote against the mainly parties, but in China people can only help the mainly party to work. Because of every party has the chance to get the power in the government in Germany, every party has the similar aim to develop the own country, but in China CCP is the only regime party. In addition, the German political system gives more power to the parties, because they can make a decision on which candidates to place on the list from which the parliamentarians will be drawn. But China's one-party system could formulate a long-term plan for national development and ensure stabilization of its policies without being affected by the alternation of parties with different positions and ideologies. Parties finance the election campaigns, but in China, the costs of elections are paid by the state treasury.

There are also many differences between the two countries in their electoral system. Most importantly, Germany adopts mixture of proportional and majority systems in order to guarantee that the proportion of parliamentary seats a party obtains is the same as the proportion of voters favoring that party. However, the China's electoral system are relatively sample compare with Germany, which based on a hierarchical electoral system, whereby local People's Congresses are directly voted by constituencies, the higher levels of People's Congresses up to the National People's Congress, the national legislature, are indirectly elected by the People's Congress of the level below And all political parties and mass organizations may have rights to recommend candidates to be deputies. Candidates may also be recommended by a minimum of ten voters directly and ten deputies in an indirect election. In the process of both direct and indirect elections, the number of candidates must greater than the number of delegates to be elected and the elections must be competitive.

Simultaneously, it has to be mentioned that parties in both countries differ in the manner of selecting president. In China, the President and the State Council are voted by the National People's Congress. And governors, mayors, and heads of counties, districts, townships and towns in turn elected by the respective local People's Congresses. China is a unitary state in which the central government has power to create or abolish lower governments. By contrast, the Chancellor in Germany is elected by the parliament, the Bundestag, which means that a majority is behind him and most every law he wants to enact will pass, because of the above mentioned party discipline. It is quite clear that Germany's political establishment of federal parliamentary republic increases opportunities for the general public of the Germany to participate in politics at the national, state, and local levels. It also increases the possibility that a citizen's personal participation will have some practical effect.

2.4 Dimension of comparing media system between Germany and China

International comparative research rapidly has gained relevance in the social sciences during the past years, since Four Theories of the Press as the starting point for comparative studies. In fundamental research's foundation, Hallin and Mancini's path-breaking work explicitly focused their analysis on the stable democracies of Western Europe and North America and are only now create the fourth, model—authoritarian corporatist—that can be used for China (Hallin & Mancini, 2004). In view of main similarities and differences between both countries' media landscape, the study has made the quite thorough comparative discussion and research based on the dimension provided by Hallin and Mancini. The conceptual framework developed in this study makes contribution to the field of the comparative media systems research in a given society.

2.5 Media system in China

China as the largest developing country with 1.3 billion populations, media landscape is considered one of the richest in the world. Media system of the People's Republic of China mainly consists of traditional media industry such as television, newspapers, radio, and magazines, as well as new-coming media especially for the Internet. Since

2000, the Internet has also emerged as one of important part in the modern Chinese media system along with the rapid growth of information technology. In the past decades, Chinese media system has experienced a tremendous shift, from a stiff structure to the government-owned business models. The rise of the freedom of expression of media among Chinese people almost tracks the changes of media system, and with it, a more democratic media environment of speech and media development space.

The party, through the Central Propaganda Department, and its local branches at all levels, continues to control the content of the mass media in considerable detail. From the founding of the People's Republic of China in 1949 to the 1980s, all media, almost without exception in China were state-run. Independent media only existed in the media world since the onset of economic reforms, and some state-run media outlets (namely Xinhua, CCTV, and People's Daily) continue to hold strong market share. However, independent media in China are no longer told to act strictly follow journalistic guidelines set by the government.

The developmental trajectory of Chinese media started when China initiated reforms and market economy in1979, which supplied the new development space and a much loosen media environment for Chinese media. As Hong notes, not only did the media made great progress and expansion, but also the content of media became much bolder than before and the restrictions on the media was much relaxed (Hong, 2013). After that, it encountered a significant obstacle in the aftermath of the 1989 Tiananmen Square Protests, in the meanwhile media control were tightened by the government. Next, China started reforms since the year of 1992, the process was renewed at an even faster pace. After opening to Western countries and enacting reforms in its economy (Hallin, 2004), substantive changes have happened in China's media structure. To put it specifically, the media have changed from being concentrated in the national capital to being dispersed to cities; they pay more attention to average peoples' lives instead of focusing on transmitting the Party's will; more media rely on market competition for their survival rather than their connections with the state.

In contemporary society, Chinese media system is gradually taking on the features of commercialization with increased competition, diversified information contents although which is that still under the control of the Communist Party. As Sparks wrote "With China's two decades of economic changes, market entrepreneurs have moved into the government's previous business monopolies. China's media systems, formerly owned and controlled by the Communist Party, now represent persistent competing forces between capitalism and Communism" (Sparks, 2008). This change indicated that China's media system gradually shifted from an "a tightly controlled party propaganda machine to a multi-faceted social institution" (Hong, 2013), under which the media has been endowed with greater autonomy and freedom than ever.

2.5.1 Newspaper industry in China

China owns one of the biggest newspaper industries in the world, and not only that, newspaper circulation is actually growing in recent years with the failing newspaper industry and declining revenues on a world scale. Between 2008 and 2012, circulation in America suffered its decline by 15 percent to 41 million along with advertising revenue decreased by 42 percent. In Europe, circulation and print advertising revenue have both fallen by 25 percent. However, circulation in Asia has risen by 10 percent (Economist.com, 2013). With 114.5 million daily newspapers, China has passed India as the world's biggest newspaper market, according to The World Press Trends report (Economist.com, 2013). As a significant branch of media industry, during the past three decades, China's newspapers have undergone profound changes, resulting in more dynamic and colorful contents covering on a wider range of topics than ever before. Meanwhile, Chinese newspapers have gone through a gradual evolvement from the mouthpiece of the government and the state to professional reporters in the fierce market competition.

As Scotton and Hachten claimed, "in the past three decades, newspapers in China have been operating on a dual-track system. They are regarded as enterprise, but they are not placed under the supervision of industry and commerce authorities. Instead they are direct under the propaganda departments, which may issue a lot of dos and don'ts over specific newspaper content and operations simply because newspapers can swing ideological orientations in China" (Scotton & Hachten, 2010, p. 51). Against this special political backdrop, Chinese newspapers play dual roles that not only represent the voice of the government as elite media as well as on the behalf of the marketplace and the public. However, newspapers have changed their business model, without further alteration of their ownership structure. There is still no private ownership of broadcasting channels and newspapers (Zhao, 2008).

Newspaper industry has leapt forward since the policy of reform and opening initiated in the late 1970s by Deng Xiaoping, who implemented media reforms by reducing government subsidies to the media and making publications and broadcasters more depend on its own business operations (Beach, 2004). In 1992, the important speech of Deng Xiaoping, delivered during his inspection tour to southern China (Goodman, 2002, p. 6) and the 14th Conference of the Central Committee of the CCP held at the same year established 'Socialist Market Economic Structure' in China (Wan & Yuce, 2007). The development of the market economy resulted in an unprecedented media boom. From 1979 to1996 the number of titles grew from 186 to 2235, a growth of nearly a twelve-fold (Davis, 2009, p. 604). In 2005, there were totally about 2,200 national and provincial newspapers, nearly 40 newspapers for national minorities (Hays, 2012).

Generally, Chinese newspapers can be divides into three categories: party newspapers, city newspapers, as well as newspapers for specific professions (Rong, 2009). Party newspapers are on behalf of the interests of the CCP, with aiming to propagating party's positions and points of view under the direct jurisdiction of Party propaganda committees. For example, The People's Daily is a kind of party newspaper as the official organ of the Central Committee of the CCP. Compared with city newspapers and specific professional newspapers, party newspapers have a greater obligation to publish political news, while non-party papers think more in terms of their readers' needs. However, under the highly competitive pressure, the party newspaper, which is always the mainstream of China media, has suffered a serious of problems in the reality, such as audience interest in reading decreased and the drop in advertising revenue. Despite all this, the party newspapers and city newspapers still have a strong share of the newspaper market, by contrast, the newspapers for specific professions are confronting with serious challenges of limited audience (Liu, 2006).

Now, the Chinese government officially owns the media, and content of newspaper is controlled by them through different level of propaganda offices. All the newspapers are supervised at the central level by the Ministry of Press and Publications. At the local level, newspaper publish is inspected by the local Party propaganda committees (Goldkorn & Danwei, 2013). Meanwhile, newspapers are requested to abide by the regulation of government directives and self-censorship. As Scotton and Hachten argues, Chinese newspapers, by contrasting with other media outlets such as radio, television and the Internet, are widely viewed as elite media due to they are an essential and powerful platform used by Chinese political departments to influence politics in China (Scotton & Hachten, 2010, p. 43).

2.5.2 TV and Radio industry in China

With the changing political economic climates and the continuous progress of transmission techniques, as well as the impetus of the accelerating the convergence of the telecommunication, Internet and broadcasting networks, radio and television have expanded rapidly since the 1980s as important means of mass communication and popular entertainment in Chinese society. According to the latest figures, in the five years through 2013, advertising revenue for the TV and Radio Broadcasting industry is expected to be annual growth rate of about 12.5%, and advertising and cable network services have become two major revenue sources for the TV and Radio Broadcasting industry in China (Francisco, 2013). The rapid growth of radio and television stations boosts the media industry commercialized development, while it also brings audience to crease drastically with numbers at levels never seen before. In 2012, the national broadcasting and television comprehensive population coverage of 97.51% and 98.20% respectively, increased by 0.45 and 0.38% respectively. Now China has set up radio and television agencies 2579, of which 169 radio stations, television stations183,42, education television stations 2185 (Li, 2013).

Television

Television broadcasting began in China in 1958, and color transmissions were firstly used by Beijing, Tianjin and Shanghai stations in 1973. But Television developed rather slowly due to economic reasons and the Cultural Revolution, during this time from 1958 to 1976, television only used as a simple political and educational instrument with fairly small social effects. The turning point was marked by the 11th Chinese Radio and Television Conference, which defined a series of new principles and policies for the acceleration of the development of the Chinese television system. As a result, from 1983 to1988 the number of television stations proliferated from 52 to 422 along with Chinese government support (Li, 1991). However, it's worth mentioning that in the context of a broad intellectual and cultural ferment in the 1980s, television became a powerful forum for promoting the liberal ideas favored by increasing numbers of the Chinese intellectual elite. And the relatively liberal political environment of the early and mid-1980s provided the space for reform-minded Chinese intellectuals to explore television as a serious medium of political communication (Wasko, 2009).

After undergoing phases of development in past decades, now altogether there are 3,000 television stations across the country, as well as their satellite and ground network systems, constitute the largest television network in the world. China's television industry has developed its own complex structural feature: it is a complete system along with high-tech program production, message delivery and coverage. As Hong argues, "China's television represents a highly complicated communication system, a most powerful ideological machine, a unique social manifestation and the largest and one of the most advanced media institution in the world" (Hong, 1998). The significant characteristics of Chinese television are that it is state-owned with a single profit model—the funding comes from the market. As the figure shows, the State Administration of Radio, Film and Television (SARFT) not only directly controls state-owned enterprises at the national level such as China Central Television and China Educational Television, but also inspects and supervises any program productions across the China TV industry that in violation of government censorship rules. As the name suggests, Provincial Administration of Radio, Film and Television (PARFT), is set up in each province upon the entrustment of the SARFT. Accordingly, there is also similar organization "city administration of Radio, Film and Television" (CARFT) for governmental supervision at the municipal level in each large and medium-sized city (Figure 2.2).

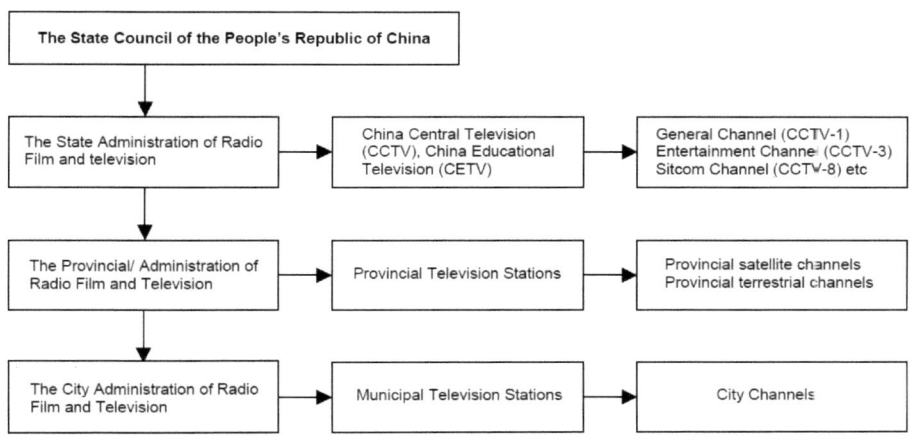

Figure 2.2 Structure of China's TV System (Marianne Friese Consulting, 2013)

In recent years, the development of a market economy in China, and especially within the Chinese television system itself, is gradually undergoing an unprecedented metamorphosis, evolving from a means of publicity of the government and party to a market-driven mass medium. In the process, pursuing its own professional goals and interests makes Chinese television expanding their influence rapidly and win greater audiences at home and abroad. In the meantime, Chinese television gained unprecedented freedom and independence. For example, China Central Television (CCTV), China's largest and most powerful state television broadcaster, which possess a network of 22 channels broadcasting diversity programs and attracted more than one billion viewers (Barboza, 2008). In addition, the television's dominance as the primary mass medium in China has been challenged over the years by new communication channels with more and more young people spending as much time on tablet computers and smart phones. And China's transition from a planned to a market economy has forced the television system to reform in fundamental ways.

Radio

Chinese broadcasting services, was first launched in 1926 in Harbin under the support of a local warlord support with providing contents such as news, music, speech and prices report. Meanwhile, private commercial radio started to take root to germinate in Beijing, Shanghai and other places in China. Due to the poorly-equipped station, the limitation in listening range, especially for the high price of radio made it have little power of influence in regard to economic, political and social situations during the initial set up stage. Later, those newly developed broadcasting station suffered seriously destroyed after the outbreak of the Anti-Japanese War. It is only since the accession to power of the Communist Party that radio has entered into Chinese life as a widely felt force. When the Party came to power in 1949, there were already 49 "Red" stations in China (Howse, 1960).

Between 1949 and 1978, radio had already become an important media and the main source where people can obtain news surrounding the government announcement through millions of loudspeakers. In the 1955 Broadcasting Conference, the government identified each person are capable of accessing Central People's Broadcasting Station. Since then, making great efforts to develop the building of broadcasting stations and expanding the scope of the radio transmission became the developing objective of the Party. Then, China's reform and opening-up in 1978 had brought unprecedented development and prosperity to the radio industry. The number of radio stations increased dramatically, from 1981 to 1991 alone, number of station from about 114 to 1363, a more than ten times increase (Scotton & Hachten, 2010, p. 74).

However, the phase of radio's rapid development draws to an end in the late 1980s, with more and more people can afford the Television sets as outcomes of the country's market-driven economic development. Some of that decline was because of radio ownership rates have reached saturation and could not increase further. Based on this data, radio ownership had already reached 251.2 million in 1990 (Lee, 1994). In the early 20th century, China's radio industry showed a strong competitive advantage. Compared with other traditional media advertising, radio advertising prices are reasonable and the effect will be terrific, especially some very good new interactive programs gathering a large audience. From 2000 to 2006, radio adverting growing was at nearly 35% yearly (Scotton & Hachten, 2010, p. 76). In 2005, there were 1,000 radio stations. The main radio station in China is the Central People's Broadcasting Station (CPBS). China Radio International (CRI) broadcast in 43 languages and has one of the largest broadcasting staff's in the world. Meanwhile, the continued urbanization drive changed people's way of life, with the quickening pace of modern life and the increasing pressure make entertainment programmers an instant hit with audiences in the aftermath of relaxation of state control. Attracting private and foreign capital brought new vitality to the radio station in China. The year of 2003 was known as "The year of radio development" (Jin, 2003) because of the greater development of China's radio industry.

At present, with the high-speed development of net communication and digital compressing technology, radio industry has been changed to a great extent. At the same time, due to the imperfect system of radio station, make the development of radio appear all sorts of problems. To face those problems as well as the challenges, digital radio has become the trend of development of the domestic radio industry in China.

2.5.3 Internet and other media outlets in China

With the development of the times, the modern media just like Internet, cell phone have grown fast and influencing people's lives in ways and thoughts few things have done before.

Internet

Since the establishment of the Internet on the mainland of the People's Republic of China in 1987, Internet has penetrated China at a surprisingly rapid. By 2000, China had 10 million Internet users and nearly 18 percent of households in four large cities could access to the Internet (Quick, 2003). Thirteen years later, the number of Internet users rose to 564 million at the end of 2012, increased of nearly 50% compared with 2000. Meanwhile, based on sixty thousand surveys found a slightly higher number of a Chinese men (56%) online than women (44%), according to a report released by the January 2013 China Internet Network Information Center (CNNIC, 2013). The Internet has created a system of two-way communication, which bores very little resemblance to the China's traditional indoctrination-oriented propaganda system. A distinguishing feature of the Chinese network is that Chinese government possesses online access routes instead of private enterprises and individuals.

At the same time, the rise and utilization of the network has brought new Internet applications appearance in public in view. The popularity of blogging, instant messaging, and social networking services and RSS aggregation tools, is leading a wide-range revolution in mass communication field among Chinese Internet users. With more government agencies and officials registering, China's microblogging services strengthened the relation between the public and the governments. Moreover, China's domestic social networking sites provide a broader platform for people to acquire information, enhance communications and speak up their concerns and feels. Among them, Weibo (the Chinese Twitter), and WeChat, a new kind of social media, become the top two fastest growing applications, with 300 million users each. The Chinese Facebook (Renren) also takes a big share online among the young (Bohua, 2013).

Despite under government control, the Internet constitutes the most freewheeling media space in China because the speed and decentralized structure of online communication present an insuperable obstacle to the censors (Shirk, 2010, p. 15). Internet could quickly delivery a big event topic for discussions and transmit multiple sources, and the topic for discussion changed with the progress of the event. Consequently, "people are not just the consumers, users and beneficiaries of the, but also their participators, researchers and promoters" (Mi, 2013). Mi argued that the revolutionary emergence of new media realizes the "all people to all people" communication mode, equality of broadcaster and receiver and the perfect blending of multi-media (Mi, 2013).

Cell phone

The mobile phone industry in China has grown to become a large industry since a nation-wide network was completed in 1988 in China. As early as 2001, the number of cell phones far exceeds the U.S. to have the most cell phone users in the world. Now, the mobile phone user base grows to nearly 1.17 billion in China, according to China's Ministry of Industry and Information Technology (Epstein, 2013). Digital telecommunication technology has broaden the potential of the cell phone to empower the public, enhances the democratic degree of information communicating with disclosing the operation of the government and the business community.

In addition, mobile media enables users to ignore the gatekeepers to spread the updated information. The flexibility of propagation mode of mobile communication enables mobile phone access to the Internet burgeoning in China. At the end of 2012, China has nearly 422 million mobile Internet users. And 74.5% of all Internet users in the country, use mobile phones to get online (CNNIC, 2013). The rapid growth has given rise to contact with social media networks through the mobile Internet. A good case in point is the widely used of mobile Weibo information transformation in China. Not only so: 34 % of China's mobile Internet users access the cyber blog sphere through a mobile Twitter account, which offers them another way to obtain uncensored information in China's government scrutiny (Wei, 2013).

Multi-media Groups

After China's entry to WTO, Chinese media industry appears the tendency of media globalization, grouping and networking finally in order to face the fierce competition of the external media group. The government has announced plans for setting up multimedia news group across the region in 2001. That same year, the China Radio, Film and Television Group established, combined with various beneficial resources of central-level radio, television and film organization as well as the radio and television Internet companies, forming the strongest multi-media group structure in China.

The convergence of traditional media, Internet and mobile services is changing the foundation of media business structure, but is also creating new revenue sources. Actually, as early of the mid-1990s, China's traditional media have joined hands with new media and of China's 10,000 traditional news media across the whole nation, 2,000 have gone online (Naisbitt & Naisbitt, 2010, p. 109). When people can watch TV shows on mobile phone in 2005, China Mobile has recruited over one hundred thousand subscribers to such services. At the same time, Chinese media do not feel content with the development of trans-region, many embarked on cooperating with overseas media groups. Since 2003, about 30 overseas television stations, consisting of Phoenix Satellite TV, Bloomberg Finance, Star TV, Euro Sports News and China Entertainment TV have entered China with conditions (China.org.cn, 2001).

2.6 Media system in Germany

Germany is the most populous country located very much in the center of the continent of Europe, with 81 million inhabitants. Along with German reunification in 1990, it has been a federal republic including of 16 states with the implementation of parliamentary democracy and multi-party system. The division of administrative power between the federal government and the federal state government has a significant impact on for the German media system for decades to come. As Hallin suggested, Germany is situated in the regions of the "north European or democratic corporatist model: characterized by high newspaper circulations, external pluralism of the press, a great level of professionalization among journalists, and state regulation particularly with regard to the public broadcasting system" (Hallin, 2004, p. 74).

Media system in Germany not only includes TV, radio, newspapers and magazines, Internet, but it also includes strong music and cinema industry. Most of the media are controlled by big profitable companies who rely on commercial business to survival. Germany owns a 'dual system' of both public and commercial media, meanwhile, emphasis on the federal sovereignty in cultural exchanges and broadcasting. Unlike China, the press in Germany is not belonged to the government or parties, but rather in the hand of private media companies.

Germany has a long history of mass media. Due to the invention of printing press by Johannes Gutenberg around 1450, Germany known as the birthplace of the modern mass media. About four hundred years ago, the first newspaper was produced in Germany, gradually followed by the emergency of other media. However, mass media became propaganda tool of the dictatorship during the Nazi period. The Allied victors opened the new period of the German media system in 1945. In the three western zones the occupation authorities attempted to establish a liberal democracy media system. In contrast, in the Soviet occupational zone the media were used as the propaganda tools of the party according to the Marxist–Leninist theory. As a result, the western authorities issued licenses for newspapers to private investors while in the Soviet occupational zone it was impossible.

From 1945 until 1990, Germany was divided into two separate countries for more than four decades. The promulgation of The Basic Law (constitution) of 1949, to ensure the freedom of the press, had very important functions. During those periods, the media system of the former German Democratic Republic (GDR) was still highly controlled by of the Communist Party. As reunification happened in Germany, this older patterns gradually fade away. Now, with the integration of East and West, the big media production centers are founded in the old West of Germany with mass media of the former GDR controlled by Western companies.

In Germany, the freedom of the press and speech, as a basic right of people is protected by Constitution. Media censorship came out at the beginning of the 16th century, however, the freedom of publication legally was ensured until 1874. German's tightly controlled mass media happened when the Nationalist Socialists seized power in 1933, but the situation was over after the Second World War. Now, the media supervision mainly depends on supervisory councils, which scrutinizes and oversights both the public and private media organizations. All broadcasting companies are managed by an independent Broadcasting Council, whose delegates are be endowed with right to reflect the "socially relevant groups", according to relevant provisions of Federal Constitutional Court's. Along with an era of reform and commercialized media in the 1980s, news supervisory organization were founded, each group with a council like the public broadcasters. Until 2009, in total there were 14 supervisory organizations are set up across the nation.

2.6.1 Newspaper industry in Germany

The most important feature of the German newspaper market is there have numerous publications and regional differences. Whether the local newspaper market, or the regional newspaper market, both are powerful and significant in the society of Germany. There are many different kinds of newspapers, including 335 local and regional daily newspapers, ten types of national dailies, ten quality publications and nine popular newspapers aiming at the public's interest events (Groebel, 2013).

The development and expansion of the newspaper industry has brought enormous revenues. Until 2008, total newspaper circulation reaches up to 20.2 million, among this, local newspaper subscription press amount to account for 95 percent about 14.3 million (Thomass, 2013). By contrast, national newspapers have the limited circulation, such as BILD, Süddeutsche Zeitung, Frankfurter Allgemeine Zeitung, Die Welt and so on. These national newspapers have their own features: independent of the parties and coverage style freedom and conservative. The most influential and biggest of them in Germany is BildZeitung, which is published by Axel Springer Verlag with the largest circulation in Germany society. However, with the rise of the digital press, paper-based newspapers from all sides of the impact of the existence of circulation decline since the early 1990s. According to related survey data shows, the penetration of daily newspapers has dropped from 79.1 percent to 72.4 percent in 2008 (Thomass, 2013).

In order to fit the development of Internet days, meet the reader's demands for online news, German newspapers immediately went to the Internet and offer customers free online news. Spiegel.de, bild.de and FAZ.NET unveiled new-look websites, thus, these online version newspapers won a large number of customers quickly. And not only that, they also established 'an unfathomable spectrum of news and opinion sites'. Although the integration trend of Newspapers and network, this may mean a mutual cannibalization between print and online, to some extent ensures diverse sources of news.

In addition, the press is characterized by a high but decreasing dependency on advertising income and a significant degree of economic concentration. The German newspaper industry is mainly managed by a small number of publishers. It's worth mentioning that the Axel Springer Group has the largest share of the market, followed by Verlagsgruppe Stuttgarter Zeitung and WAZ Group and DuMontSchauberg in Cologne. The 10 big publishers of dailies together accounts for 44.8 percent of the market (Thomass, 2013). Another type of publication, for example weekly newspaper with more in-depth analysis and background reporting became popular after 1945.

Moreover, German newspapers provide the platform for political communication. A variety of editorials, political celebrity interviews and a serious of political statements occupied the layout of German newspapers. At the same time, protecting free speech with the force of the German Basic Law, has created a free developing space and proper chance for the diversity of newspaper industry. German newspapers and other news media as the fourth estate in Germany's political platform, will therefore play a significant and increasing role in the future media market.

2.6.2 TV and Radio industry in Germany

Since 1980s that private media turned up in Germany media system and commercial television stations started broadcasting, the German radio and TV landscape system of Germany transformed into a double structure: public service and commercial system both coexist. Before that, broadcasting and television was only controlled by public broadcasters. With the development of private media, the birth of a competition between public and commercial media. Private media mainly depends on entertainment programs such as TV serious and soap operas to draw enormous audiences, while public broadcasting clearly has an advantage of focusing on political coverage. All German radio and TV station are supervised by broadcasting councils and required to obey the fundamental rules with offering real information to audience.

Radio

After the end of the Second World War, the allied forces was in control for all radio stations across the nation in Germany until the West Germany founded a new media infrastructure. During the middle of the 20th century, German radio stations' rapid rise and obvious has been witnessed to shape a new media system. In order to ensure without repetition of the type of state control in 1949, each state was required to administer its own radio and television stations under the federal constitutional provision. It influenced the formation of diverse roles of radios and televisions at the different sixteen states in the later.

Before1981, the German radios were controlled by public broadcasters. The traditional public service broadcaster included independents and non-commercial organizations, subsidized mainly by license fee (Kleinsteuber & Thomass, 2007, p. 114). As early as 1954, the first public sector broadcasting corporation, Arbeitgemeinschaft der Rundfunkanstalten (ARD), was born as a consortium of all regional corporations. The key feature of the public service broadcasters was that, besides producing regional news, ARD also paid attention to culture coverage and educational programming. Seven years later, the second public broadcaster, ZweitesDeutschesFernsehen (ZDF), was established in Mainz as a separate corporation with an agreement with all states to offer national programming service.

This monopoly was gradually disappeared when private broadcasters emerged in the society of Germany. In 1987, the sixteen states granted broadcasting licenses to private companies by law, which became a symbolic event with deep influence of the German media system. Along with this legislation became the provision throughout Germany, radio use has increased as more private corporations have opened their owned radio stations. However, German radio starts to slide in the twenty-first century. Based on this data, only 6 percent of the public obtain their news information from the 77.8 million radios in Germany (Kalvani, 2010).

Now, radio is a popular medium in Germany with about 500 radio stations for the most part local and regional in character. They generally provide program, deliver announcements, or gives running comments on important events based on a region to meet the different tastes of the audience. Additionally, there are three nationwide public radio stations with public funding on the agreement of the states. Although commercial radio is licensed by all sixteen states with a regional pattern, national broadcasters do not yet exist. In sum, the radio industry in Germany is extremely diverse due to the regulation different in each state.

Television

Television system can also be divided in two different levels: national and regional. As early of 1950, the first regional broadcaster was founded by all regional public broadcasters and was famous for its oldest and the first nationwide Television channel "Das Erste". Follow that, the Second German Television ZDF started based on an agreement of all states, which was a centrally organized channel with the focus only on television programs. In addition, ARD and ZDF together provided a number of specialized programs: such as Arte, Kika and Phoenix to cater to general and specific audiences. Apart from these largest public broadcasters such as ARD and ZDF, Germany also owns some of private television stations across the nation and the pay-TV channel Sky. At present, with nearly 40 million TV households and 365 TV channels as well as entire market volume up to € 9,615 million in 2008, Germany possess one of the biggest and most diversified TV industry in the world (German TV

Market Report 2009, 2009).

Moreover, public radio stations typically play double duty in the Germen scciety by broadcasting legally defined programs and maintaining independent of political, economic. But since commercialization has become so important, those public network broadcasters are facing stronger competition with the private stations. Beyond that, the emergence of Internet and mobile communication makes more young people turned their gazes toward online news information and programs.

Now, German commercial television is controlled by two powerful media groups named 'Senderfamilien'. One of the groups was formerly owned by Leo Kirchfrom the earliest times, but later it was took over by the Anglo-American investment funds Permira and Kohlberg, Kravis & Co. (KKR). Another one is managed by the German media corporation Bertelsmann, which is known as one of the largest media company and book sellers in the world. Then, more and more regional private stations were set up in some large cities such as Berlin, Hamburg etc. The audience for broadcasting has been attracted by multiple channels programs, which hits advertising revenue. Data show the television advertising market participates in the total advertising market with a share of 43.7 percent, among them, the radio advertising share account of 6.2 percent (Thomass, 2013). As a final note, the only pay-TV company in its initial period was owned by Leo Kirch. In 2009, shortly after it collapsed, it was controlled by Rupert Murdoch with a brand-new name Sky. However, because of too much competition of freely accessible channels result in this pay-TV company is not ideal.

2.6.3 Internet and other media outlets in Germany

Since 2000, economic and technological developments have pushed German traditional media channels to adopt towards the online medium as a news platfcrm. The appearance of the new media such as net and mobile phone have blurred the distinction between the newspaper and broadcast news. At the same time, with the constant increase of the new media user, network and cell phones increasingly show their importance in public life in Germany.

Internet

Like many other countries all over the world, with the rapid popularization of the Internet and sharply increasing of Netizens throughout in recent year, the traditional media landscape in Germany has been broken. There were total 71.7 millions Internet users in Germany, which means 88.6% of the population access to Internet in mid-year 2014 (InternetWorldStats, 2014). At the same time, Internet users' online needs and preferences are gradually diversifying, especially for the young, the social network such as Facebook, MySpace, StudiVZ and SchülerVZ, as well as blogs appears to be more credible and more attractive with its emergence and development rapidly impacting on the mass. In addition, over the past few years, the relatively cheap and easy accession to Internet also drives the popularity of Internet usage.

In some districts in Germany, cable TV connection makes both telephone and Internet available users to access. A great amount of providers provide a service which is restricted to certain regions of Germany except for Kabel Deutschland. In 2006, Deutsche Telekom possessed up to over 10 million DSL customers in Germany, making Germany become one of the top DSL nation across the regions of European Union (Kleinsteuber & Thomass, 2007). Now, the development of network makes nearly all German traditional media such as newspaper and magazines appear on the Internet with their own websites. However, many of the media organizations in the beginnings worried about going this way due to fear of competition.

Cell phone

The history of mobile phone in Germany can trace to the first half of the 20th century. Even as early as 1918, the Deutsche Reichsbahn had conducted the first experiments about mobile phones. Later, the mobile network services was established and mainly used in port, train and city service. In 1958, the first national mobile phone network was created by the Federal Post Office. A network had moved its development so fast that it became the largest public mobile phone network on a global scale at the end of the 1950s.

Since the 1950s, the number mobile phones have risen exponentially in Germany, as the mobile phone technology advances and diverse functions appear. Now, cell phone users can select from over four major providers and lots of sub-providers as well as special prepaid card providers. But before this, the government had the right to control telephone services. There are different kinds of telephone services with landline access in Germany. According to the data, today more than one in ten households or over nine percent of German households use a mobile phone instead of the landline (Informationszentrum Mobilfunk, 2012). Now, the opening up of telephone market and the rapid growth of affordable mobile phone have influenced the expression and exchange of public opinions between different people.

2.7 Conclusion

Since the 1920's, some Chinese intent to save their country with new political system and choose the Communist Party. In the west, the development of German's media system shows that German shares much of the characteristics attributed to the Democratic Corporatist Model. Because of culture, political of two countries and something else, the medium of two countries play the different roles in the people's political life. The difference between the Germany and China media system is presented in the following:

Firstly, the primary dissimilarity is that Germany and China have the different media ownership and ownership rules. The media and communications industry in mainland China is owned and administered by various government agencies and regulators though the laws proposed that the public are the owner of the media in China. And these front runner medium are all State-run, such as the People's Daily, Beijing Daily, Guangming Daily. However in Germany, the media can be owned and controlled by the government, political parties, private people or institutions and some organizations. And large media are owned by private companies in Germany, such as Axel Springer AG is one of the largest newspaper publishing companies in Europe. Consequently, difference of media-ownership between both countries leads to differences in media political content with accordance to the ideologies and orientations of the people, the government, the political parties and the institutions.

Secondly, another big difference between these two media systems is government censorship and other restrictions on media, especially, censoring on political news and information. In China, a one-party regime carries out tight censorship over traditional media and new media to maintain the rule of the Communist Party of China, although the relative freedom of expression available via Chinese social media. By taking a series of security measure such as closing publications or websites, establishing media monitoring systems, Chinese government prevent any harmful information to threat national political stability and information safety. However, a high degree of civil freedom has created more conducive atmosphere for people expressing their public opinions freely and participating in political affairs in Germany. The Article 5 of the German constitution guarantees the Germans have the right freely to express and delivery public opinion, and freedom of the press and freedom of reporting by radio and motion pictures are also guaranteed. In the context, censorship of publications in Germany is permitted when these publications causes the harm to the young users. In addition, the powers of management broadcasting are given exclusively to the states according to the German Constitution, which also assures that the television and radio industry has power in advancing freedom of expression in Germany.

Thirdly, the differences in Germany and China are mostly manifested in the disparity of the role of mass media orientation and social ideological and political propaganda. As Zhao proposed, China's one-party-predominance is different from multi-party democracies with political pluralism (Zhao, 2012). In China's case, the Chinese Communist Party possess shares of the news media, and the majority of the press is affiliated with the party structurally, so that media landscape in China can be deemed as a "media as mouthpiece" system combine with party-press parallelism (Zhao, 2012). In contrast, the media industry in Germany is characterized by the early development of press freedom with high circulation acted as for a propaganda tool and instrument for expression of social, religion and political issues for decades. With the historical development, the high period of political parallelism in Germany was faded a lot. Hallin pointed out that, German media now is characterized by a commentary-oriented journalism combined with increasing emphasis on neutral professional and information-oriented journalism (Hallin, 2004, p. 74).

Fourthly, as we will see in chapter three below, the results reveal the differences between the China and the Germans young people political participation. Generally, the media system and regulations in China is toward ensuring government tight control with the result that it actively discourages people's political participation in China. However, in Germany, the freedom media environment freedom makes people who are more likely engage in political activity.

As can be seen, because of the different political context, the two media systems have some differences as noted above, but there is some common points in the China and Germany media system should not be underestimated. First of all, both countries have experienced long-term and abundant media development histories whether the traditional media such as the press, the broadcasting and Television, or the new media such as the Internet. The media landscapes in two countries have been improved considerably due to introduction of the commercialization media during the twentieth century.

Next, with the development of the globalization, the trend of homogenization and internationalization make media systems in both countries facing the same challenge and transformation issue across the world. Meanwhile, the force of homogenization and internationalization lead to the concentration of media ownership and emergence of large media groups with both pressure from the interior integration and exterior competition in Germany and China. Such as Germany's Axel Springer Corporation is one of Europe's largest multimedia companies, with over 80 publications in 36 countries including Germany, France and Spain.

Finally, the appearance of new media in Germany and China already caused the two country's traditional medium development to come under the influence and the impacts, especially for the shock of the 4th medium-the Internet. With the widespread availability of Internet, political information become very easy to access and share across a wide population in both countries. Social networks such as Twitter, Wikipedia, blogs, and Facebook influence and even change the political regime. In addition, the media's growing autonomy in the digital time has been reflected the growth diversification of media content catering to different general and target audience in Germany and China. In sum, the comparison between China and Germany suggests that the distinct differences of media systems can spring from the different political context, because of political system characteristics are displayed more or less directly in the media landscape (Hallin, 2004, p. 296).

Chapter 3 Forms of political communication and participation in the context of different political system

3.1 Introduction to political participation

Forms of political participation, such as electoral voting, political lobbying, and civil disobedience, have triggered a series of studies in democratic societies. These behaviors, however, may not represent political participation in societies with other types of political systems, such as China, where people express political opinions through various patterns of participation or non-participation that are different from those in western countries. Meanwhile, the advent of Internet has made many academics and experts raise hopes that Internet has become an important way of youth participation, especially statistically usually shows that young population are more likely to engage in the social media space (Holt, *et al*., 2013). All of these encourage us to explore differences and similarities of political behaviors among citizens between Germany and China, and whether the Internet has become a key factor for enhancing youth political participation in those two countries in consideration of the differences in political context, economy and culture of both countries.

This chapter probes into modes of political participation among young people from four aspects. First, this part explores the definition of political participation, placing special emphasis on the measurement of political participation. Second, this part attempts to explain the differences of political participation between Germany and China based on the theoretical analysis method. Third, the chapter discusses about the development of political participation in different society and draws a conclusion about the cause of different political behaviors. In the end, this section demystifies the unfound area of comparative research and makes a conclusion.

3.1.1 The definition of political participation

Political participation is now considered by many scholars to be any kind of behavior which targeted at directly or indirectly influence of the government's the process of decision-making (Conge, 1988; Salisbury, 1975). One of such classic studies has defined political participation "as all voluntary activities by individual citizens either intended to influence directly or indirectly political choices at various levels of the political system" (Verba & Nie, 1972). Generally, patterns of political activities are divided into conventional and unconventional political involvement. Traditional political participation is most often thought of as those patterns that were related to the institutions of government and party, such as voting, becoming a member of a party, or contacting a government official (Conge, 1988).

Then, as time goes on and the change of participation forms, such patterns of unorthodox, aggressive, extreme political behaviors as well as illegal activities that influence who has access to and standing in political arenas. In addition, the age of the Internet has created new modes of political participation that did not exist before such as online election campaigning, reading about politics online, online petitioning via letters or calls, online monitoring, etc. Due to these advantages of ease of access, low cost, strong influence and interactivity, online political participation has lately aroused interest from researchers, government officials and ordinary people (Di Gennaro & Dutton, 2006; Hsieh & Li, 2013; Tolbert & McNeal, 2003).

However, mainstream research on political participation has been criticized that the only focus on traditional types of participation conceals much of the new patterns of participation, method of political expression, new political topics as well as political targets (Stolle & Hooghe, 2005). So, it is need to renew the definition instead of adopting institutional and traditional conceptions for decades. In youth research, the concept of participation is a very broad one ranging from young people's participation in the shaping of their own lives (Diepstraten, 2007), the co-shaping their of their direct environment such as schools and local communities, to young people's tries to influence political decision-making processes and to challenge authority relationships (Spannring, Ogris, & Gaiser, 2008).

Thus, the definition of political participation not only as all voluntary activities by private citizens either aimed to influence directly or indirectly political choices at various levels of the political system (Verba & Nie, 1972), but more generally actions of enhancing consciousness of certain issues and acts of influencing social, economic as well as political practices (Spannring, *et al*., 2008, p. 17). Under this wider definition, political participation it is broad enough to consist of a wide range of traditional, institutional forms of political behaviors such as voting and party membership in political organization as well as informal forms participation in some social movements, political communication, political protest and political communism (Spannring, *et al*., 2008, p. 17).

3.1.2 Theories about political participation

In consideration of forms of participations in different countries, scholars have already done a great deal of theoretical and empirical researches on the impact of political participation factors (Brady, Verba, & Schlozman, 1995), and formed a consensus conclusion for the multidimensionality of political participation (Dalton, 2008). By and large, political communication scholars offer various classifications of the forms of citizen participation in solving social problems (Koopmans, 1996; Marien, Hooghe, & Quintelier, 2010). Although researches are divided about the most efficient of political activity and related system of improving the level of participation and the participation rate, most of them postulate citizen political participation as an integral part of a democracy (Forbrig, 2005). As Zittel and Fuchs noted that, democracy is inconceivable without citizens' political participation (Zittel & Fuchs, 2006).

Post-modernization theory as one of the main explanatory perspectives on cross national differences in regard to citizen's political participation (Demetriou, 2012, p. 227) would give some hints about comparative political communication study. The main argument of post-modernization theory is that democracy shows more stability and effectiveness in social economic developed area in a general way. Specifically, the process of modernization along with its key elements such as industrialization, urbanization, rationalization and secularization would bring about some reforms of the social political and economic structures. Those changes result in the improvement of people's living standard, the growth of employment, the national education level increases and the expansion of information exchange (Demetriou, 2012, p. 227).

In addition, the core point of post-modernization theory is that the socio-economic development links with the increase of political participation. For example, Nie, Powell, and Prewitt have demonstrated that economic development is associated with a sharp increased in the general level of people's political participation (Nie, Powell, & Prewitt, 1969), and Orum found that cumulative economic impoverishment eventually creates the dissatisfaction necessary to make people participate in a political protest movement (Orum, 1974). Beyond that, there is a great deal of research shows that the degree and level of civil participation in politics in established Western democracies is higher than Post-Communist countries (Letki, 2003; Norris, 2002; Van Deth, Montero, & Westholm, 2007).

Moreover, post-modernization theory deems that the processes of modernization increase citizen's resources and their cognitive mobilization, which boosts the formation of a "participatory" political culture (Inglehart, 1997). Political culture is deemed as another factor which affects patterns of political participation between different countries. Verba and Almond argued that, "nation vary in the degree to which they manifest participant, subject or mixed political culture, and these variation are assumed to influence on patterns in political participation in important way" (Verba & Almond, 1963, p. 58).

Taking China for example, China's political culture today may be best generalized with the terms of a quasi-familistic or native term-Guanxi network. A quasi-familistic or Guanxi political culture is deemed as a way of relating to the development and maintenance of a family-like network of personal ties. The primacy of personal ties and reciprocal obligation has offered the significant foundation of Chinese citizen's political life (Zhou, 2013, p. 13). In concrete terms, the quasi-familistic character of contemporary Chinese political culture includes two levels. On the elite level, the quasi-familistic networks and values strongly influenced and imposed restrictions on the patterns of authority, the decision-making process, official recruitment, and the like (Hamrin & Zhao, 1995). On the popular level, network values and practices strongly affect the Chinese individuals' thinking and behavior toward to political affairs (Chu & Ju, 1993). By contrast, "Germany's political culture today is a member of the "extended family" of liberal western democracies, and it has the reputation of being one of the most stable among them" (Leggewie, 2013). Since the sixties in particular, extensive democratization has transformed the legacy of an authoritarian state into an open, participative, civil society in Germany.

3.2 Measurement of political participation

In research practice, political participation can not be measured directly, but only by asked for behavior intentions or self-reports of past behaviors. To overcome these problems above, the study adopts the differentiated approach. Specifically, three different dimensions of political participations served as dependent variables in estimated different levels of political participation in the survey. Meanwhile, political factors of political participation are investigated such as political efficacy, political knowledge and political trust, which have been argued that these important political variables are indicators of political participation.

3.2.1 Three dimensions of political participation

Base on the Europe comparative research made by Spannring, *et al* (Spannring, *et al.*, 2008, p. 56), political participation was divided into three different dimensions as following:

The first dimension is political engagement, it referring to interest in politics, following politics in different kinds of media and discussing politics with friends or family. Here, interest in politics as an important political behavior in people's life. To get an even more complete picture of political media use, following politics in the media (such as television, newspaper, radio) will be analyzed. Meanwhile, discussing with friends is as another indicator for political engagement among young people.

The second dimension is participation in the representative democratic system, which consists of voting and membership in traditional political organization. In this dimension, young people's participation in conventional institutionalized forms will be investigated by analysis their participation in elections and in political parties. From the point of view, voting represents the most significant right and responsibility of a citizen in a democracy society (Agran, Arden, & MacLean, 2014). Partisanship shapes voters' opinions on a range of issues, motivates citizens' involvement in politics and ensures the stabilization of the political system as well as political order.

The third dimension is participation aside from representative democratic structures, which concludes membership in social movements, political communication, action and protest as well as political consumerism. Before the 1960s political participation was confined within election and party related behaviors. Until 1970s activities outside and beside political institution becoming increasingly widespread, and what used to be unconventional participation has become part of mainstream political repertoire of citizenry. The term social movement was defined as "a network of individuals loosely linked through an institutional base, multiple goals and actions, and a collective identity that affirms members' common interests in opposition to dominant groups" (Taylor & Whittier, 1992, p. 107). By contrast with traditional political organization, social movements have diverse and dispersed organizational structures, and the distinctions between social movement and non-institutionalized forms of participation becomes pretty muddied.

Besides, due to the young people's reservation toward conventional forms of participation, the spontaneous, single acts of political expression and communication are becoming more accepted and welcomed by young people than continuous participation in political organizations and social movements (Spannring, *et al.*, 2008, p. 8). Thus, in addition to social movement, other forms of political communication will be assessed in the study such as attending political meeting, sign petitions, contacting a politician and so on. Moreover, legal demonstration, illegal and violent forms of participation also is measured. Life politics as an important element related to young people's political consciousness, which has become an interesting topic in recent years. As Giddens noted "While emancipatory politics is a politics of life chances, life politics is a politics of life style" (Giddens, 1991, p. 214). Despite recent claims that such behavior has become more widespread recently, political consumerism has not been explored systematically in survey research on political participation (Stolle, Hooghe, & Micheletti, 2005). When citizens take participate in boycotts or buycotts with the aim of using the market to express their political concerns, they are deemed to engage in the act of political consumerism (Stolle, Hooghe, & Micheletti, 2005).

3.2.2 Political factors of political participation

As research continues, based on the analysis to three political factors of political participation below, the author will put propose three hypotheses about the association of students' political variables (including political knowledge, political efficacy and political trust) with their political participation in Chapter 4.

3.2.3 Political efficacy and measurement

Campbell, Gurin, and Miller defined the concept of political efficacy as "the feeling that political and social change is possible, and that the individual citizen can play a part in bringing about this change" (Miller, Campbell, & Gurin, 1954, p. 87). Thus it can be seen that, political efficacy is a determinant for political participation because only citizens believe that one's actions are capable of affecting change, can they have incentives to participate in politics (Abramson & Aldrich, 1982). Generally, political efficacy includes two different contrasts: internal efficacy and external efficacy. Niemi*et al.* defined that internal political efficacy as "beliefs about one's own competence to understand, and to participate effectively in, politics" (Niemi, Craig, & Mattei, 1991, p. 1407), whereas external political efficacy was described as "beliefs about the responsiveness of government authorities and institutions to citizen demands" (Niemi, Craig, & Mattei, 1991, p. 1408). By contrast, integral type of political efficacy is more closely related to political participation because it refers to participation effectively in politics.

While describing political efficacy as a whole concept, internal and external political efficacy respectively have their own distinct dimensions, and these dimensions linked differently with other political variables (Balch, 1974). When taking consideration of socio-demographic variables, previous investigations have demonstrated that Internet access and online access to political information are significantly and positively associated with these important political variables: political knowledge, political participation, political efficacy, especially the internal efficacy (Kenski & Stroud, 2006). In addition, Morrell found that internal efficacy beliefs are positively related to education, motivation and political involvement, but not to trust in political institutions

(Morrell, 2003). Moreover, some research suggests that the Internet could enhance political efficacy because it help citizens interact with public officials, apply pressure to political institutions, give citizens easy access to obtain political information, and involve in the political process (Tedesco, 2007).

Measuring of political efficacy

In order to enhance the validity and reliability of our measures of political efficacy and related constructs, to explore levels of political efficacy and examines the link between efficacy and media use, many research applied six internal political efficacy items and four external political efficacy items (Lee, 2006). And some studies measured political efficacy using Likert scale items to measure political efficacy in its components through the asking of particular statements. The measure is based on asking respondents to respond to each of the following statements on a 5-point scale ranging from agree strongly to disagree strongly.

Internal political efficacy by asking individuals questions such as: "I consider myself well-qualified to participate in politics; I feel that I have a pretty good understanding of the important political issues facing our country; I feel that I could do as good a job in public office as most other people; I often don't feel sure of myself when talking with other people about politics and government" (Morrell, 2005). Meanwhile, the external political efficacy questions includes four items: "There are many legal ways for citizens to successfully influence what the government does; Under our form of government, the people have the final say about how the country is run no matter who is in office; If public officials are not interested in hearing what the people think, there is really no way to make them listen; People like me don't have any say about what the government does" (Morrell, 2005).

3.2.4 Political knowledge and measurement

As Mondak noted, political knowledge has emerged as one of the key variables in political behavior studies, with numerous scholars devoting considerable effort to explaining variance in citizens' levels of knowledge and to understanding the consequences of this variance for representation (Mondak, 1999). Moreover, the level of knowledge about politics is a key predictor for involvement in politics has been demonstrated by a large body of previous studies (Carpini, 1996; De Vreese & Boomgaarden, 2006). Several studies and researchers deal with political knowledge includes two distinct dimensions, factual knowledge and structural knowledge (Genova & Greenberg, 1979). As the first dimension, factual political knowledge often refers to the ability to mesmerize or recognize bits of information that can be determined by observers to be true or false (Carpini, 1996, p. 11). Factual political knowledge is maybe the most commonly investigated part of political knowledge, and it is generally circling round certain knowledge, such as knowledge of the names, officials, and their different position in the political system, knowledge about political reform and process, state leaders, as well as other political topics. Another dimension of political knowledge is structural knowledge. It is mainly about the way in which factual political information is organized by people (Carpini, 1996, p. 11).

Normally, political knowledge can be obtained through formal education, interpersonal political discussion, traditional news media as well as social media, etc. With a large body of studies examine political knowledge as a dependent political variable, recent research have generally demonstrated that levels of political knowledge affect the acceptance of democratic principles, attitudes toward specific issues, and political participation. On the other hand, some scholars examined media effects on political knowledge and political participation in political communication field and obtained conclusion that traditional news media use is positively associated with political knowledge (De Vreese & Boomgaarden, 2006).

Measuring of political knowledge

A number of studies have operationalized differently ranging from political information, political party, political leaders, to the current political alignment, or accurate or sufficient information that can facilitate individual's political decision making such as voting (Carpini & Keeter, 1993). Due to political knowledge cannot be directly measured, it is generally assessed via test scores or grades by a serious of questions. Verba, Schlozman, and Brady noted that political knowledge can be measured by asking respondents the names of public officials and by testing their political knowledge about government and politics, is a significant predictor of time based political activity (e.g. working as a volunteer for a political candidate, contacting government officials), voting, and political discussion (Verba, Schlozman, & Brady, 1989).

Today, the measurement of political knowledge through asking survey participants the scores of open-ended questions concerning political facts: "Who is the contemporary prime minister in your country?" and "how many memberships of Parliament/Federal Parliament are there in your country?" in order to know if people answer the right answer. In addition, the respondents were also asked about some national and international political leaders who have been in the news recently and whether they know them or not, for instance: Barack Obama, Angela Merkel and so on. Moreover, the participants were asked about their general knowledge of institutional fact: such as "in your country, whether national election (or elections for the national leaders) must be held every 3 years?" For each correct answer, respondents received one point, with the number of correct answers summed up to establish the variable of political knowledge (Jung, Kim, & de Zúñiga, 2011).

3.2.5 Political trust and measurement

Political trust can be defined as "the belief that political system or some part of it will produce preferred outcome even if it untended" (Shi, 2001). Thus, political trust is not only deemed as a significant indicator of political legitimacy embodying citizens' political support for the state and government, but also treated as scarce resource which is beneficial for political institutions and actors to improve their performance. Yet previous empirical studies have not always been clear regarding Internet use and political trust, because some studies demonstrated that there existed the positive relationships between the intensity of social media use and political trust (Valenzuela, *et al.*, 2009), whereas other research failed to find such a link (Kaid, 2002). Still other studies found that the positive or negative influence of news media use on political trust is relay on both the news source and citizens' existing level of political trust (Avery, 2009).

Although many scholars have paid attention to the concept of political trust from different aspects, there is still no consensus on how to measure it. The earliest study adopted a political trust index comprised of five questions (Citrin, 1974). The measurement method came from the original battery of five questions in the National Election Studies (NES) in 1958: by asking "trust the government to do what's right, whether the government is run by a few big interests, how much tax money the government wastes, whether those running government are crooked, and whether those running government are smart" (Gershtenson & Plane, 2007).

After that, a large number of research on political trust has applied a "standard" four-item NES index. However, the measurement method is controversial. In addition, some scholars have used two or three items of related questions to establish their measure (Hetherington, 2005), but these simple methods are not comprehensive and can't reflect the total dimensions of political trust. According to the methods and theories researched above, the concept of political trust was measured in the study by asking college students "In the following there are some names of different bodies such as the government and the European Commission. Please indicate how much you trust each of them?" These questions have the advantages of measuring the latent definition of a citizen's general orientation to government more concretely and more comprehensively.

3.2.6 Other political factors relevant

The final political relative variable the author needs to consider is party identification. The term of party identification refers to "a sense of personal, affective attachment to a political party based on feelings of closeness to the social groups associated with the parties" (Goren, 2005, p. 881). In other words, individual's politics may be shaped by aspects of their social identification with a group exhibiting partisan.

Party identification is significant because empirical studies of political actions have established a connection between party identification and vote behaviors (Miller, 1991), in addition, it enriches the democratic process, as well as links to political efficient and political trust (Lambert, Curtis, Brown, & Kay, 1986). Party identification can lead to greater political trust and increased confidence in government when an individual's party is in power. Individuals with a strong sense of identification with a party are more likely to take part in politics than those with weak party attachments.

3.3 Situation of political participation in different society

Reference to participation can be interpreted as key concept for an understanding social integration in modern and late modern societies in which the actions and choices of individuals-in their role as citizens play an essential role in terms of influence, involvement and active citizenship (Muniglia, Cuconato, Loncle, & Walther, 2013, p.

2). Political participation as a very dynamic and evolving social and political phenomenon, in different social context, people are more likely to be more or less politically active.

3.3.1 Political participation in Chinese society

In China, which has been undergoing a series of political transformations with the progress of social economy in the past three decades, the importance topic of political participation in China has triggered interest among many Chinese and foreign academics in the past years. Meanwhile, these changes in regard to economic, political and social situations might exert a great and profound influence on the ways of political participation for citizens, especially college students who are often characterized as apolitical in the society.

Past studies of political participation in China have established that, since the outset of the economic and political reform in the late 1970s, more and more ordinary citizens have been reportedly participating in public affairs and politics across both urban and rural areas of China. For the purpose of the section, political participation in China can be broadly defined as "political participation of ordinary citizens is the political behavior of public political life which directly or indirectly affects the government's decisions or government-related activities in a certain way" (Xi, 2013). Here, political participation is not only a form of new politics expression for individuals, but also a way of achieving democracy society which is beneficial to link the party and the masses society in China today society. From village level, Eldersveld and Shen deemed that political participation is thus a channel that the lowest classes in Chinese society can use for expression of views and for working together with others for collective goals (Eldersveld & Shen, 2001, p. 119).

In democratic society, elections and group-based activities are often two ways people can use to exert influence on government policy. Heberer and Derichs made more elaborate classification compared with the prior to the study of others, he divided general forms of political participation into six modes (see Table 3.1) and each type of political participation belongs to three different regions: legal, greyzone, illegal respectively. It's not hard to see that legitimate political participations political and involvement in election and institution are for the sake of effecting political process. Because in China many governmental policy outputs are assigned to the grassroots from top to the bottom, which means that certain political processes are open to political participation of individuals or social force which have a say in decisions and polices that directly impact on them (Lye & Hofmeister, 2010, p. 31). Social networking participating is a new tool for civilian anger and participating in politics. At the same time, some illegal political participation forms such as political violence, which is not allowed by the Chinese government due to the dangers of social stability and personal.

Although the enriching forms of political engagement with the progress of the political and the popularity of network, the desire of the Chinese political participation enhances unceasingly. However, not in coordination with high participation desire is actual political participation level is not high (Zheng, 2013). Chinese people's low level of participation in policy has been confirmed by the report issued by Chinese Academy of Social Sciences. In light of the questionnaire survey carried out in 10 provinces including 7000 samples across the Chinese mainland, the report reached the conclusion that the overall performance of Chinese people in political participation is only 4.21 point out 10. It's worth mentioning that 'acceptance Policy' is a basic feature of political participation. Meanwhile, there is a big discrepancy between "high willingness to participate" and "low actual participation behavior" for the contemporary college population (Xi, 2013).

Legal	Grey zone	Illegal
Citizen participation • Elections at the village and neighbourhood level	**Social networking** (Establish and employ close personal and social relationships) • Clan networks • Nepotism • Patronage • Other kinds of informal relations	**Popular resistance** • Illegal demonstrations • Strikes • Refusal to pay taxes • Foot-dragging • Forming clandestine organisations
Institution-orientated participation • Membership in CCP or other parties • Delegate in national or local legislatures or consultative conferences • Membership in mass organisations • Engaging in registered social organisations	n.a.	**Political violence** • Violence against property or persons
Problem-specific participation • Letters to the editor • Visits and complaints • Contacting functionaries • Legal demonstrations •	n.a.	n.a.

Table 3.1 Forms of political participation in China (Heberer & Derichs, 2008, p. 85)

Since China's reform and opening up, China's citizen political participation roughly has gone through four stages development according to Chinese political participation report (Chang, 2011). 1979-1981 is the first stage, during the period China's citizen political participation with the obvious "turning point" feature, the political participation changed from the blind political movement of 'cultural revolution' to the rational, institutionalized political participation—"taking economic construction as the center". The second stage is from 1982 to 1994, Chinese citizen's political participation with important "routing choosing" characteristics. In the third wave of democratization worldwide, the path of political participation in China is faced with three choices: the first path is through large-scale demonstrations, parades, and other forms of participation, put pressure on the party and the government calling for political reform, and some people definitely require development of western-style democracy in China. The second path is carefully groping for the suitable road for the situation of China political participation. The third path is the fully restriction of the development of political participation so as to resist the influence of the "bourgeois liberalization". Finally, drawing lessons from the change of the socialist countries in Eastern Europe, China choose the second path (Chang, 2011).

1995-2003 is the third stage, China's citizen political participation with obvious characteristics of "innovation". First, the emergence of a series of "election innovation", innovative election pilots was chosen from country level to the state organ. Second, created some new participatory platforms, such as village affairs, urban community building and "Network participation". Since 2004 until now is the fourth stage, the Chinese citizens' political participation in the scientific concept of development under the guidance of the "institutionalization" and "rule of law" development, participation in the election, people's organizations and mass self-government organizations, policy participation, contact participation in areas there have been some important changes (Chang, 2011).

Recently, in order to improve the enthusiasm of political participation of the mass, the party and the government have also made a series of efforts. "We must ensure that all power of the state belongs to the people, expand the citizens' orderly participation in political affairs at each level and in every field" (Li & He, 2007). In this way the political report to the 17th National Congress of the Communist Party of China (CPC) which was held in October 2007 has upgraded the level of the orderly public participation in politics (Li & He, 2007). Beyond that, China has continuously improved and developed of several systems which are all important elements of China's democratic system: the People's Congress system, the Multi-parties Cooperation and Political Consultation, the National Regional Autonomy and the Villagers' Self-government System (Li & He, 2007). Moreover, the administrative bodies at all levels have established the Press Spokesman System to transparent with the whole process of the government's regulations and policies to the mass.

Furthermore, with the rapid development of computer technology, especially for the arrival of social media, which has raised the possibility that discussion among different Chinese Internet users can bring out citizens with new ideas and more informed, thereby, more people involved in politics (Keller, 2013). The Chinese government authorities are also making an energetic stab at Internet construction, pooling public voices and opinions more effectively and widely. These measures are very effective in student groups, relevant data shows that, the current network has become a main tool for college students' political participation, 58.7 percent of them express their opinions through online (Xi, 2013). Under the background of the progress of politics and the development of the network, "the Chinese people, having taken the Internet over as a replacement for physical civil society, have become seemingly more attached to Internet discussion than some western countries have (Keller, 2013)".

3.3.2 Political participation in German society

Voting as the most common and extensive types of political participation among the masses in Germany which is tensely focused on. Voting gives the power to the German citizens and acts as the major means of impact on the forming of policy operation (Conradt & Langenbacher, 2013, p. 183). However, in a few years after the World War II, beyond the limited and hardly taxing act of voting, there have been relatively low rates of participation in activities such as party organizations, election campaigns, and public causes (Conradt & Langenbacher, 2013, p. 103). Much of this was mainly due to political contradiction and clash of Weimar party under the control of the Third Reich. Against that backdrop, German citizens hesitated to participate in politics was deemed to a negative activity. So, both East and West German states consciously attempted to encourage political participation of the masses. The government of the Federal Republic built upon the public's developing acceptance of democratic politics and encourages them to involve in the political process. Meanwhile, the East German government also promoted the pubic to participate in developing socialist democracy.

After that, the change of perceptions of politics and the citizen's roles in politics brought about a dramatic increase in political involvement. From 1972 to 2009, turnout in national had ranged from 91 percent to 70.8 percent, averaging about 80 percent over seventeen postwar election (Conradt & Langenbacher, 2013, p. 103). And the overall pattern of political participation focused on private matters, with little political involvement except for voting throughout the 1950s and 1960s (Conradt & Langenbacher, 2013, p. 104). But this condition was improved due to the economic development and the promotion of education in the sixties and seventies of last centuries. Germany seems to have transformed from the traditional top-down relationship between the citizens and the state to toward a more participatory system.

In the first democratic elections since unification in December 1990, elections Eastern turnout reached 74.7%, compared to 78.6% in the West, and this continued in the general elections that followed. It's worth mentioning that, the reunification seems become a turning point for voting, because since that turnout appeared relatively low compared before: 1998 – 82.3%; 2002 – 79.1%, 2005 – 77.7% (IDEA, 2011). The relatively low number of voters can be seen as an indicator of relatively small interest in political sphere. Now there are still substantial differences in citizens' involvement in politics in the east and west regions of Germany. Compared with the east part, the voting rate appeared quite stable in Western part, in Eastern part it decreased in the large.

However, in 2009 the final turnout dropped substantially in both west and east regions of Germany (71 percent overall)—the record low levels in the post-war Germany election. A number of scholars and politicians attribute the drop in election to a lackluster campaign by the political parties. Moreover, a majority of German citizens expected the eventual outcome, so the lack of competitiveness was another factor. In addition, young voters of 21 to 24-year-olds only accounted for 59.1 percent and ranked the lowest of all age groups (Egeler, 2010). This phenomenon may be explained by the fast pace of the online world leave youngsters feeling out of touch and loss interest in politics.

Today, patterns of political participation in Germany have expanded to include protests, demonstrations, and other direct actions among citizens. Among them, participation in campaigns such as working for a party, attending campaign conferences, convincing other people of voting, becoming a member in a party or political organization can be an effective way of citizen influence (Verba & Norman, 1978), due to such political actions in campaign have more intense and direct impact on political elites. At the same time, as political interest and sophistication have grown among the Federal Republic's electorate, the forms of people's participation in politics have shifted toward more emphasis on citizen-initiated activities and unconventional patterns of political action (Dalton, 2009). The growing citizen-action groups and the way of directly involved in politics make the German people have greater control of political participation by themselves. As Conradt and Langenbacher notes "these groups represent new patterns of political participation that contradict the traditional characterization of German as political passive, relying on intermittent, indirect participation through voting or formal contact with the state bureaucracy" (Conradt & Langenbacher, 2013, p. 105).

In addition, the emergency of the network politics participation among German citizens is another new political phenomenon for the individuals who take part in the social and political activities over the network. In Germany, the most common technology to connect to the Internet is DSL. As early as in 2005, the median of DSL availability have reached 78 percentage (Czernich, 2012). That the same year, the German Bundestag started using an online platform that provide users easy access to post and co-sign petitions directed at the German parliament online (Jungherr & Jürgens, 2010). With the growing importance of the Internet in the field political communication, German society seems to be in a state of transition: not only parties and the states are increasingly taking advantage of personal homepages, social networks, blogs etc. to publicize their points of view, but also traditional media online version (online newspapers, online magazines etc.,) have entered the political life of people with providing information on politics and politicians.

3.3.3 Conclusion

As Asher, Richardson, and Weisberg noted that "comparative political research involves analysis of political participation among mass publics in different nations" (Asher, Richardson, & Weisberg, 1984, p. 57). This means that comparative political participation across different regions is an integral part of the comparative political study. It seems that compared with high political participation in Germany, political participation among Chinese citizens is not high in the whole population. Based on the above classification, the study uses Table 4.1 to show the different forms of political participation between Germany and China.

By contrast, we can see some of the obvious different aspects in terms of forms of political participation between Germany and China.

1.   Elections appear distinctly different between two Countries. Although voting plays an important role in China, direct elections only occurs from lower government levels such as in villages, communities, neighborhoods or districts. And the entire candidate or candidates' proposals must be approved by the next higher party bodies or organizations. By contrast, German voting has more freedom and openness.

2.   The formation of parties or political organizations that challenge the Communist Party's rule can result in penal consequences. There is the power monopoly of a single party, demonstration, strike, protest movements, petitions or the free formation of associations be approved by the government. And illegal demonstrations and protests are forbidden in China.

3.   At the informal and individualized participation level, Guanxi participation is obviously one of the distinctive features of China's political participation. In China, Guanxi participation includes production or use of close personal or social relationships about clan associations, nepotism, networks, cliques, patronage, bribery, forms of corruption economic benefits etc. With the rising of the political democracy in China, the corruption of public officials has been put more and more attention on, thus Guanxi participation appears to be emerging.

Main forms of political participation	Germany	China
Political engagement	Interest in politics Discussing politics	Interest in politics Discussing politics
Participation in a representative democratic system	Election in the national parliamentary level Membership in political parties Membership in traditional political organizations (youth, trade and political organization etc.)	Election at the village and neighborhood level Membership in CCP or other parties Delegate in national or local legislature consultative conferences Membership in mass organizations (trade unions, youth association, women's association, etc.) Engaging in officially registered social organizations (e.g. Professional associations)
Membership in social movements	Membership and voluntary work in non-government organizations and social movements	Membership and voluntary work in non-government organizations and social movements
Political communication, action and protest	Contacted a politician Contributed to a political discussion on the Internet Wrote for forward a letter or email with political content Wrote an article, e.g. in a student's newspaper or Internet Attended public meetings dealing with political or social issues Wrote political message or graffiti on walls Worn a badge with a political message Donated money to support the work of political group or organization, Collected signatures Held a political speech Signed petitions Participated in a legal demonstration Participated in a strike Illegal and violent forms of demonstration: such as wrote political message or graffiti on walls Participated in a political event where property was damaged Participated in a political event where there was a violent confrontation with the police	Internet and microblogging Letters to petitions or at official complaint institutions Letters to / prospect for officials / inside Letters to the editor Negotiations behind the scenes Held a political speech Petitions in state institutions Approved demonstration Strike For bidden illegal demonstrations and protests: such as refused to pay taxes, inefficiency, refusal, etc. Education of illegal interest organizations (illegal unions and interest groups, Secret societies , country teams) Geographically-administrative: Regionalism / communalism political violence such as violence against property or person Guanxi participation: such as production or use of close personal or social relationships (Guanxi)

Table 4.1 The different forms of political participation between Germany and China (building on Derichs, 2014, p. 112; Spannring, *et al.*, 2008).

The specific differences of patterns of political involvement in Germany and China can be explained by those aspects:

First of all, political participation conditions and their influence mechanisms in different political context are really different. The election mechanism and measure is not perfect, which let a lot of people have no interest in politics even have negative perceptions of the Chinese political context (Yu, 2010). Meanwhile, the Chinese government and the party take the greatest efforts in keeping stability (Yu, 2010), mass media are prohibited from publishing some content that jeopardizes the security of the nation, divulges state secrets and disturbs the social order are prohibited by Chinese authorities. In this political and media context, there are very few political opportunities for people involvement in politics freely and the express their opinions. However, Germany as a democratic society owns a more robust mechanism of political participation.

Secondly, the development of economic-society as well as the level of education seems to positively influence participation. Because China is a developing country, the whole economic development level is not high, so that more Chinese citizens normally pay more attention to practical problems such as working income, housing etc. instead of concerning with politics. Besides the low level of education level especially in rural and remote areas, which make Chinese people short of opportunities to participate in politics.

Thirdly, the different political culture in Germany and China society influence patterns of political participation. One can refer to political cultural factors resulting from the history heritage, especially for the quasi-familistic character of contemporary Chinese political culture make individuals lack of understanding of politics of their own. Compared with Germany, although Chinese have changed their culture and minds a lot, this change is not big enough to influence their political participation. For example, men are more likely to take participate in politics than women (Yu, 2010), which means that the influence of tradition still exists.

Finnally, although the popularity of information and communication technology which is represented by Internet has created a new way of political participation—electronic participation in China, network supervision system make quite a number of people don't dare to express their true thoughts. Meanwhile, some Chinese netizens have the techniques to bypass the Internet censorship by using anti-blocking software and mirror sites (Endeshaw, 2004; Lacharite, 2002), people in China still have relatively limited opportunities to participate in politics. By contrast, German citizens have more free and open network environment, thus, the network political participation among citizens appears more effective.

3.4 Young people's political participation

Youth participation in politics is the significant symbol of measuring the level of a country's social modernization, democratization and legalization. However, for more than two decades, indifferent with politics, disenchantment with political commitment and political affairs are labels frequently attached to the political involvement of young people. For instance, only 19.32 percent of Chinese youth report that they are interested in political issues according to a poll on the awareness of political participation was carried out among the Shanghai youth (Gang, 2013). A similar disinterest in the conventional political participation in and increasing participation in unconventional forms has also been noted in Germany (Feldmann-Wojtachnia *et al.*, 2010).

However, looking beyond involvement in formal political engagement, a different picture of involvement can be seen: young people tend to choose new patterns of political participation. These political activities are considered to be new forms of political involvement such as political discussion through the Internet, attending political meeting via social networks and so on. Horvath argues that "the nature of political actions has changed significantly: they have become more individualized, ad-hoc, issue specific and less linked to traditional societal cleavages" (Horvath, 2013). Young people today tend to emphasize on their individual needs while ignoring the collective interests of the whole community. Moreover, the processes of globalization (Bauman, 2001), and guidance of consumption and competition (Kestilä-Kekkonen, 2009) in the reality, make the pattern of young political participation different from their parents' generation.

Moreover, with the penetration of new information and communication technologies, various scholars and politicians view the Internet as a new source of political socialization and a way to bring youthful practitioners closer to the political process. It appears that groups of young people tend to use Internet to express their voice and involve in politics. Emmer, Wolling, and Vowe found young population segments with high affinity for political communication via Internet might develop habitualized online political communication patterns more quickly (Emmer, Wolling, & Vowe, 2012).

3.4.1 Theories of media use and political participation

Here, we use three theories of political communication, including mobilization theory, reinforcement theory and theory of diversity and democratic culture, to consider how media especially the Internet could influence on people's political participation.

Mobilization theory

"Mobilization theory argues that a combination of rising educational levels and easier access to ever larger amounts of political information have helped to mobilize citizens, both cognitively and behaviorally" (Newton, 1999). It can be seen that definition of mobilization theory highlights that media as provider large amount of easily accessible political information, which decrease costs and facilitate political participation in the public lives. As Tang and Iyengar note that, mobilization theory seems to distinguish the network from traditional media in accordance with relatively simple quantity of information disseminated in the media system and the users' information costs, disregarding the possible content change (Tang & Iyengar, 2013, p. 36).

In addition, Norris argued that, mobilization theory assumes that the usage of that Internet will boost new patterns of political activism. And he pointed out the strongest claims of mobilization theories are that Internet activism represents distinctive types of political participation which are dissimilar with traditional political actions like working for political parties, organizing grassroots level of social movements, or persuading elected officials (Norris, 2000). Meanwhile, as many scholars continue to explore individual participation, other researcher begin to turn their eyes on whether Internet as a means for collective action (Margetts, John, Escher, & Reissfelder, 2009; Zheng & Wu, 2005) due to net help people strengthen their social connections and coordinate and organize their behaviors to cope with joint concerns. In China, based on conclusion from scholars, the Internet has been demonstrated the potential to shape social organizations and act as a means for collective action (Yang, 2003; Zheng & Wu, 2005).

However, previous multiple studies on various political and scientific issues have come to the mixed conclusions. Some scholars found there was a positive association between Internet use and political participation, others found a very limited relationship. Gerhards and Schäfer found only minimal evidence to support the idea that the Internet is a better communication space as compared to print media in Germany and USA (Gerhards & Schäfer, 2010). Although the theory is based on the notion that resources: such as time, cost, organizational skills, and certain social or political opportunities which are important elements to the social movements, mobilization theory has been criticized by investigators for empirically invalid because of degrading social characteristics of the Internet users (Lei, 2011). For instance, Klandermans argued that mobilization theorists have almost overlooked social-psychological approaches of social movements (Klandermans, 1984).

Reinforcement theories

In contrast to the theory of mobilization, reinforcement theory argues that increased Internet use will not fundamentally change existing patterns of political communications and political involvement. The main reason was due to the digital divide, or the split between people who access to the web and those who do not (Larson, 2004). Basically, this argument is considered based on two significant aspects. The first aspect is that unequal exists around the world in terms of access to and use of Internet information and communication technologies at different socioeconomic within specific regions (Norris, 2003a). Citizens with high economic and social status have greater access to Internet and become more involved in politics activities. As a result, the poor are becoming groups of political inactive, as the unequal strengthened by the Internet (Norris, 1999). And the second aspect is the theory generally states politics online activities will only attract people already developed opinions, interested and took participate in offline political actions.

In addition, reinforcement theory as one of the oldest theories of motivation (Redmond, 2013), which has aroused the interest of some scholars to further explore the importance of motivation in determining the people's usage of the Internet for political purpose. The Internet would provide an alternative platform for the politically motivated, active and engaged citizens to do what they have always done (Hill & Hughes, 1999). Grönlund pointed out that the most motivated citizens are also most likely to use the political opportunities of the Internet (Grönlund, 2007). This is may can be used to explain why the Internet affect participatory behavior among the young citizens. Carpini found out the Internet provide new channels for tapping existing interest in particular issues and using this interest to motivate and boost action (Carpini, 2000). However, the theory of mobilization and reinforcement appear the essential distinction in stressing out the Internet in shaping citizens' political activity online. The reinforcement theory, by contrast, deems the Internet more as a new way for the politically motivated, active and engaged citizens to involve in familiar political activities.

Theories of Diversity and Democratic Culture

The diversity and democratic culture theory proposes that the Internet enables the production and dissemination of information that is much less likely to emerge and circulate without the Internet. In advanced capitalist democracies, the rise of the Internet could raise the difficulty for market players or power elites to dominate public spheres (Lei, 2011). This means that ordinary citizens are able to express their diverse voice and opinion without afraid of prohibited by gatekeepers.

In terms of the cultural dimension, Balkin argues that, democracy culture is a culture in which individuals have an equal chance to express themselves and it concerns each person' ability to take part in the production and distribution of the culture (Balkin, 2004). According to Taubman, the possibility of introducing more diversity to political communication in authoritarian countries could have huge democratic impacts as the Internet could create conditions of ideational pluralism and lead to a loss of hegemony in authoritarian states (Taubman, 1998). Recently, "the Internet is an inherently emancipatory tool, a device that necessarily and inevitably promote democracy that by giving voice to who lack political power, and in so doing undermine authoritarian and repressive government" (Warf, 2013). Jay also agreed with Warf's opinion that the Internet could weaken the capacity of authoritarian regimes to monopolize sources of public information (Jay, 2013).

All in all, the view of culture dimension as a ground-breaking analytical tool, such a 'cultural turn' in media engagement and participation analysis might be the most attractive angle of view to interpret the ongoing changes and to shed light on the meaning, behaviors, communication and identities (Dahlgren, 2006). This study that applies theories of diversity and democratic culture, offsets the deficiency of mobilization theories and reinforcement theories. Such as mobilization theory mainly center on quantity of political information renders it ill equipped to thoroughly analysis how evolution of the media system may facilitate political change especially in authoritarian countries (Lei, 2011).

3.4.2 Mass media and youth political involvement

Issues related to the relationship between various forms of youth political involvement and media use have been at the center of political communication research field for decades. Political information and political content in a range of mass media from newspaper, television, radio, Internet to other mass media, are delivered to young people by journalists, pollsters, and political consultants. Those political content provided by the mass media play very important role in facilitating young citizens' political knowledge, political engagement, and political awareness (Norris, 2003b). As Cantijoch notes, being informed about politics is highly correlated with political attitudes and participation, young citizens use the media to access the political issues concerning them and gain political knowledge, which in turn allows them to feel more motivated to engage in political activities (Cantijoch, 2008).

The news media always pays attention to hot political topic, thus attract eyeballs and shape the young people's political opinions about them. Besides, young people also can actively take part in politics through different kinds of mass media. Moreover, mass media act another critical role of making ordinary citizens know what other individuals think and letting political leaders gain a large numbers of audiences (Duignan, 2013, p. 82). Thus, the media expanded political influence among young people and make public opinion cover a large numbers of individuals across different regions.

Previous research has consistently shown various types of public affairs media exposure, such as reading newspapers, listening to news on radio, and watching news on TV is positively related to young people's political knowledge and political participation (De Vreese & Boomgaarden, 2006; Shah, 1998). Hoffman and Thomson even demonstrated that watching late night television and local television news have a positive and important effect on high school student's political participation (Hoffman & Thomson, 2009). Given the differences in information presentation and in the impact on people's information processing, there is a higher positive link between a variety of Internet use and different forms of political participation than the relationship between most uses of traditional media and participation (Bakker & de Vreese, 2011). The latest studies have found that social media news about political candidates had more of an impact on affect potential voters' views by contrast with traditional political news (Robertson, Semaan, Douglas, & Maruyama, 2013).

Although mass media remain an indispensable vehicle for political expression and political engagement of individuals, in some areas of where media are strictly controlled, word of mouth such as Twitter and text messaging, thus become the channels for underground public opinion (Duignan, 2013, p. 83). China is a good example, due to the mass media in mainland China are administered and controlled by government agencies and the authorities imposes restrictions on press freedom. The central government exercises strict control on the reporting content relative with disasters, accidents and calamities; especially for "extra-territorial" news reporting and monitoring are not allowed for these types of topics (Shan, 2013). Although the traditional media in China society is still the major sources of information for ordinary citizens, more and more young people tend to vent their feelings and obtain their news online with the popularity and convenient characteristic of Internet (Shan, 2013).

3.4.3 The effect of Internet on youth political participation

Recently, studies have repeatedly shown that teens and young adults are more likely to be active and communicative on the Internet, compared to older generations. Because youth have grown up with the Internet, from their communication with friends to raise their voice on the Internet, from play games to finding a partner, Internet is increasingly becoming the taken-for-granted platform where their daily lives are increasingly embedded. Geck labeled next generation who were born and saturated in digital environment coincide with the introduction of the graphical web in the 1990s "Generation Z" (Geck, 2007, p. 235). It seems that, with the wide application of Internet, Internet has become an indispensable part of present college students' social life today.

As Bakker and de Vreese noted, the Internet is a natural channel for alternative and digital forms of political involvement for young people (Bakker & de Vreese, 2011). In the network information age, the low cost of media outlets like Facebook, the instant political information access as well as the low-cost forms of involvement Internet provide to young citizens are the main reasons more young people have been especially keen to take part in politics. It can be witness by the following relevant data. For example, there are a total number of 591 million China web users by the end of 2012, the Internet penetration in China is around 42.1%, whereas this was 54% for the age group of 10 to 30 and only 6.2% is older than 50 years (Zhu, 2013). In Germany, younger people also belong to the group of heaviest Internet users. In the mid-year 2012 the overall percentage of Internet users' percentage of population Online is 83.0% according to Internet World Stats (Internet World Stats, 2013).

Recently, the topic of young people's online political participation has drawn a great deal of attentions from various scholars when they exam the role of Internet as a potential arena for civic and political participation. Young people use the Internet intensively, but not everyone uses it in the same way: some use it as a source of information or for seeking entertainment, whereas for others, the Internet has a more social function. The most frequent online activities of Chinese Internet users are still to read news and to access entertainment (Guo, 2007). By contrast, the Internet functions mainly as an 'information expressway' in western countries (Guo, 2007). In addition, prior work within political communication research divide political Internet use into active usage and positive usage based on the lines of specific active and passive forms of political Internet usage. Active Internet usage refers to create or contribute to online content such as writing comments on blogs or engaging in online conversation via social networks. Passive Internet usage is defined as consuming online content, for example, reading online comments or watching online videos (Muntinga, Moorman, & Smit, 2011). The current literature shows that active forms of Internet usage appear to have a bigger impact on political outcome variables than passive forms of Internet political usage. For example, a recent results obtained from a panel study demonstrates a positive relation between two particular forms of political use and voter turnout of election (Kruikemeier, van Noort, Vliegenthart, & de Vreese, 2013).

In terms of civic and political engagement with Internet, research has also focused on the decline of traditional political participation among the young people in the West continues, and this decrease has been accompanied by a pronounced increase in activities which differ from traditional ones. Due to that young people are the most avid information and communication technologies users and the most susceptible to the influence of various socialization experiences (Quintelier & Vissers, 2008), they tend to involve in politics via new media and express their political opinion. Bringing in recent survey in relation to youth people and online political participation, many scholars enthuse about Internet is having an immensely positive impact on young people from personal development such as knowledge gains (De Vreese & Boomgaarden, 2006) to the character of civilization such as promote participation, even monitor politicians and government officials (Zhang & Chan, 2013). In China, "Weibo anti-corruption" is arguably one of the important grass root campaigns in China, where young Internet users expectedly highly involved, in driving public sector more transparent (K.-w. Fu, 2013). Although the force fields of optimism are often visible in discussions and research about it, the conclusion of the effect of Internet on youth political involvement is still mixed. For example, Calenda and Meijer found the Internet reinvigorates political participation field but does not trigger young people away from 'old' to 'new' politics (Calenda & Meijer, 2009).

With the diffusion and development of social network sites (SNS) such as Facebook, blog and MySpace, more empirical researches pay attention to whether social media can boost political participation online among young groups. In the Germany context, a recent survey found that the very popular among young people were social online services and pages with user-generated content. Students ranked social media such as YouTube, schülerVZ and Wikipedia highest in this respect (Feldmann-Wojtachnia, *et al.*, 2010). In China, the speed with which information is diffused in the social media sphere has helped young users to deliver their discontent with problems who encountered in their real lives, especially for the negative consequences of economic growth, income inequalities and corruption and mismanagement by government officials corruption (Sullivan, 2013). Today, more researchers have found that the use of Internet is related positively to both online and offline political engagement (Zúñiga, Puig-I-Abril, & Rojas, 2009; Quintelier & Vissers, 2008).

In the end, online media, of course, are as a core component of the larger social and cultural world, intertwined with the offline lives of young people as well as with the functioning of different groups, organizations, and institutions (Dahlgren, 2011). Thus, Internet use and engagement of young citizens with embracing the opportunities new web technologies should be understood base on the given social and cultural background. Especially for China, which is essentially a collectivistic nation, thus social communities and opinions expression of individual seem to be very important for young people. Social media transforms these communities to a new digital level and enables young people to handle their 'Guanxi' (relationships/connections between people) much more effectively (Snobmonkey, 2013). When the legal or established ways of political expression is constrained, people seek alternative ways or use social media and personal relationships to contact political actors, either to express their opinions in a safe way or to bypass Chinese government repression (Shyu, 2009; Zhang & Lin, 2014).

3.5 Unexplored area of comparative research on political participation

With the diffusion and integration of digital media in social and political life, new forms of political organization and new opportunities for political participation are created (Castells, 2009). In addition, the rapid development of global communication systems and processes have become beyond the scope of the region and the borders. Moreover, online political behavior shows ripe for comparative research (Anduiza, *et al.*, 2012, p. 86). However, most of the comparative political communication research centered on established democracies such as the United States and Western European countries. By contrast, the comparison between Western democracies and transition countries still belongs to those unexplored fields of cross-country research which deserves attention (Pfetsch & Esser, 2004). Therefore, there is an urgent need for the pioneering research with the important innovative significance to fill this gap.

While political communication research in Western countries has entered its mature stage, in China study on political communication is behind the starting line, and far away from a systematic and comprehensive study on this field due to its late initiation. Communication was born after the Second World War, but it was not until the early 1980s was introduced into mainland China (Chu, 1988). After that, the pro-democracy movements of 1989 in China impelled scholars focused on political and traditional culture. Beginning early in the twentieth century, Western academics focused on the effect of electoral institution on political behavior in the field of political communication research (Asher, *et al.*, 1984, p. 26). At this point, comparative political participation research has appeared with a more general sociological interest in comparing political performances in different social contexts. For example, Gosnell's "Why Europe Votes", as the first study to compare political participation behavior in the field of political communication with his fellow researchers across different European countries (Gosnell, 1930).

By contrast, the Chinese field of political communication studies is still less advanced than in Germany. Since the first political communication studies appeared in the early 1980s in China, the earlier research political communication studies focused on descriptions of the interactions between the mass media and the state, not only that, the number of researches in media effects and public opinion increased slowly that in the past ten years (Kaid, 2004, p. 479). The explanation for the small number of political communication studies originating in China lies in three reasons. Firstly, the Chinese political context which makes it difficult to apply theories of political communication developed in Western democracies. Secondly, many research results of political communication are not published in English and are confined to release in local area, which often makes China's communication studies is not recognized by scholars of other countries. Thirdly, due to limitation of freedom to conduct political communication studies in China, there is lack of sufficient financial and institutional resources support for political communication research (Kaid, 2004, p. 480).

Beginning from the early 1980s Chinese scholars increasingly focused on examining political communication. Chinese studies on political communication can be characterized by four distinct features. Firstly, the present researches in this field are limited on a narrow range and have many defects. For a long time the media is deem as apolitical tool in Communist China, then it renders specialized academic area of political communication research of much less significance and most public communication shows signs of political propaganda. It's also worth pointing out that scholars in China always use politically correct jargon, vague tongue vague euphemism, and Marxist terminology to cover up the true meaning of their researches out of worry their own security interests (Willnat & Aw, 2009, p. 4).

Secondly, existing researches on political participation in China just rest on concepts and qualitative analysis, theories and methods of quantitative researches are few. It can be seen from articles and research materials on political communication researches in China that a majority of them are only qualitative analysis and center on the conduct descriptive (Hu, 2012; Li, 2012). For example, Xie investigated old Chinese people's participation in voluntary associations, communities, and politics, based on qualitative analysis of interviewing members of a senior-oriented computer training organization in Shanghai. He found that the Internet can boost the civic engagement of these Chinese seniors (Xie, 2008). At present, there exist some reasons why the domestic scholars in the study of political participation in China are lack of in-depth empirical methods analysis. According to He, the political environment in mainland China, the Chinese way of examining political communication, the lack of suitable theories, and a general short of empirical research have severely impeded the development of political communication studies in China (He, 2009).

Thirdly, with the reform and opening and economic development, political communication study in China has undergone major changes from studying and rethinking of propaganda to focusing on the influence of the economic development in politics. Political communication takes mostly the form of propaganda due to the lingering Communist framework still controls the public discourse universe in early stage (He, 2009). China's economic developing and social progressing make more and more available studies focus predominantly on the relationship of economic development and political democracy, the impacts of economic development on social structure, people's political attitudes and political behaviors by comparing China with other Asian countries. For instance, McCormick compared and assed the political aspects of Chinese and Vietnamese states, he argued that economic reform has profoundly changed both societies such that their traditional Leninist institution are increasingly lose effective tools for building popular legitimacy or managing society (McCormick, 1998).

Fourthly, the popularity of information and communication technology which is represented by Internet has promoted the development of political communication research, especially the emergence of international comparative study covers the void of domestic research in China. For example, Xie and Jaeger compared the social impact of the Internet on political participation among older Internet users in America and

China, and found that older adults are not only lagging behind in terms of physical access to the Internet but also in engaging in political participation on the network (Xie & Jaeger, 2008). Fan examined the linkages between regulatory regimes, market environments and Internet access in both China and Australia (Fan, 2005).

In contrast, political communication has been researched a great deal in Germany and scholars have already published many books and articles on the subject. In the West, the research into comparative political communication has been more than 80 years, and has formed more systemic theories and more mature scales. As noted that "European political communication research has always been nationally orientated and produced single-country studies" (Holtz-Bacha, 2004, p. 469). From coming into being, the political communication research has brought very deep influence especially on the empirical studies of political campaign, voting behaviors and political participation across different regions. Jay Blumler as one of the founding fathers of political communication research in Europe, has been a long-term advocate of broadening the perspective across countries and also among the first to undertake international comparisons in this field. In 1978, his investigated audience expectations of election campaign information in Belgium, Britain and France in this study as a point of departure for the comparative analysis of different political communication systems (Blumler, Ewbank, Cayrol, Geerts, & Thoveron, 1978).

By the end of the 1980s, for Europe, this means that the perspective for political communication has indeed broadened; in many cases, however, it is the comparison between European country and the United States, not between European countries. Different approaches have been taken to cross-country research. For example, Farrell & Wortmann used of a political marketing framework to compared modern party election campaigns in German, British and Irish. They found that that the CDU were the only party to have communications policies which closely matched their product policy and that distribution activities appear to be where future campaign developments are likely to concentrate (Farrell & Wortmann, 1987).

A number of different aspects in the field of political communication have been taken to cross-country research. Some scholars focused on political institution, political mobilization activities by parties or elites and social groups among major European countries. Examples of this studies that include Lewis-Beck examined economic voting in several Western European countries (Lewis-Beck, 1986), Dalton investigated political parties and political representation party supporters and party elites in nine Western European Nations (Dalton, 1985). Helms analyzed and compared the most significant features of constitutional provisions relating to the chancellor and the prime minister in Germany and Britain since 1945/49 (Helms, 1996). Among those researches, the very party advertising in Germany was subject to a number of analyses in a comparative perspective (Cwalina, Falkowski, & Kaid, 2000; Holtz-Bacha, Kaid, & Johnston, 1994; Kaid, 1999).

Simultaneously, the role of mass media and their relation to people's political participation in different countries has attracted a great deal of scholarly attention. For instance, Semetko compared news on television during recent national election campaigns in the United States, Britain, and Germany with focusing on television news professionals at election time. Through content analysis, observation as well as interviews, he found that that television news professional is different in each country based on data during the recent election campaign (Semetko, 1996). In addition, still some scholars centered on the psychology of political participation and political culture. For example Hayes and Bean used comparable survey data from the United States, West Germany, Great Britain and Australia to clarify the dimensions of political efficacy and their relationship to socio-demographic factors (Hayes & Bean, 1993).

Moreover, the Internet technological developments of recent years have influenced political communication patterns in profound ways. By now, the field of online political participation study has inevitable become one kind of new research tendency. For example, Cinalli and Füglister focused on networks that are built in the field of unemployment in three European states: Britain, Germany, and Switzerland. He found that network variation is matched against cross-national differences of collective action (Cinalli & Füglister, 2008). Lusoli examined European citizens' use of the Internet for electoral information regarding the 2004 European voting turnout in 25 countries (Lusoli, 2005).

In general, studies on political participation in Germany bear its own characteristics that make them differ from literature studies in China. Firstly, research scope is not only confined to Europe political election, the Americas and other countries are also involved. Meanwhile, the result of study is diverse, and the content is abundant. Secondly, the multidisciplinary nature of intercultural political communication entails multidisciplinary approaches to intercultural communication studies. The research methods of quantitative content analysis, surveys, and experimental analysis are widely used among research on political participation study in Germany. Thirdly, the origin and development of comparative political communication as a special area of media studies came much earlier in Germany due to its political background. Fourthly, the impact of new technologies especially Internet on political communication now is a dominant topic in Germany. Germany scientists have been publishing more research findings about online political participation than Chinese researches. However, as Holtz-Bacha wrote that "theoretical diversity and different academic and research cultures are the main obstacles for comparative research, particularly when countries or researchers from outside Europe are involved" (Holtz-Bacha, 2004). At the moment, in view of some differences in the political tradition and the economic or cultural background as well as language barriers between Germany and China, there is no comparative political communication research about these two countries.

Chapter 4 The role of social media in political participation area

In recently years, researches from Germany and China over the past years have shown an increasingly positive relationship between social media use and levels of political engagement (Cheng, Liang, & Leung, 2014; Tumasjan, Sprenger, Sandner, & Welpe, 2010). Although the effect may be little at times (Zhang, *et al.*, 2010), it is rarely contested that social media has played an important role in connecting citizens to civil society. However, the mechanisms by how social media use makes political participation more probable among groups of young people is somewhat elusive. This question is particularly important in consideration of some recent studies in Chinese society, where mixed results in citizen-led revolutions online have provoked different opinions about social media use for democratic politics (Zhang & Lin, 2014; Chan, Wu, Hao, Xi, & Jin, 2012). To better understand the role of social media in connecting individuals to political participation, the contributors of this study are probing into related aspects of this relationship with research model and measurement methods for political participation in two different political contexts.

Firstly, the chapter investigates how different patterns of social media affecting political involvement among citizens with analyzing three specific social media: Facebook (Renren), Blog and Twitter (Weibo) in associating with political participation and citizens. In addition, the section proposes a research model to generalize several contextual factors such as political system, media system and political culture in conditioning the relationship between social media use and political engagement. Secondly, the part explores how social media brings about changes in the field of political participation. Thirdly, the study gives a conclusion and puts forward its hypothesis.

4.1 Social media as a new tool for political participation

Unlike traditional media, using Facebook or other social media does not refer merely to exposure to content, it also refers to the active participation of networks, the establishment of personal profiles, consumption or production of shared information, and giving some comments on or simply 'liking' other people's postings. Therefore, online political activities represent different forms of political communication in other way. In addition, each type of web-based communication has a different primary goal. Given these distinctions, it seems to consider that dissimilar forms of online political communication may have different political potential for influencing citizens' political participation.

4.1.1 Facebook and political participation

Since its founding in 2006, Facebook has sprung up from being a university network service to being one of the world's most popular online social networks in recent years with over 727 million daily active users on average (Noyes, 2013). The popularity of

Facebook enables users to interact with each others by sharing political information and discussing political opinions via personal profiles especially among younger generations and college students. Likewise, it offers a highly visible channel for political parties and organizations to advertise themselves, express their political standing, and keep in touch with citizens through some online applications.

As Yousif and Alsamydai noted that "from a resource perspective, these affordances also offer affordable opportunities to develop civic engagement skills with little to no additional time costs for users of Facebook, while simultaneously having access to a potentially large enough 'public' to develop civic skills" (Yousif & Alsamydai, 2012). The advantage of political information delivery makes Facebook seem to be well suited for enhancing political participation, improving political knowledge, as well as increasing political interest. Over the past few years, prior studies have demonstrated the intensity Facebook use was associated with increased involvement in civic and political life among citizens (Feezell, Conroy, & Guerrero, 2009; Valenzuela, et al., 2009).

Recently, scholars have started to examine the use of Facebook from comparative perspectives. Some of these studies focus on how users in different political systems used social networking sites differently. For example, although Facebook achieved great success around the world, in China, it was over taken by the local website Renren which adapts to Chinese cultures and political regulations. Li found there are some differences between Facebook and Renren network: firstly, Facebook users diversify the sources in contrast with Renren users have a single source (Li, 2011). Secondly, Facebook has more widely audience than Renren (focusing on 18-34 years old users). Thirdly, Facebook users are similar to men-to-women ratio, but Renren users are mostly women (Li, 2011). Based on this study, Chen et al. investigated Facebook usage in the Germany and Renren in China. Their analysis reveals that the Chinese users have more virtual friends than German while German users connect with friends more often in real life (Chen et al., 2013).

However, the relevance of Facebook and Renren for political participation in both Germany and China is unclear. Part of the reason is that most politicians are might refuse to use social networks in their political lives (Stieglitz, et al., 2012). For example, researches have shown that a majority of German politicians do not endorsed political communication over the social network (Christmann, Melcher, Hagenhoff, Gissendanner, & Krumbein, 2010). For Chinese users, due to political regulations and self-surveillance, their Renren use is only enjoying the apolitical does not challenge the Chinese state.

4.1.2 Blog and political participation

Now the surge of attention to the blogosphere has made some researchers are enthusiastic about the political potential of Internet in terms of its increasing opportunities for political discussion and political involvement. Their ability to facilitate active interaction, help mobilize political opinions, and set the agenda for political elites, while offering citizens effective channel to involve in politics (Woodly,

2008), all of those make political blogs become an interesting research subject. In addition, the unique structural characteristics of blogs may have various benefits to both citizen consumers and elite users that are distinct from traditional news media (Woodly, 2008).

Since the middle of the 2000s, blogs in China have expanded from the elite to the mass. There are different patterns of blogs, for example, personal blogs written by citizens, group blogs for organizational purpose, or official blogs serves for the government. Due to its widespread use, personal blogs are known to dominate the Chinese political blogosphere. However, the key blog's political value in China is not to be discovered in politician presentations, but in the online political discussions on recent political events and public issues among millions of bloggers (Zhou, 2009). The phenomenon of officials being involved in blogging is just emerging in Chinese society, until 2006 during the two sessions in China, many government officials began to set up their own blogs.

In Germany, political blogs have been paid attentions to blog content and users' motivations by scholars. For example, by providing insight into the qualitative textual analysis, Greuling and Kilian discovered that the social interaction with other bloggers is the main motive for blog users in German blog sphere together with the desire for the further exchange and discussion about political information, and the expression opinions in terms of this topic (Greuling & Kilian, 2013). Meanwhile, blogs appear to offer a more personal image of candidates and increase the interactive capabilities of a political campaign during the 2005 campaign. Presently there are lots of independent German political blogs, office holder blogs, and sites for German political parties. Although compared with China, blogs in Germany are starting to be involved in political campaigns with encouraging users with seemingly unfiltered information a little earlier. There is still a significant research gap in how and why people are actively participating in political blogs using different methods to be able to derive more implications for political participation (Greuling & Kilian, 2013).

4.1.3 Twitter and political participation

Twitter is a novel microblogging website where users read and write short messages with up to140 character on a variety of topics each day online. In Germany, currently the role of Twitter has been used as a user-generated communication for political deliberation, political participation. Online messages on Twitter validly reflect offline political sentiment is also examined by some studies (Tumasjan, et al., 2010). Thus, Twitter is rather seen as a platform for self-promotion and facilitating direct political communication between official members and citizens.

However, Twitters are banned from using in China alongside with Facebook, YouTube and other western social networks due to the Great Firewall since mid-2009. But Twitter still can be used by the virtual private network (VPN) software that only a small number of dedicated users to 'scale the wall'. By contrast, the Chinese domestic microblog service (Weibo) had dominated the microblog market, which has the same functions as Twitter and contains more features. Weibo is one of the very few platforms can be used by Chinese citizens to exchange political opinions and discuss about officials and political themes. Among them, Sina Weibo as the mainstream microblog has developed into political platform through unveiling political scandals and mobilizing online political opinion by users (Sullivan, 2012).

Twitter/Weibo has become a free space for tweeting a consciously political decision, attracting a congregation of like-minded activists, bloggers, lawyers and other people critical of the state in both Germany and China. In sum, Twitter's important political potential lies in that it not only as a direct communication channel between politicians and citizens but also as an alternative ways of political communication and mobilization (Kim & Park, 2012). Now, a number of studies have explored the adoption and application of Twitters in some Western contexts. For a more balanced and overall comprehending of the role of different patterns of social media usage in the field political communication in non-western contexts is still need to be considered.

4.1.4 Other social media forms and political participation

Apart from the above-mentioned social media networks, there exist some other patterns such as YouTube, Linked or Flickr, which can be categorized as microblogging or SNS, and they are always characterized by significantly different functionalities based on target users. However, there can be overlap among the different kinds of web services. For example, Facebook has the function of microblogging with their 'status update'. Flickr and YouTube share the same comment characteristics with blogs. Those overlapping of functions of social media might affect the investigation the influence of different forms of social media on the public to some extent.

In addition, with the rapid development of smartphones and high-speed data transmission technologies, major social media services are all mobile device-capable and affect citizens' political attitudes and behaviors. But little attention has been paid to how social network sites affect political participation, even though it seems clear that social networks are engaging people in the democratic process. Moreover, few studies published in the major communication journals has yet touched on the mechanism of social media use within non-western political contexts and its cultural implications for relationships and networks (Zhang & Leung, 2014). Such as the Asian culture, which is deeply rooted in Confucianism, laying stress on long-term relationships, the personal influence, humanism, loyalty, benevolence, order, and harmony (Zhang & Leung, 2014).

Thus, the study provides an approach used in investigating social media political participation from multilevel analysis by situating individual characteristics within a large social and institutional context (Figure 4.1). From the macro level, political system, media system and political culture constitutes the social media use environment, which effect individuals' social media usage differently between China and the West. From the microscopic level, individual's factors including demographic factors and related political factors also influence social media usage according to the discussion in the previous chapters. Here, political factors mainly refer to political efficacy, political knowledge and political trust. As Jensen and Anduiza noted that "even though the architecture of the Internet remains common across contexts, the motivations for use—that is, the attitudinal, socioeconomic factors, and the institutional environments that give rise to different forms of participation—may vary considerably on the basis of contextual features" (Jensen & Anduiza, 2012, p. 86).

In fact, the effect of social media on students' political participation is depended on how they use it. So in the study the varied functions of social media serves have been considered in accounting for media influence on individuals' political participation. Although social media use has been divided into four dimensions: information exchange and instrumental use, relational and social media use, recreational or entertainment use, and social media based political activities (Zhang & Lin, 2014). But not all the four dimensions will result in the improvement of political participation in the previous studies. For example, recreation-oriented use like visiting chat rooms and playing games are consistently and negatively associated with civic engagement (Shah, 2001). In contrast, informational uses of the Internet (i.e., searching for information and sending e-mail) was found to have a positive impact on citizens' civic engagement (Shah, 2001).

Level of investigation	Institutional environments	Socioeconomic factors	Culture and psychological factors
From micro (individual) level	Political variables such as political efficacy, political knowledge and political trust.	Socio demographic factors such as age, gender, income, education background and networks.	Individual's motivation, perceptions and socialization.
From macro (system) level	Political system including electoral system and party system.	Social structure including media system.	Political culture, social capital and trust.

Figure 4.1 Approaches of investigation on political participation in cross-cultural studies (building on Gabriel, Keil, & Kerrouche, 2012)

4.2 Social media platforms change online political communication field

In recent years, social media services deemed to have an impact on the public discourse and public sphere in the society. Not just are the channels of political communication are becoming more diversity, complexity and fragmented, from the deep layer meaning, political power relations among main message providers or creators and receivers or audiences are being reconstructed and rethought (Brants, 1998), but also "the new social network service has caused structural change in the theory of communicative action of Jurgen Habermas called public sphere and this has turned out to be a change in the communicative system and an act of political communication" (Kweon & Kim, 2010). More scholars and experts are gradually coming to realize that the transformative effects of the social networks revolution on online political communication field which brings a huge reform to the society and politics in civil society that may different from its previous media change.

As Riaz notes, "President Obama's election campaign was the beginning of a new era of political communication and it opened new doors for researchers and media scholars to study the effects of new media technologies on society" (Riaz, 2013). Emruli and Baca defined political communication which depends on new information and communication technologies' 'new political communication' (Emruli & Baca, 2011). Under digital media context, online political communication is changing—in part due to the development of computer technology—and these changes produce a series of new concepts and elements in the modern political communication realm. Such as politics 2.0, e-government, e-participation, web 2.0, which are emerging terms in the political communication field and these incessant new concepts, words, medium broad and expand the scope of modern online political communication research domain. New media provides a new vision of a possible interaction between the senders and recipients in the process of communications, supplies people with low-cost channels of accessing huge amounts of information, and furnishes a more human-friendly communicative forms in accordance with the will of politicians and the mass, beyond that, the constant feedback online that makes a continual transmitting of messages among all the users (Ward, 2009, p. 43).

Moreover, web-based social media such as Twitter, Facebook are deemed to promote the political exchange and share of political information, thus having the potential for increasing political communication effectively. While Twitter is an ideal platform for users to spread not only information in general but also political opinions publicly through their networks, political institutions have also begun to use Facebook pages or groups for the purpose of entering into direct dialogs with citizens and encouraging more political discussions. More specifically, the social media has been discussed as a major agent of change for political communication and participation. Two scholars find that new forms of political communication are mainly a complement to existing forms with few substitution effects through panel survey data (Emruli & Baca, 2011). Kweon and Kim attempted to measure the change in modern the political communication process by applying O1-S-O2-R model in the new media age. They found that there is a link between variables on the predisposition of web users to online activity in the online political activities (Kweon & Kim, 2010).

Political communication change can be mainly explained from three aspects including new communication environment, politics changes and power citizens. Media environment as the key elements in the political communication process, as McNair notes, "the effects of political communication of whatever kind are determined not by the content of the message alone, or even primarily, by the historical context of in which they appear, and especially, the political environment prevailing at any given time" (McNair, 2011). The online political communications environment is constantly changing with the development of computer and information technology during the past decades. Meanwhile, the political use of social media is almost changing and influencing the action of politicians, governments and related authorities all over the world. "Not only has Internet become the vital aspect of campaign strategy, but it has revolutionized the way analyst, candidates, and ordinary citizens think about and deal with politics" (Panagopoulos et al., 2009, p. 3). Blog, Facebook, Microblog, Twitter that are all being used in politics today, and social media use in political field is gradually becoming significantly more complicated (McGoveran, 2013).

The introduction of social network webs into political communication domain has been extensively studied by numbers of scholars during the past decades. Normally, those studies have tended to explore how social media might boost new possibilities for politicians, parliaments, candidates and political parties. In the early 20th century, Internet had been used by political party in the U.K. for intraparty democracy and interparty competition (Gibson & Ward, 1998). However, the use of the Internet as an influential political tool in cyber protest and campaign all over the world until 2004 (Donk, 2004), and the 2008 Obama presidential campaign demonstrated that information and communication technologies, in particular burgeoning social media, have become an integral part of online political communication. Recently, a lot of research study digital media use is positively related to political participation in American (Bimber & Copeland, 2013; Hemphill, Otterbacher, & Shapiro, 2013).

For China, although the Chinese state's firm control in the traditional and new media, well development local social webs still release information and mobilize cyber users to act. Yang noted there is a new communication revolution taking place in China, and this is "expanding citizens' unofficial democracy" (Yang, 2009). Some scholars studied the transformation of political communication influences political change (Coutaz; Esarey & Qiang, 2011). Others have probed the political power of social media to liberalize political discourse and advance public supervision of the Chinese Communist Party (Sullivan, 2013; You, 2013; Ziccardi, 2013). Still others explored the transformation of political communication in China, mainly depends on two factors technology and commercialization (Lin, 2008; Tang & Iyengar, 2011). Although scholars have different views on what change has happened, there has been few systematic study to produce representative evidence to address change, and some of parts of political communication has not been well untapped.

For Germany, political communication field presents more extensive and diversified compare with China, with the issue political communication on the social media is a hotly debated issue in the growing and predominantly online community in Germany. It's worth mentioning that there has been much written about political campaigning, use of information and communication technology especially social media in mobilizing and influencing citizens (Lilleker & Vedel, 2013; Saleh, 2005). Some scholars seek to gain insight into the political communication based on social media in Germany by conducting an analysis of social media presence of German political parties, campaigns, politician, as well as a survey of members of the German parliament regarding their social media use (Albrecht & Verboord; Stieglitz, *et al.*, 2012). Others take consideration on social media monitoring in political context as well as research implications in information systems (Zerfaß, Van Ruler, Rogojinaru, Vercic, & Hamrefors, 2007). Yet another school of thought—explores the changing field of political communication with understanding technologies, political, social, and economic transformations in the new media society (Bennett & Iyengar, 2008; R. Koopmans & Zimmermann, 2003; Saleh, 2005).

Despite local social media still be controlled and manipulated by the authoritarian state to some degree, China's social media revolution has radically transformed the relationship between state, societal actors and citizens from the net from the net, from fictitious China's cyberspace to reality. In a rapidly development media area, people have imagined and created new political possibilities through traditional and social media, as well as face-to-face communication. Social media has made it possible for both countries' media communication to undertake a new, albeit some scholars pointed out social webs can be something of a double-edged sword for politician mainly meaning every with his millions of followers, there are thousands of examples of politicians very publicly falling flat on their digital faces.

4.3 Conclusion and hypothesis

With more recently scholarly attention has shifted to the effects of social media, research has often measured political participation by using some questions for political knowledge, trust, or efficacy in politic activities to examine the relationship between social media and political participation. Although they generally confirmed that there are significant positive relationships between the use of social media and political participation and in broad terms (Gaiser, De Rijke, & Spannring, 2010; Zhang & Lin, 2014), the old measurements of political participation might underestimate or misrepresent the scope and degree of participation in politics. In addition, there is only little research investigating how college students navigate between the traditional and social media for political participation. Furthermore, most research in this area has been done in the United States, which makes the generalizability of results unclear.

Against this background, the purpose of this study is to examine the use and effects of different forms of social media on students' political attitudes and behaviors. More specifically, this study investigates (a) the effects of frequency of social media use on political participation, (b) the interplay between social media and traditional media political news use in terms of political participation, (c) the association of political variables including political trust, efficacy and knowledge with political participation, (d) the different levels of political participation between German and Chinese college students.

Thus, this section use the following hypotheses to examine these four aspects of research according to the following research model 4.2, which is concerning college students' social media use activities and their effects on several political variables, as well as political participation. Based on this research model 4.2, this study hypothesizes that both the frequency of accessing social media will be positively associated with political participation. More formally, focusing on questions from chapter1, the author proposes the following other six hypotheses:

RQ1: Why and how do college students engage politically via social media in Germany and China?

Hypothesis 1: The frequency of social media use will correlate positively with their political participation.

Hypothesis 2: Social media use for political news will correlate positively with their political participation.

In order to find out the different level of political participation behind uses of new technologies, particularly Facebook, Blog and Twitter, these social media shall be compared to traditional media concerning association with political participation among college students. Thus, the author proposes RQ2.

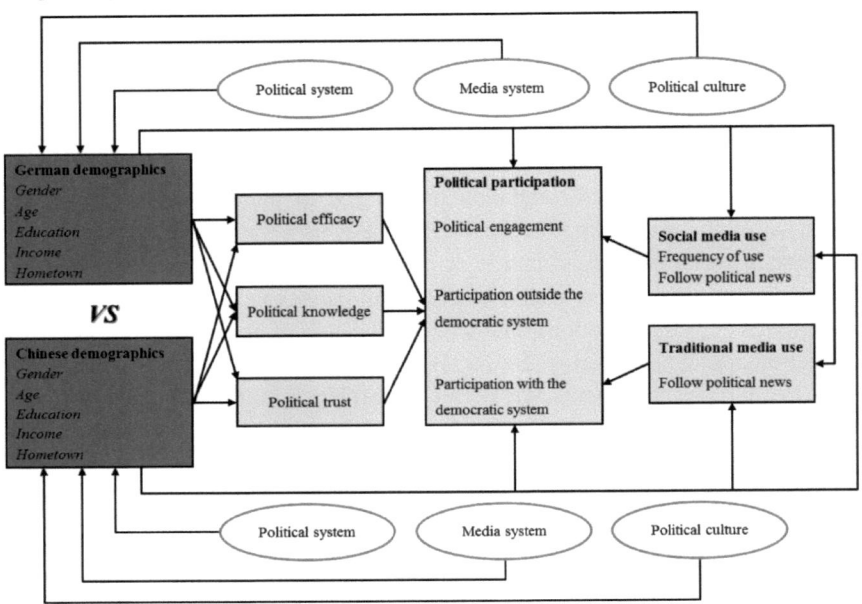

Figure 4.2 The research model

RQ2: To what extent do college students use social media to engage in political participation, comparing to traditional media?

Based on the literature analysis above, the author also proposes the following **Hypotheses 3: Use of social media for political news correlates more strongly with political participation than traditional media.**

Concerning the web's indirect effects in contributing to the development of participation via the enhancement of civic agency, knowledge, practices and identities (Dahlgren & Alvares, 2013); we have RQ3.

RQ3: Are students' political (including political knowledge, political efficacy and political trust) associated with their political participation?

In the above section of 3.2.2 Political factors of political participation, the study has explained and reviewed related literature, thus the study gives hypothesis 4, hypothesis 5 and hypothesis 6.

Hypothesis 4: Students' political knowledge is positively correlated with their political participation.

Hypothesis 5: Students' political efficacy is positively correlated with their political participation.

Hypothesis 6: Students' political trust is positively correlated with their political participation.

Moreover, as the two countries vary significantly in their contextual features (political system, cultural, and media system), this study hypothesized that the different social media environment in different countries would affect political participation. More formally, the question is as follows:

RQ4: How do university students in China and Germany differ engage in politics through social media uses?

To answer RQ4, according to the theories of Diversity and Democracy Culture, the social media may diverse information and communication and diminish the power of the state, in China, one of such transitional societies, while the ruling Communist Party continues its monopoly of the traditional media, the social media have opened up relative freedom space for political expressions among citizens. The political context for political participation in China is different from that of well-established democracies. Because China is a one-party system, the political system and promote has infiltrated the lives of college students. Meanwhile, political system as a determinant affect the different degrees of political participation in different countries has been demonstrated (Zhang, 2012).

In addition, Chinese citizens have fairly limited official channels to engage in politics (Economist Intelligence Unit, 2012). Firstly, although citizens have the right to vote local candidates, the channels for political participation are still limited, due to the nomination of the candidates are manipulated by the central government. Secondly, Chinese citizens suffer low information availability because of the Chinese government's tight control of traditional media and restrictions on access to information originated from new media (Zhang & Lin, 2014). Under such a circumstance, Chinese people may be more willing to use their local social networks to express political voices and engage in politics in a safe way or to bypass government repression. Thus, this emerges another two hypothesis:

Hypothesis 7: There are significant differences between German university students' and Chinese in the level of political participation.

Hypothesis 8: Chinese students' political participation is more closely related to social media use than German students' participation.

Moreover, whether men are more likely to participate in politics than women in both countries are also be examined. Gender differences in political participation are found throughout the literature on gender and political behavior. Women continue to lag behind men in many forms of participation in Western democracies (Beauregard, 2014; Gidengil, 2004). As a transitional democracy state, China is still a heavily patriarchal society, which results in gender imbalance in the political field. There has been a continuing low degree of women's political participation compared with men (Zeng,

2014). Therefore, here require a question and a hypothesis about women's participation in politics.

RQ5: Whether men are more likely to participate in politics than women in China and Germany?

Hypothesis 9: Men are more likely to participate in politics than women.

In the end, in order to clearly show all the research questions and hypotheses, the Figure 4.3 below, compiled by the author, gives a cursory visual guide to the general picture of research-related issues in the dissertation.

Research questions	Research hypotheses
RQ1: Why and how do college students engage politically via social media in Germany and China?	H1: The frequency of social media use will correlate positively with political participation.
	H2: Social media use for political news will correlate positively with their political participation.
RQ2: To what extent do college students use social media to engage in political participation, comparing to traditional media?	H3: Use of social media for political news correlates more strongly with political participation than traditional media.
RQ3: Are student's political (including political knowledge, political efficacy and political trust) associated with their political participation?	H4: Students' political knowledge is positively correlated with their political participation.
	H5: Students' political efficacy is positively correlated with their political participation.
	H6: Students' political trust is positively correlated with their political participation.
RQ4: How do university students in China and Germany differ engage in politics through social media uses?	H7: There are significant differences between German university student's and Chinese in the level of political participation.
	H8: Chinese student's political participation is more closely related to social media use than German student's participation.
RQ5: Whether men are more likely to participate in politics than women in China and Germany?	H9: Men are more likely to participate in politics than women.

Figure 4.3 Research questions and hypotheses

Chapter 5 Methodology

This chapter explains the methodology of the research and design used for this study. The following information relating to the sampling procedures, data gathering, data analysis, and measuring dependent and independent variables, determining reliability and validity of the instruments will be covered.

5.1 Selection of participants

As Leung *et al.* suggested that in order to ensure the validity of comparative study, the selected samples from different cultural groups must be have the same background characteristics, or else, it is difficult to indicate whether the distinctions observed are because of cultural differences or sample specific differences (Leung & Van de Vijver, 1996). To obtain similar sample data in the study involved two countries Germany and China, the sampling strategy was to select college students from the populations at TU Dresden (TUD) in Germany and Zhengzhou University (ZZU) in China. Three hundred college students from these two large public universities were drawn respectively due to that they have similar in academic fields and education backgrounds.

TU Dresden (N=300)			Zhengzhou University (N=300)		
Items of faculty	Sample number	Percentage	Items of faculty	Sample number	Percentage
Mechanical Engineering	52	17.3	Mechanical Engineering	30	10.1
Science	36	11.8	Science	50	16.7
Education	26	8.8	Education	3	0.9
Business and Economics	23	7.6	Business and Economics	42	13.9
Electrical and Computer Engineering	23	7.5	Electrical and Computer Engineering	10	3.5
Medicine	22	7.4	Medicine	45	14.9
Arts, Humanities and Social Science	22	7.3	Arts, Humanities and Social Science	26	8.6
Environmental Sciences	21	7.2	Environmental Sciences	12	3.8
Linguistics, Literature and Cultural Studies	15	5	Linguistics, Literature and Cultural Studies	13	4.4
Civil Engineering	14	4.8	Civil Engineering	9	3.1
Computer Science	14	4.6	Computer Science	27	8.9
Transportation and Traffic Sciences	14	4.6	Management Science and Engineering	20	6.8
Architecture	9	3.2	Architecture	3	1
Law	9	2.9	Law	10	3.4

Table 5.1 Student's sample in Germany and China

The survey was administered in China and Germany, and questionnaire was developed in English, German, and Chinese. In addition, in order to guarantee the accuracy and more specific of questionnaire, the questionnaire obtained some useful and helpful suggestions from professors and colleagues in the area of political communication. The author collect the data used in this study from sample of young people or university student's distributed among different faculties with accordance to the number of students in each faculty, so to be able to extrapolate and generalize the results of this study on a larger group (see Table 5.1).

In so doing, the study avoids studying a whole population or every single individual. Additionally, colleges and universities are places where the impacts of changing values and attitudes are first experienced. Moreover, for social media research, in both countries represent a large percentage of the population college students form a large proportion of users on social media networks. Social media sites have created new and non-personal platforms for students to connect with others and young adults have taken advantage of this technological trend. Compare with other age group, young people are more familiar with new-media skills, the Internet, and social media (Facebook, YouTube, Twitter, etc.). Thus, it was expected that the research could achieve better explorations of the impacts of social media on using the data from the college samples.

5.2 Data collection procedures

The data collection in Zhengzhou University was conducted from November 12-31, 2014. The research administrates the data collection processes in China. Meanwhile, several students volunteered to help with the data collection. Questionnaires were distributed in students' classroom in different faculties. Students who took the questionnaires were told to return them in 30 minutes later. Neither extra credits nor monetary incentives were provided to the Chinese respondents. They filled out the questionnaires voluntarily. The returned questionnaires were shipped back to Dresden from Zhengzhou by express courier on the first week of December, 2014.

Preliminary data examination found that responses from 35 Chinese participants were unclear or ambiguous, and those questionnaires were not qualified to remain in the data set. In total, 300 valid questionnaires comprised the Chinese sample size of the research. German data collection was conducted in the TU Dresden during the weeks of November 7 and 21, 2014. Before distribution of the questionnaires, the students were informed that their participation was completely anonymous and voluntary and that no individual information and individual answers would be released in the results. Then the questionnaires were handed out to all in attendance, and students were told to return them later in the classroom. A total of 300 copies of the questionnaires were distributed in the classroom, and participants returned the questionnaires in class. Excluding those completed questionnaires filled out by international students, the rest were usable questionnaires. After that the sample was selected randomly from different faculties representing different academic fields.

To assure validity of the questionnaire, the study runs a pilot survey to test the questionnaire on a sample of 25 students in each university first. The aim here is to detect any flaws in the questioning, correct these prior to the main survey, and ensure that all the questions are as clear and understandable as possible. To measure the time spent for each student's filling in the questionnaires, which average about 20 to 25 minutes for all samples.

TU Dresden (N = 300)			Zhengzhou University (N = 300)		
	Number	Percent		Number	Percent
Gender	300	100	**Gender**	300	100
Female	149	49.7	Female	147	49
Male	151	50.3	Male	153	51
Age group	300	100	**Age group**	300	100
18-23	164	54.7	18-23	138	46
24-29	120	40	24-29	131	43.7
Above 30	16	5.3	Above 30	31	10.3
Education group	300	100	**Education group**	300	100
Abitur oder Fachabitur	205	68.3	High-school degrees	23	7.7
Bachelor-Abschluss	70	23.3	College or bachelor degree	145	48.3
Master-Abschulss or Diplom-Abschluss or Magister-Abschluss	21	7	Master degree	111	37
Promotion	4	1.3	Doctor's degree	21	7
Personal income	300	100	**Personal income**	300	100
below € 130	40	13.3	below 1000yuan	154	51.3
€ 130 - € 399	57	19	1000 - 3000 yuan	62	20.7
€ 400 - € 799	163	54.3	3001 - 6000 yuan	49	16.3
€ 800 - € 1199	30	10	6001 - 9000 yuan	17	5.7
€ 1200 - € 1499	8	2.7	9001 - 12000 yuan	11	3.7
€ 1500 - € 1899	1	0.3	12001 - 15000 yuan	2	0.7
above € 1900	1	0.3	above 15001 yuan	5	1.7
Hometown	300	100	**Hometown**	300	100
Big city	46	15.3	Big city	75	25
The suburbs or outskirts of a big city	50	16.7	The suburbs or outskirts of a big city	21	7
A town or a small city	145	48.3	A town or a small city	98	32.7
A village or a farm	59	19.7	A village or a farm	106	35.3

Table 5.2 Overview of China sampling and Germany sampling in the survey

Therefore, the study collected information about demographic and other descriptive variables, including gender, age, education, personal income and hometown (see Table 5.2). Of the German sample, 50.3% were males and 49.7% were females. The Mean of age was 1.51 (SD = 0.598, ranging from 18 to above 30 years old). Among the 300 respondents, 68.3% obtained Abitur oder Fachabitur, 23.3% with Bachelor-Abschluss, 7.0% with Master-Abschulss or Diplom-Abschluss or Magister-Abschluss, and 1.3% with Promotion. By contrast, for Chinese sample, 51.0% were males and 49.0% were females. The age of Chinese respondents ranged also from 18 to above 30 years (M= 1.64; SD = 0.661). For the education level, 7.7% were high school graduates, 48.3% were college graduates, 37.0% were master graduates, and 7.0% had doctoral education. In terms of monthly personal income, it is obvious that Germany students (M=2.72, SD=0.969) have higher personal income per month than Chinese students (M=1.98, SD=1.328). Besides, the research also included measures of hometown, in order to assess whether different backgrounds for students would affect their social media use and political behaviors.

5.3 Design of questionnaires

Questionnaire is a research tool consisting of a number of specific questions and other prompts for the sake of obtaining information data from respondents in a survey. The questionnaire employed open and closed ended items and was designed with accordance to the theoretical background, previous studies in this field. In final format the questionnaire consists of 32 questions divided into three main parts: part one covers the subjects of media use; the amount of social media or traditional media use; how access to political information. Part two: it includes some questions to examine the effects of social media usage on political participation through measuring the level of university students' political participation, efficacy, trust, and knowledge. Finally, part three covers socio-demographics questions including gender, age, education, personal income and hometown (see Appendix).

The questionnaire was applied as self-administered or 'self-completion' meaning that all respondents filled in the questionnaire themselves. Meanwhile, the questionnaire for this survey is based on the pre-test. The analysis of the pre-test data enabled the questionnaire to present a considerably reduced and improved version for the main survey. The pre-test analysis yielded a plethora of interesting results, e.g. concerning the structure of the questionnaire, the length and phrasing of questions, the different scales, the relevance of questions, the comparability across countries and so on. The pre-test questionnaire was eventually reduced to an average duration of 25 minutes across translations (to account for the different languages that cause different durations). This master questionnaire will be applied in two countries (China and Germany).

5.4 Data analytical strategy

In this current work the researcher tries to create several indexes including some questions about political knowledge, political trust and political efficacy in order to measure related political factors. Besides, the study attempts to design a scale about measuring three different dimensions of political participation. The researcher also noted that one commonality in the rich body of several researches on political participation studying political participation, knowledge, and interest by coding the answer in as (0= no participation) and (1= participation), and subsequently sum up or compute the average of the scores. In the study, the measurement of political participation concept and related political variables in the current study took place in three steps:

Firstly, the first step was gathering all the questions concerning three political variables including political knowledge, political efficacy and political trust. Among them, political knowledge (questions 23/24/25, see appendix) in one index after re-coding to be in the same scales between (0= not correct; 1= correct). An index including political efficacy (questions 16/17, see appendix) recoded as new political variables to be in the same scales between (1= strongly disagree; 2=disagree; 3= neither agree nor disagree 4= agree; 5= strongly agree). The third was political trust by gathering all the questions

(questions 22, see appendix) in one index after re-coding to be in the same scales between (1= not at all trust; 2= not very trust; 3= somewhat trust; 4= very trust).

Variables	Questions	
Background	26.27.28.29.30.31.32	
Frequency of social media use	6	
Follow political news on social media	5	
Traditional political news use	2	
Political participation	Political engagement	1.2.3.14.15
	Political participation in the representative democratic system	8.9.12.13.20
	Political participation outside the representative democratic system.	9.13
Political efficacy	16.17	
Political trust	22	
Political knowledge	23.24.25	
The effectiveness of participation	19	
Barriers to participation	11	

Table 5.3 Questions in the dissertation

The second step is to make three index including all questions about three different levels of political participation (questions 1/2/3/8/9/12/13/14/15/20), also after that the study recodes some variables to be in the same measure scales between (0= no or never; 1= yes).

At the end, a single index includes the above three dimensions of political participation indexes into one measure of political participation. According to the theoretical part before, the dimensions of political participation can be obtained from the three different indexes (see Table 5.3).

5.5 Measure of variables

Three main categories of variables were of importance in the present study. First, various dependent variables were employed. Second, traditional media use and social media use were examined as independent variables. Finally, control variables are also be measured.

5.5.1 Independent variables

Political participation as a dependent variable will be measured by testing the following independent political variables: political knowledge, political efficacy, and political trust in addition to generate the relationships between these political variables.

Political efficacy Based on the concept of political efficacy was distinguished between "internal" and "external" efficacy in the previous studies (Kenski & Stroud, 2006). For measuring these two items, the study adapted the subscale for internal and external political efficacy of the Craig and Maggiotto's political efficacy Measure (Craig & Maggiotto, 1982). This reliability and validity of the political efficacy scales (internal and external) developed by Craig and Maggiotto in the current study with Cronbach's Alpha of 0.78.

So five internal political efficacy items (Cronbach's alpha = 0.78) and nine external political efficacy related items (Cronbach's alpha = 0.78) were selected. The internal political efficacy questions are including such as: Sometimes politics and government seem so complicated that a person like me can't really understand what's going on; People like me are generally well qualified to participate in the political activity and decision making of our country. All the participants had to answer how strongly they agreed with them based on a five-point scale (1 = strongly disagree, 5 = strongly agree). For measuring external political efficacy, the study also used Craig and Maggiotto's political efficacy Measure (Craig & Maggiotto, 1982). The external political efficacy questions consist of 9 items and students had to give their answers based on a five-point scale (1 = strongly disagree, 5 = strongly agree). Those questions are: "I don't think public officials care much what people like me think; Generally speaking, those we elect to public office lose touch with the people pretty quickly......."

Political knowledge In order to measure political knowledge, survey participants were asked questions concerning both structure and factual political knowledge. Such as who is the current prime minister/counselor in your country? How many members of parliament/Federal Parliament are there in your country? In addition, students were asked true or false questions involved some national and international public figures, institutional fact and foreign affairs. Correct responses to each item were coded as 1, and incorrect or missing responses were coded as 0 in the study.

Political trust Respondents were asked four questions to measure their political trust, questions involve that how much they have confident in the government, police, central government, political parties, People's Court, People's Congress/the European Parliament and Army. Then these related items were standardized and combined into an additive index.

Political news use for traditional media In order to tap media access and exposure to political information, the respondents were asked the following questions about the general media use: "How often do you follow politics in the news on television, on the radio, in the newspapers?" The answers were coded on a five point scale (everyday, several times a week, once or twice a week, less often, never).

The frequency of social media use In addition, they were asked: In the past week, on average, how much time do you spend on online social network sites? Respondents also answered how long they used their social media account (with a five-point scale ranging from less than 10 minutes, 10–30 minutes, 31–60 minutes, 1–2 hours, 2–3 hours, more than 3 hour).

Social media use for political news By using a 5 points scale as follows: 1=Everyday, 2=Several times a week, 3=Once or twice a week, 4=Less often, 5=Never, the participants were asked "How often do you use social networks for the following activities?" Focusing on social media use, ten items of social media use were proposed such as browse or update your social networking profile, find information about friends and so on. Among those activities, following politics on the news via social media was treated as the index of social media use for political news use.

5.3.2 Dependent variable

Political participation as a dependent variable will be measured by testing the three different dimensions as follows.

1. Political engagement was measured by three questions surrounding interesting in politics, following politics in the media and discussing politics with friends and family. In order to measure political interest, survey participants were asked questions, how interested they are in politics, the respondents' level of interest in politics were measured by four-level variables ranging from (1=not interested at all to 4=very interested; Cronbach's α= .86). In addition, the participants were asked "are you very interested, somewhat interested, not very interested or not at all interested in the following politics (Local politics, National politics, European politics, Asian politics, or International politics)? Moreover, in order to assess political discussion, the survey respondents were asked questions with whom they discuss political matters and the frequency of this discussion such as: "do you always, often, sometimes, rarely or never try to persuade your friends, relatives or fellow workers to share your views?"

2. Participation in the representative democratic system, which was assessed by participation in election and membership in traditional political organization. In terms of voting, participants were asked: "did you vote in the last general elections or village elections in 2013?" and "how often do you participate in the following political activities such as voting?" In order to measure membership in traditional political organization, the questionnaires gave participants a list of organizations and let them choose which organization they are a member as well as whether they participated in an activity arranged by this organization or whether have done voluntary work for this organization?

3. Participation aside from representative democratic structures was measured by three different dimensions: (1) Social movements. All the students were asked by question about during the past 12 months, do you participated in any youth, trade or political organizations? (2) Political communication, action and protest as well as. Respondents were asked if during the past 12 months they had involved in major forms of political activities such as attending political meeting, petitioning, protesting, contacting with political officials, and taking local action for social or political reform and so on. A respondent's score on participation is the number of yes responses he or she gave to the participation item. (3) Political consumerism. Students were asked "Have you bought/boycotted certain products for political, ethical or environment reasons?"

5.3.3 Control variables

Demographic variables were measured as control variables including gender, age education, personal income per month and hometown. In addition, in order to reflect geographic differences for social media use, all these participants were asked "which of the following do you think best describes the area where you come from?"

5.6 Validity and reliability test

The next step is to exam the quality of the questioners, which consist of testing validity and reliability of this quantitative methodology. Among them, validity is a criterion to assess the relationship between theoretical concept and empirical indicator. In the study, the validity of the questioners has been measured according to the suggestions of the experts and scholars from related fields. Based on the opinion and perspective of the reviewers, the author made some adjustments to the questionnaire concerning clear and accurate of language, functionality, structural of design, and add or remove some items, so as to ensure the trustworthiness of data. After the pre-test and reasonable adjustment to the questionnaire, the formal questionnaire for study is formed finally. Reliability in quantitative research refers to that results are repeatable and consistent (Ferketich, 1990). Normally, the most frequently-used form of reliability is test-retest-reliability. This means that the consistency of a measure the same subject after a certain interval. If the first and the second measurement lead to the same results, the corresponding instrument (code-book, questionnaire) is reliable. The degree of reliability varies between 0 (not reliable at all) and 1 (completely reliable). Without reliable measures, any conclusion or interpretation might be misleading or at least dependent on the situation in which the data was collected.

The most common method of assessing the reliability of questionnaires is to use Chronbach's coefficient alpha. Due to measures of internal consistency are a popular set of assessments with Cronbach's alpha being the most favored (Ferketich, 1990), so questionnaire data were input into SPSS, and get a high level of reliability of 0.865. Based on the guidelines proposed by Nunnally, the alpha coefficient of at least .70 to be adequate for an instrument in early stages of development and a coefficient of at least .80 to be adequate for a more developed instrument (Nunnally, 1978). In other words, Cronbach's alpha 0.7 was deemed to be the minimum acceptable reliability value. Therefore, the questionnaire meets all the requirements of stability and was able to be used by this survey.

Chapter 6 Results and analysis

For the purposes of providing answers to the concrete research questions, this chapter presents the results of the empirical analysis on social media use, traditional media use and political participation among young people in Germany and China.

6.1 Comparing uses of different media

6.1.1 General social media use

Considering that social media has exerted relatively large effects on individuals' news consumption, the time is ripe for expanding and elaborating on previous limited research based on student samples from Germany and China. The index of general social media use was created with a single item by asking respondents to state how many minutes do they spend on online social network sites. As shown in the figure 6.1.1, for the Chinese university student, the findings are revealing that more than half of students (64.7%) devote more than half an hour to using social media across a typical day. On average, Chinese young people consume one and half hours to using social media across a typical day (more than 10 hours a week) (M = 3.26, SD = 1.53) (Figure 6.1.1). This chart clearly reveals social media is the important news sources for China students to learn and keep up-to-date with local and global information.

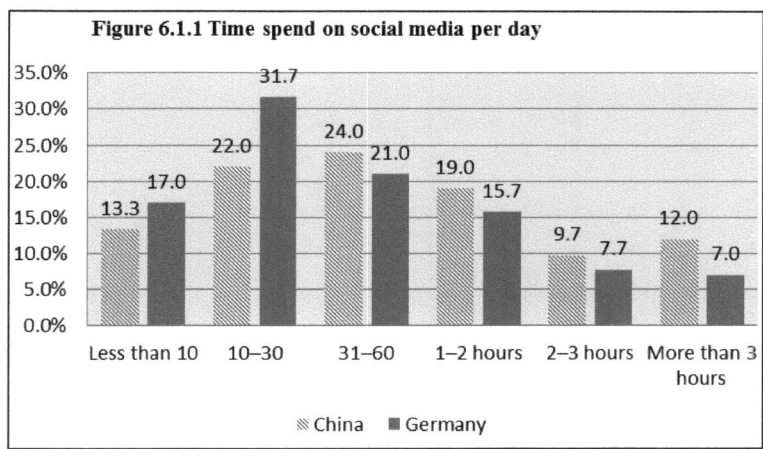

Note: question wording "On the average, how many minutes every day do you spend on online social network sites, such as Facebook/Renren, Blog, and Twitter/Weibo?" Response categories range from 1= Less than 10 minutes to 6= More than 3 hours. (China n=300, Germany n=300).

These results are in contrast with those from German university students who use social media to get information about what happens in their country as well as other countries and regions. Indeed, almost 51.4% of German young adults use social media more than thirty minutes per day. On the average, young Germans spends nearly one hour per day (nearly 7 hours a week) on the social media (M = 2.86, SD = 1.44). Besides, quite unexpectedly, the following figure displays only 12.0% of Chinese and 7.0% of Germans saying that they consume more than three hours on social networking sites.

Overall, Chinese students are slightly more likely to spend more time every day on social media compared with German students. These findings are understandable in light of Internet restrictions on global social networking sites including Twitter, Facebook and YouTube, which make China's local alternatives of these sites such as Renren and Weibo are highly popular with Chinese young netizens.

6.1.2 Traditional or social media use

The study also investigated whether young people prefer social media over traditional media in different aspects. Figure 6.1.2 shows that 86% of Chinese students and 71% German students said that they prefer social media over traditional media due to social media has a strong interaction function. In addition, 81% of Chinese students and 56% of German students stated that they also like using of social media because of its speed in delivering and obtaining news. Besides, entertainment function was also popular with students in China (84%) and Germany (50%). These results indicate that social media for its unique advantages and powerful features, particularly in the areas of exchanging information and providing entertainment are favored by students in both countries.

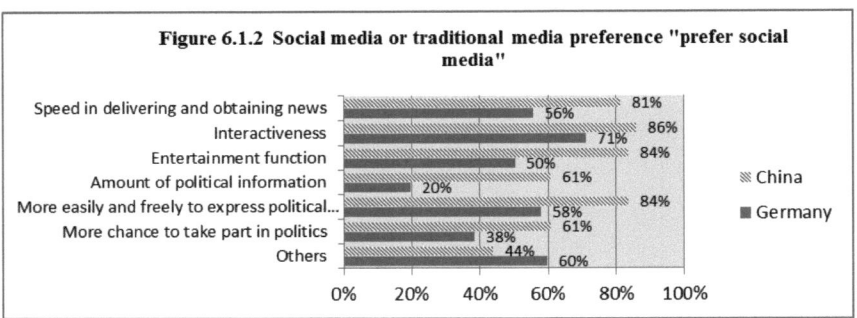

Figure 6.1.2 Social media or traditional media preference "prefer social media"

Note: question wording "In comparison to traditional media, do you prefer social media over traditional media in the following aspects?" Response categories 1= prefer social media, 2= both equally, 3 = prefer traditional media. (China n=300, Germany n=300).

In terms of the political communication field, the study focuses on whether social media has become a political tool as well as the online political discussion platform for university students. Generally, the results reveal that more than 60% of Chinese university students said they were more likely to use social media to get amount of political information, express their political views and join in political participation compared with traditional media platforms. This is in line with previous research that experimentally shows social media provides an important environment for Chinese citizens to exchange their views and develop a greater understanding of politics (Chan, Wu, Hao, Xi, & Jin, 2012).

This result stands in contrast to Germany, where traditional media remain important for German young people. They are more likely to use print publications, television, or radio to access the news. Only 20% of German young people preferred to obtain political information from social media and 38% of German students reported that social media platforms provide them with more chance to engage in politics. On the one hand, a possible reason for these different responses between Germany and Chinese students' is that Chinese citizens suffer low information availability due to the Chinese government's strict control of traditional media for a long time and the restrictions on access to amount of political content from it. On the other hand, these differences can be explained by in countries such as Germany and the USA, freedom of the press and freedom of political opinion are widely guaranteed. Therefore, print and other traditional media communication is relatively open and balanced (Gerhards & Schäfer, 2010).

6.1.3 Interrelations between media use and political information

Moreover, as will be seen below, the author examines the political news consumption among university students. The results suggest that 26.0% of the Chinese university students reported radio is the most important media for them to get recent happened political events. Television was a close second, taking 21.0% of the vote, and then newspaper with 16.7%. These data and conclusions are in contrast with those from German university students, 24.0% of them believe radio to be the most important media for them to get information about what happens in their country and the world, followed by and newspaper 19.0% and Facebook 17.0% (Figure 6.1.3). In general, the proportion of 36.7% Chinese students selected social media as the most important media to go online for news was a little higher than that of German students' 30.7%. Also, the results show that 61.7% of Chinese young people still would likely to use traditional media (consisting of newspaper, television and radio) compared with 61.0% of Germans (Figure 6.1.3).

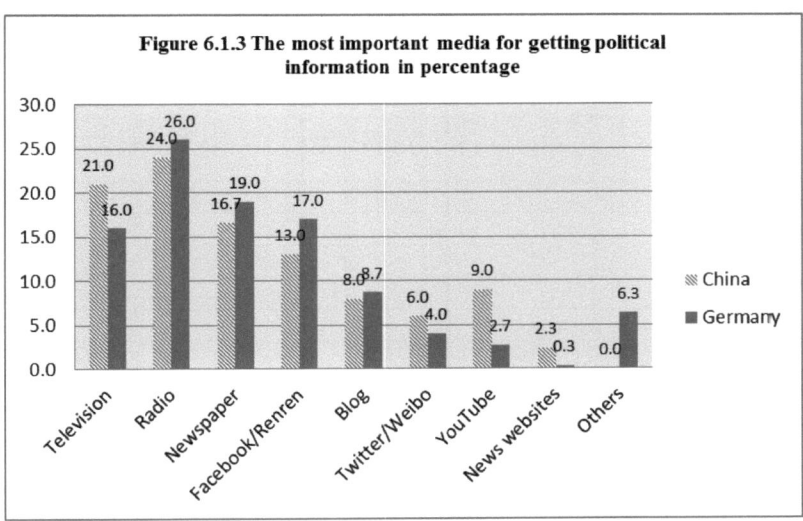

Note: question wording "If you want information about a recent happened political event, how important are the following media to you? Please rank by giving number 1 to the most important, number 2 to the second most important, and so on". (China n=300, Germany n=300).

Moreover, as the table 6.1 shows, in terms of mean rank of all the medium, the top three medium for German students to obtain political news are Facebook (Mean=3.4, SD=2.20), Radio (Mean=3.51, SD=2.49) and Newspaper (Mean=3.55, SD=2.30).

However, for Chinese students, the top three medium for them to get political information are YouTube (Mean=3.61, SD=1.79), Renren (Mean=4.34, SD=2.38) and Radio (Mean=4.44, SD=2.65).

Table 6.1 Descriptive statistics of Mean rank

Items of media	Germany (N=300)		Items of media	China (N=300)	
	Mean	SD		Mean	SD
Facebook	3.47	2.2	YouTube	3.61	1.79
Radio	3.51	2.49	Renren	4.34	2.38
Newspaper	3.55	2.3	Radio	4.44	2.65
Blog	4.16	1.97	Newspaper	4.57	2.5
Twitter	4.9	1.79	Weibo	4.63	2.13
others	5.23	1.63	Blog	4.8	2.3
YouTube	5.66	1.35	Television	5.84	2.85
Television	5.72	2.93	News websites	6.99	2.71
News websites	8.8	0.88			

From this result, we can see that although social media has become an important channel for students to get political news, traditional media is still popular today in both countries. So, to conclude, what we can infer from these preliminary data is that social media are becoming more and more used in political practices and increasingly being perceived as either more useful than traditional media or as important interrelated tools that provide additional means of engaging with politics in China. It is important to note, traditional media is challenged severely by social media, while its role as political content provider can't be changed easily in both countries.

Table 6.2 Activities of young people on the social media in percentage

Items of activities on the social media	Germany (N=300)			China (N=300)		
	Never	Less often	Often	Never	Less often	Often
Keep in touch with friends/ family	5.3	7	87.6	0.7	11.7	87.8
Read new contributions	4.7	12	83.3	1.3	9	89.7
Obtain information for study	10.7	21.3	67.9	1.3	12.3	86.3
Find information about friends	6.3	26.3	67.4	1	9.7	89.3
Follow news on social media	13.3	27.3	59.4	3	13	84
Browse or update social networking profile	10.3	40.7	49	4	33	62.9
Discover new music, books, and other entertainment	14.7	38.7	46.7	7	35.3	57.7
Express opinions explicitly on politics	27.3	40	32.7	16	48.7	35.4
Join groups on a social networking sites	16	56.3	27.7	10.3	44.7	45
Organize political activities	57.7	31.7	10.7	54	33.7	12.3

Note: question wording "How often do you use social networks for the following activities?" Response categories range from 1=never to 6=daily. The percentage of often includes percent of (once or two times a week, several times a week and daily).

Compared with most surveys are limited to the examination of frequency of social media use. Furthermore, in this part the author measured several broad categories of activities on social media that university students might engage in. The finding is that the most popular activities for German students seem to be keeping in touch with friends or family, reading new contributions and finding information about friends or studies (see Table 6.2). Following news via social media is also rather frequent activities and, as we have seen in the literature, might enhance the political participation of young people. However, the organizing political activities are much less frequent among young Germans with only 10.7% have often done so via social media.

The results are slightly different from Chinese university students, nearly 90% of them often use social media to read new contributions or find information about friends. Besides, the Chinese people are significantly more likely than Germans to get political information through social media, with 84% often did this. Organize political activities is also the least frequency in China, where only 12.3% of Chinese respondents have often performed it. In generally speaking, the results indicate that Chinese students joined in different types of activities via social media more frequency than Germany students, most likely due to the lack of censorship from government in the contemporary Chinese society.

6.1.4 Conclusion

The comparative study found that the general media use habits and preferences are clearly different in both countries, Chinese young people prefer to use social media and spend more time on it than young Germans, especially in the area of political communication. Whereas traditional media still dominate their news consumption per day, young people have realized the importance of it in Germany and China. Thus, the conclusion are in line with earlier studies showing even when computer skills and Internet access become more widespread in the general population, use of the World Wide Web as a news platform seems unlikely to diminish substantially use of traditional news media by a survey of 520 undergraduate students from a large public university (Althaus & Tewksbury, 2000).

Meanwhile, this study contributes to the growing research in political communications in terms of underscoring how social media use help political participation among Chinese students when traditional media still function as a state propaganda tools and freedom of the press is out of the question. The underlying assumption of the civic and political impacts of media use is that, media are the primary provider of political information, through which citizens are informed, discuss with others, and finally reach a basic agreement on social facts (Swanson, 2000). In China, however, Chinese citizens have limited channels to get political information due to the Chinese government's strict control of traditional media and restrictions on access to political content originated from international social media such as Facebook and YouTube. Under such a circumstance, by disseminating uncensored news and information originated from users, Chinese local social media platforms have opened up new spaces for multiple modes of expression, discussions, and various forms of political actions in an authoritarian country. Therefore, social media platforms seem to fill the void and fulfill the political information needs of millions of Chinese young people who aspire to take an active part in politics in China.

6.2 Compare the levels of political participation

Young people are often perceived as disengaged from the formal political process and from democratic institutions. However, a number of recent studies have suggested that while young people may have little interest in formal politics, this cohort are more likely to take part in differing forms of less institutionalized methods such as demonstrations, boycotts and direct action (Dalton, 2008; Norris, 2003c). So, in the following sections the author examined three levels of political participation in Germany and China, including political engagement, political participation within the representative democracy as well as participation outside the representative system.

6.2.1 Political engagement

Political interest

This part cares about individual's level of interest in politics in both countries because is a component of the conception of a democratic citizen and associated with other political variables. The author examines how the social media's potential as an instrument for increasing university students' political interest, which is considered as the a prerequisite for autonomous involvement in politics. The results show that there is no great difference between Chinese and German university students' level of political interest. More than a third of Chinese (32.3%) and German (36.0%) young people claimed to be very interested in politics. Besides, around half of the respondents in the survey said they are somewhat interested in political affairs, the percentage is 47.0% in China and 50.7% in Germany.

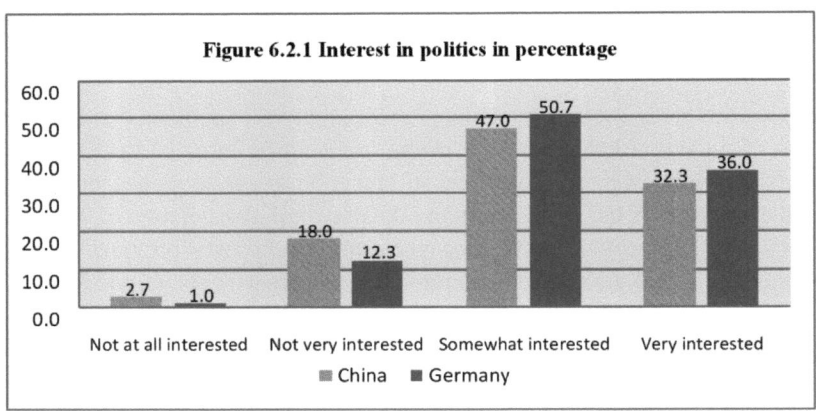

Note: question wording "How interested are you in politics?" Response categories range from 1= not at all interested to 4= very interested. (China n=300, Germany n=300).

While 18.0% of Chinese and 12.3 % of German university student's indicated that they are not very interested in politics. Overall, the evidence shows that levels of interest in politics amongst Chinese young people are slighter lower than Germans. Especially in Germany, the rate of young people who are very or fairly interested is quite high. In China the rate is slight lower, but still come to nearly one third. Whereas adults as a whole most commonly claim to have somewhat interest in politics, they are not likely to report having not at all interest of politics.

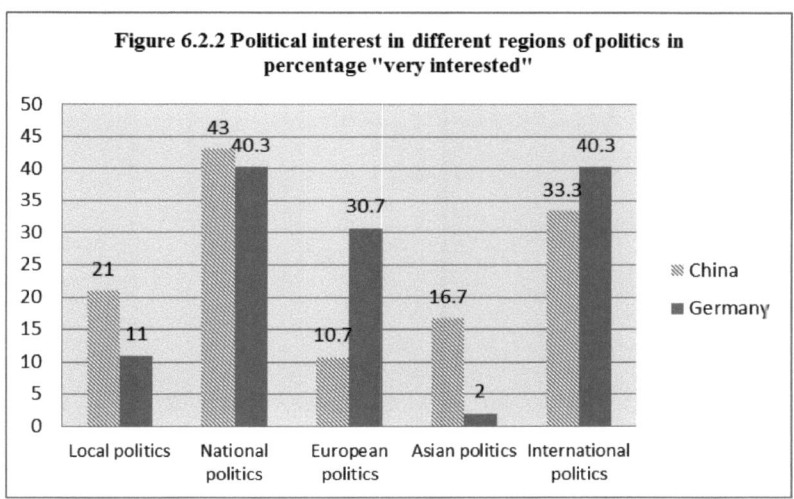

Figure 6.2.2 Political interest in different regions of politics in percentage "very interested"

Note: question wording "People's political interest sometimes varies across different regions of politics. Are you personally very interested, somewhat interested, not very interested or not at all interested in......?" Response categories range from 1= not at all interested to 4= very interested. (China n=300, Germany n=300).

In addition, university students were asked another question concerned their political interest in different types of politics. Seen from the figure 6.2.2, national news and international news are both the most interested types of news for Germans, closely followed by European and local news. By contrast, with respect of different kinds of politics, the most interest is articulated in national political information in China with 43%. Unlike Germany, in China that interest in national politics is somewhat higher than interest in international politics. In addition, for young people of China, European politics ranks below national politics and certainly below international politics (See Figure 6.2.2). Thus it can be seen that the political issues young people are interest in and get active for are not confined to the nation level in both countries. Nowadays, as the Internet integrates the functions of traditional media, people can read news at home and abroad and get as much foreign or international information as they can more conveniently. In fact, many young people in China prefer to pay close attention to local news because this is to do with their everyday life and the things that happen around them.

Following politics in the news in Germany and China

In line with the national differences in the degree of political interest, flowing politics in the news displays differ slightly between China and Germany. The proportion of Chinese and Germany students who use media to track political news or issues daily are both high. More than half of the student samples in the survey said they have used different kinds of media to follow news about current events, public issues, and politics, the percentage is 56.7% in China and 52.0% in Germany. Besides, German students are more likely to get political information through media several times a week: 30.3% of the young Germans did this, compared with 21.3% of Chinese young people. Overall, as seen in the figure 6.2.3, 82.3% of Germany shows the slightly higher rate of daily consumption or nearly daily consumption, compared with 78% of China.

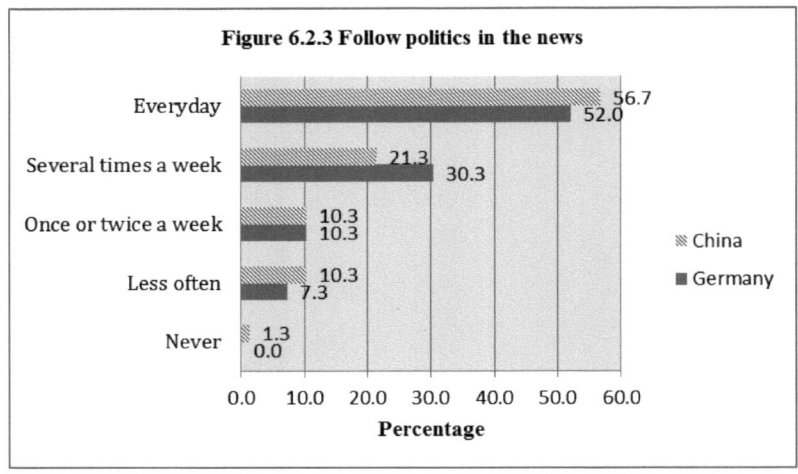

Figure 6.2.3 Follow politics in the news

Note: question wording "How often do you follow politics in the news on television, on the radio, in the newspapers?" Response categories range from 1= never to 5= everyday. (China n=300, Germany n=300).

Discussing politics with friends

Citizens' discussion about politics plays a major role in boosting rational political decisions, orientations and attitudes formation as well as political behaviors (Huckfeldt, 1995). The results for this survey show that there are slight differences between Chinese and German students in their frequency of political discussion with friends: firstly, a sizeable 47.7% of Chinese and 43.0% of Germans reported that they sometimes discuss political matters when they get together with their friends. Followed by 17.0% of Chinese and 30.0% of Germans who said that they frequently discuss political matters with their friends. So, German students talk political issues with friend more often than Chinese students. There is one more important thing worth mentioning, young people tend to would like to take the time to share and communication their political views with others (See Figure 6.2.4).

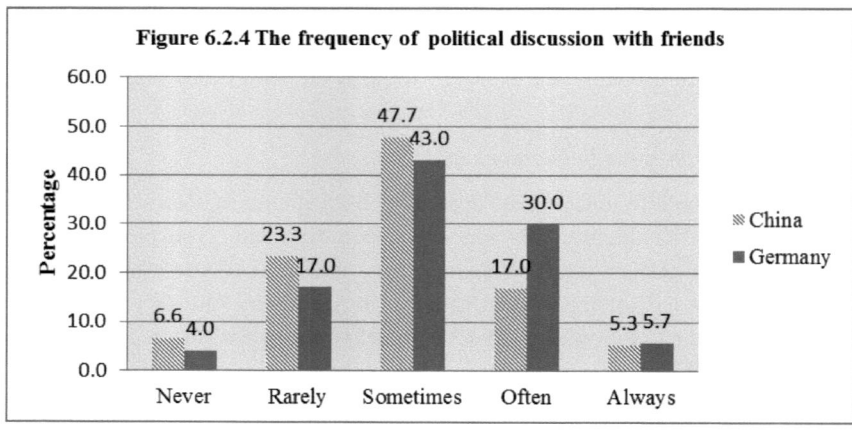

Figure 6.2.4 The frequency of political discussion with friends

Note: question wording "When you hold a strong opinion on a political issue, do you always, often, sometimes, rarely or never try to persuade your friends, relatives or fellow workers to share your views?" Response categories range from 1= never to 5=always. (China n=300, Germany n=300).

Besides, when it comes to discuss current political event with friends, family, coworkers as well as other people, the data suggested nearly 18% of the young Germans discuss politics with their friends and family daily, 6.7% with their co-workers and acquaintance. Strangers are less frequent discussants in Germany. Therefore, in Germany, the most important partners are friends, colleagues as well as teachers. In China, friends and family also play prominent roles as discussants, even more so than co-workers and acquaintance. In sum, family, friends play an important role for young people's daily political communication in both countries (see Figure 6.2.5).

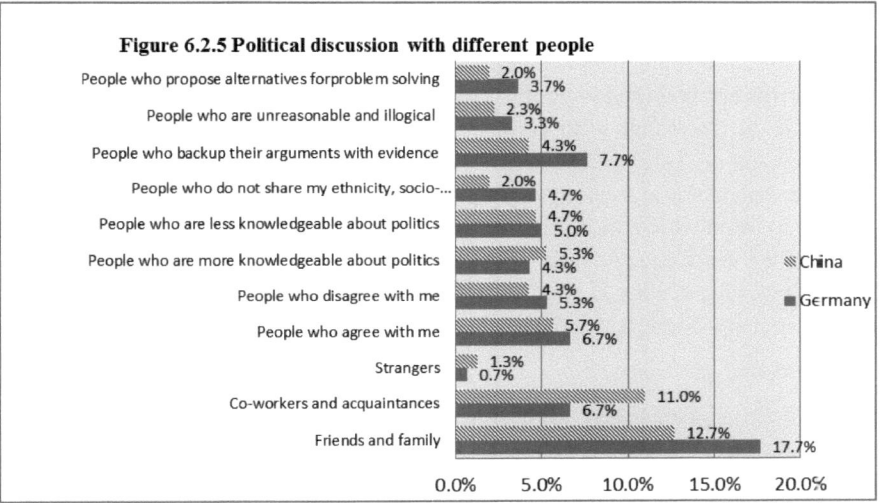

Note: question wording "How often do you discuss political issues when you get together with the following people?" Response categories range from 1= never to 6= daily. (China n=300, Germany n=300).

Conclusion

The concept of political engagement is measured by three indicators: young people's political interest, tracking political news on the media and frequency of political talk in China and Germany. The results portray a rather positive picture of young people's political engagement in both countries, and reveal that the young people are able to develop their engagement nowadays. Our findings suggest that, in general, there is no great difference between Chinese and German university students' level of political interest. However, in terms of university students' tracking political news on the media and frequency of political talk, there are some differences between Chinese and German students. Firstly, Chinese university students are more likely to focus on local news than German students. In addition, academic pressure and future employment drive them to pay more attention to what's happening around them. These two major reasons lead Chinese students to focus more on the local news. Secondly, German students discuss political issues with friends more often than Chinese students. One reason may be that Chinese contemporary political communication is very much influenced by traditional Chinese political thought (Lu, 2002). Especially Confucian norms of conformity and collective mentality still subconsciously affect the communication behaviors of many ordinary Chinese (Lu, 2002).

Therefore, today Chinese people do not like to openly express their different views on these issues nowadays in public situations. Even at their own social media spaces, Chinese students prefer watching others' reactions to political issues and keeping silent themselves (Zheng, 2011). They simply sought to avoid speaking of sensitive subjects with friends in order to avoid conflict and Internet censorship. With web-based services especially social media facilitate the transmission of large amounts of political messages, which make political information such as public petitions to government officials can be shared more effectively and easily through social media than through in-person communication.

6.2.2 Political participation in the representative democratic structures

In order to measure young people's participation in traditional forms we focus on their participation in elections and in political parties in China and Germany. In this section, the key task of this study is to compare these two institutional forms of political participation among young people in different countries based on survey data. From the angle of the democracy system, Spannring, *et al.* explain that "these two forms embody the crucial basis on which the representation of people's will as well as legitimacy and functioning of the elite rule test" (Spannring, *et al.*, 2008, p. 62). Moreover, in consideration of the decline in mainstream political participation has been ongoing for some time in many countries all over the world (Norris, 2002).

College students' participation in elections

Here, university students were asked some questions concerned voting in elections. Figure 6.2.6 shows that 84.0% of the German sample said that they voted in national election, compared and only 16% of the Chinese young people have voted in the national and village election in 2013. The results show that the participation rate in China is much lower than Germany (Figure 6.2.6). Besides, the findings in this study suggested that although Chinese college students use the Internet and social media to gather and obtain political information, it does not encourage them to keep using those medium to engage in political election, thereby decreasing the media's usability for political purposes.

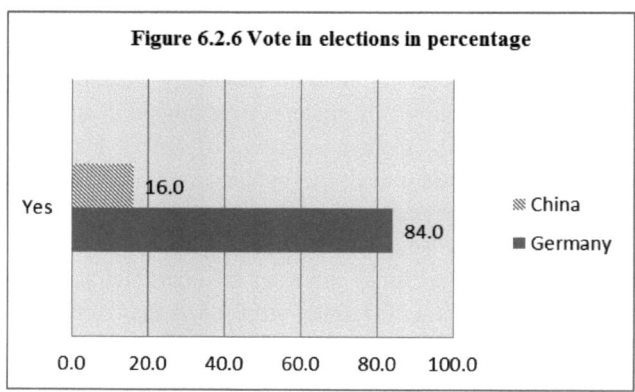

Note: question wording "Did you vote in the last general elections or village elections in 2013?" Responses recoded as follows: (0= no, 1=yes). (China n=300, Germany n=300).

Our study does not find a high level of the election in the university context in China. A possible explanation is that Chinese university students do not have the necessary channels to vote. Firstly, there are plenty of problems in election process in China such as "Central authorities are not elected through free, open, and competitive general elections" (Zhang & Lin, 2014). At the local level, the venues for students' participation are still limited, due to the nomination of the candidates and students' eligibility are still manipulated by the Chinese government (Li, 2011; Zhang & Lin, 2014). Secondly, the CCP (Chinese Communist Party) restricts the political information circulated on social media directly on university campuses. As Wang suggests the Chinese Communist Party organizes a team of web administrators to monitor and report students' online political speeches that are at odds with the government (Wang, 2013)

Political identification

A voter's identification with a political party is intimately associated with to the alignment of his political views as well as his voting behavior (Campbell & Valen, 1961). In other words, if a person identifies with one political party, the person may most commonly support this political party by voting or other activities on some level. The sample was asked one question about whether they identified with a political party or not. As shown in Figure 6.2.7, nearly half of young Germans reported that they identify with the SPD (46.3%), followed by the FDP (43.3%). The CDU/CSU reaches 7.3% of identification, the Green Party only 2.3%. And just 0.3% of young Germans have no any political identification.

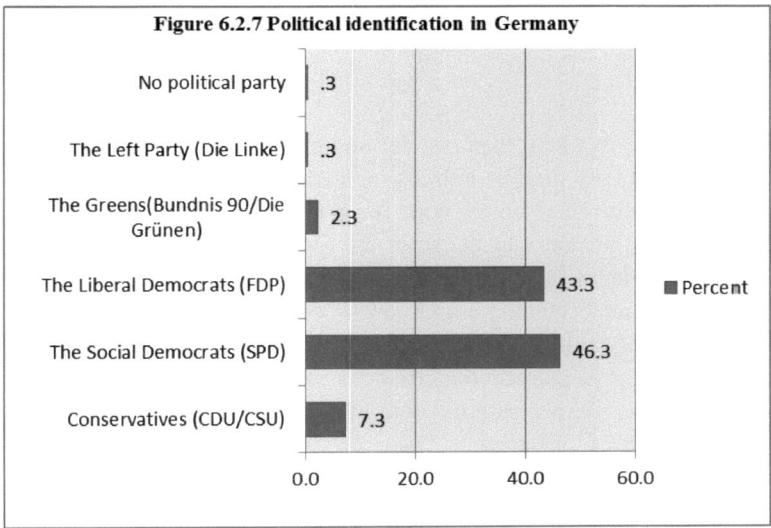

Note: question wording "Which political party do you identify with?" Responses recoded as follows: (C= no choose ,1= choose). (China n=300, Germany n=300).

The more striking difference arises when we compare with China: there is more than two thirds of Chinese university students (65.3%) said they identify with the Communist Party, whereas 28% people who do not identify with any party. At the same time, there is also 6% that feel identification with other party (see Figure 6.2.8). On the whole, we can see that the level of political identification of young people in Germany is higher than in China. For these difference seems mainly to be due to the character of party systems differs greatly between the two countries. Meanwhile, by these differences at least, it sometimes appears that today more young Germans are willing to participate in the election than Chinese

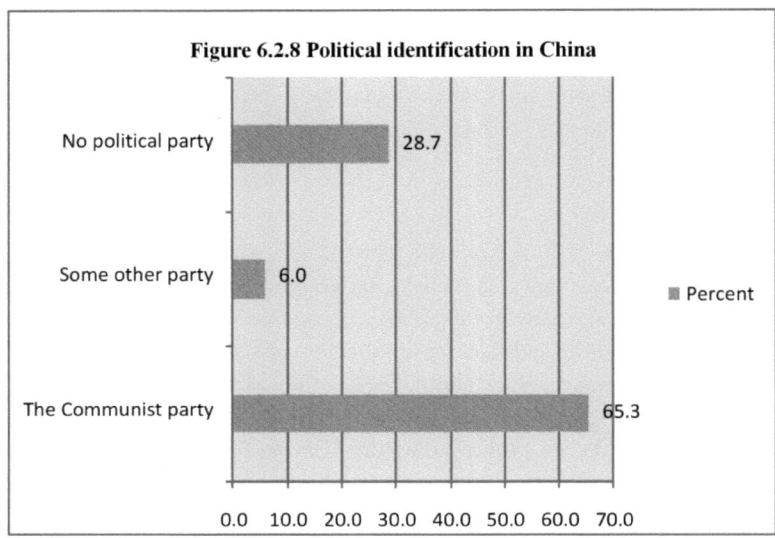

Figure 6.2.8 Political identification in China

Note: question wording "Which political party do you identify with?" Responses recoded as follows: (0= no choose ,1= choose). (China n=300, Germany n=300).

Party membership

Party membership is often seen as an important vehicle for citizen's political participation. It not only impacts citizens' political opinions on a range of issues, but also stimulates political activities such as voting choice and political campaign. Furthermore, party membership is one of the central variables in understanding our modern electoral democracy (MacKuen & Rabinowitz, 2003, p. 115). Thus, the measure of party membership is a question by asking whether the respondents are a member for several political organizations during the last 12 months. The survey indicates membership in political organizations among the German respondents seems disappointingly low. Membership in youth organizations linked to political parties is 9.7% in China and 6.7% in Germany. Trade unions have a similar low membership rate as youth organization, in Germany, where trade union membership is 6.0% and China where it is 9.0%.

However, membership of the political parties is a little higher in China: 21.3% of Chinese students participated as members in party, compared to only 9% of the Germen students. This particular high level related to the fact that becoming a party member is a resume booster that can get a Chinese graduates won better position and promoted more rapidly within government or state-owned-enterprises (Yuen, 2013). But taken as a whole, the results reveal that students in both countries are disinclined to join in these political organizational of their own country especially for trade union, mainly because of their low level of membership in these traditional party organizations (see Figure 6.2.9).

Note: question wording "Please indicate for each organization if you are a member. Also, please indicate if during the last 12 months, you participated in an activity arranged by this organization or if you have done voluntary work for this organization?" Responses recoded as follows: (0= no, 1=yes). (China n=300, Germany n=300).

Participation in traditional political organization

In addition, another issue that should be taken into consideration is participation in activities among Chinese and German university students. The results reveal that students in both countries are disinclined to participate in any activities organized by those political organizations in their own society, in particular because their level of participation in activities in these organizations was very low. For example, trade union have lower activity rate in both countries, joining in an activity of the organization only reaches percentage (5.3%) in China and (6.7%) in Germany.

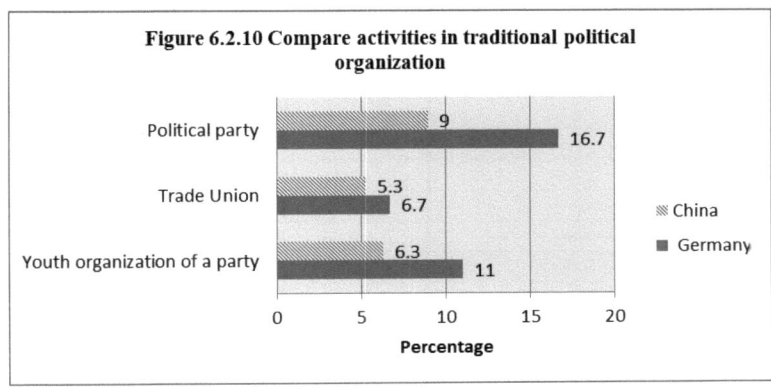

Note: question wording "Please indicate for each organization if you are a member. Also, please indicate if during the last 12 months, you participated in an activity arranged by this organization or if you have done voluntary work for this organization?" Responses recoded as follows: (0= no, 1=yes). (China n=300, Germany n=300)

Besides, the analyses show that students in both countries tend to have different activities preferences from each other, for instance, 9% of Chinese students had took part in the any activities of the party, followed by 6.3% youth organization of a party. However, 16.7% of German students reported that they had joined in the any activities of the party, followed by 11% of them said they had joined in activities in youth organization of a party. The interesting thing is that although more than 20% of Chinese student are members of political party, only few students (9%) keep high enthusiasm and actively take part in the activities in the party. In terms of the level of volunteered in these political organizations, the results seem that it even lower rate in both countries (see Figure 6.2.10).

Participation at university

In addition to supplying basic knowledge and skill, university also plays an important role in offering opportunity structure for students' involvement in political activities (Spannring, *et al.*, 2008). It can be seen from Table 6.3, the opportunity structures for participation at school differ significantly. Since the 1990s party organizations at all the Chinese universities and colleges have greatly stepped up their efforts at ideological and political work (Guo, 2005). Consequently, today China has both a relatively more formal and explicit representation system and a well-defined official role of a speaker for the class. This is why more Chinese students joined in participation than Germans: nearly 48.7% of Chinese student having been council members and the 67.3% having ever been in the role of a speaker for the class in their university. An explanation for this is that because the decline of political control over college students was deemed a crucial contributor to the 1989 Beijing student movement (Zhao, 2000), the CCP now strives to control the ideology of university students through a series of measures such as encouraging the college students to join the Party, recruiting the best students to serve as the CCP cadres, and propagating the Communist ideology in college classrooms.

Table 6.3 Compare participation at school in percentage

Items	Germany (N=300)			China (N=300)		
	Percentage	Mean	SD	Percentage	Mean	SD
Participation at school		0.17	0.197		0.4	0.253
attended a students' meeting	42.3	0.42	0.495	77.7	0.78	0.417
participated in a protest movement	34	0.34	0.475	10.7	0.11	0.309
joined a political group online though social media	15	0.15	0.358	12.7	0.13	0.333
organized a political event	10	0.1	0.301	13.7	0.14	0.344
taken an active role in such a meeting	9.7	0.1	0.296	52.3	0.52	0.5
had a function as a speaker for the class	5.3	0.05	0.225	67.3	0.67	0.47
have been a member of a student council	4.3	0.04	0.204	48.7	0.49	0.501

Note: question wording "And have you ever done any of the following at school?" Responses recoded as follows: (0= no, 1=yes).

Besides, because the party organizations hold meetings on a regular basis at university, this is why 77.7% have ever attended a students' meeting with almost half of them being in an active role in such meeting. By contrast, it is found that German pupils or students participated in protests more often, 34% had ever did it. Political protest as sensitive words in China, students' protest behaviors are not supported and encouraged by university concerning pupils safe. In terms of joining a political group online, German students more prefer to do this through social media. In general, due to great differences between Germany and China in both the system of representation in university and the understanding of the key words in the questions about political participation at school, the results indicate Germans were very different from Chinese

Conclusion

This section reports a comprehensive overview of new data on the levels of young people's participation in traditional institutionalized forms in contemporary China and Germany society. As these data clearly reveal, parties in contemporary society are rapidly losing their capacity to engage the youth people in both countries. Meanwhile, the survey seems to indicate that the preference of students to get activity individually rather than within various organization in both countries. A comparison between Germany and China also suggests different organization structures and different meanings of membership as well as political activities. In China, for example formal membership in the party may participate in some activities of the party at school, but they do not recognize it. Nearly in each university in China has a department of party committee, they regularly organize some lectures, meetings, other activities for university students. Students often think these activities are held by the school not the political party. In contrast, Germany has a low membership are, but high activity and volunteer rate.

6.2.3 Political participation aside from representative democratic structures

Political participation is an issue that is often discussed in the political communication field. However it tends to focus mainly on one subject—constitutional reform—with rather less attention being given to other forms of outside the well-established representative system among citizens. Therefore, the purpose of this section is to investigate young people's participation outside the political institutions of the representative democracy system. The following chapter will compare young people's engagement within these forms in between China and Germany: membership and voluntary work in non-government organizations and social movements, participation in political communication, action and protest as well as in life style politics.

Membership in NGO

The membership in NGO is examined by asking young people whether they are members in non-government organizations such as peace organizations, human rights or humanitarian aid organizations, environmental protection as well as animal rights or animal protection groups (see figure 6.2.11). It can be seen that there are no significant differences between Chinese and Germany respondents in those three four forms of non-government organizations. The percentage rate of membership in peace organizations is equal in Germany and China with 6.7% respectively. Similarly, environmental organizations have the same rate with 9% in both countries. Besides, concerning the other forms of unofficial organizations, date on human rights and humanitarian aid organizations show a little different: this form attract 9% Germany and 6% Chinese respondents. In addition, Germany (8%) has slightly higher membership rate of animal rights or animal protection than China (6.7%). On average, membership in NGO is somewhat lower in China, while more young people in Germany tend to become members, especially in human rights and environmental organizations.

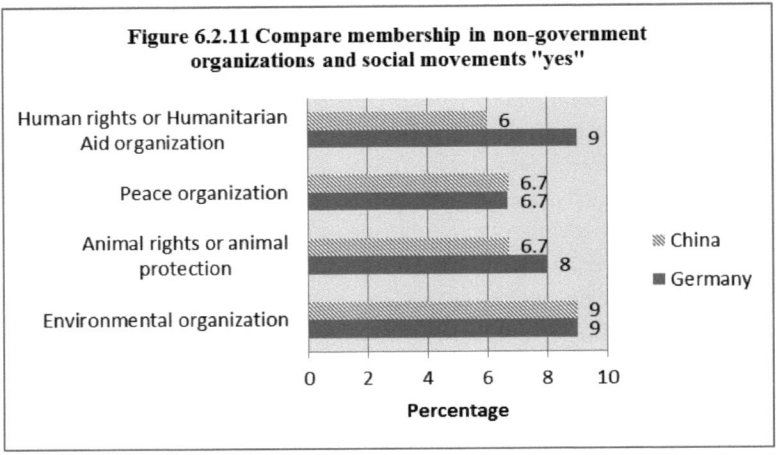

Note: question wording "Please indicate for each organization if you are a member. Also, please indicate if during the last 12 months, you participated in an activity arranged by this organization or if you have done voluntary work for this organization?" Responses recoded as follows: (0= no, 1=yes). (China n=300, Germany n=300).

Political discourse

This study proposes a question for understanding individual's unconventional political activities. The respondents were asked the question of "During the last 12 months, how often have you done this?" (see Table 6.4). The comparison between Germany and China indicates substantial differences in their levels and styles of political communication action and protest. These differences are mainly resulted from the difference of the political system, political culture as well as opportunity structures.

The results indicate that, in general, German students' participation in political communication more often than Chinese. In Germany, signing petitions and attending public meetings dealing with political or social issues is very common for students. Only 19.3 % of the respondents stated that they never sign any petitions, and 21.3% reported they never join in public meeting. Other political activities are popular in Germany are contacting a politician, contributing to a political discussion on the Internet and donating money.

In Germany, around 50% of the respondents have already contacted a politician. The least likely activity is holding a political speech with more than 80% people never did this. However, contributed to a political discussion on the Internet achieve the highest rates in China with nearly 60% of Chinese students had talked about political issues with other person online in the past year (see Table 6.4).

Table 6.4 Compare political discourse between Germany and China in percentage

	Germany (N=300)								China (N=300)							
	Never	Less than once a year	Less than once a month	Less than once a week	Once a week	More than once a week	Mean	SD	Never	Less than once a year	Less than once a month	Less than once a week	Once a week	More than once a week	Mean	SD
attended a public meeting	21.7	30.7	26.3	13.7	6.3	1.3	2.56	1.22	76.3	14.7	6	1.3	0.7	1	1.38	0.85
signed a petition	19.3	34	32.7	11.3	3	0	2.44	1.02	81	15.7	1	0.7	1	0.7	1.27	0.72
contributed to a political discussion on the Internet	40.3	21.3	21	11.3	3.3	2.7	2.24	1.32	42.3	21	20.3	8	5.3	3	2.22	1.37
wrote or forwarded a letter/an email with a political content	53.7	17	16.7	6.7	4.3	1.7	1.96	1.28	64.7	19	9.3	3	1.7	2.3	1.65	1.13
donated money	50.3	32.7	12.3	4	0.7	0	1.72	0.88	65.7	21.3	10	2	0.7	0.3	1.52	0.85
collected signatures	60	23.7	11.3	4	0.3	0	1.6	0.87	81.7	14	1.7	1.3	1	0.3	1.27	0.71
contacted a politician	62	23.7	11	2.7	0.3	0.3	1.57	0.86	77.3	15	4	1	1.3	1.3	1.38	0.9
worn a badge with a political message	74.3	12.7	6.3	2.3	1.7	2.7	1.52	1.12	82.7	12	3.7	0.7	0.7	0.3	1.26	0.67
wrote an article e.g. in a students' newspaper	74.3	11.7	7	4	2.3	0.7	1.5	1.02	69.7	19	7	2	1.3	1	1.49	0.93
distributed leaflets with political content	79.7	11.3	6.3	1.3	1	0.3	1.34	0.79	86	10	1.3	0.7	1	1	1.24	0.75
held a political speech	81	12	5	1.7	0.3	0	1.28	0.67	87.3	9	1.3	1	0.7	0.7	1.21	0.68

Note: question wording "There are different ways of being politically active. How often do you participate in the following political activities?" Response categories range from 1= never to 6=more than once a week.

Political protest

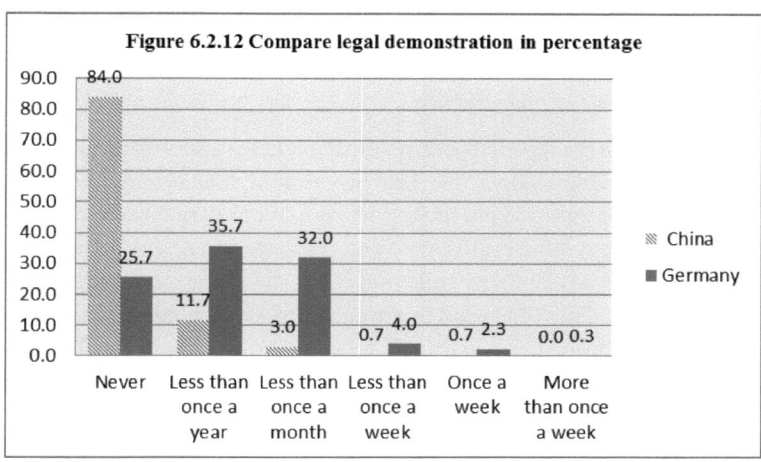

Figure 6.2.12 Compare legal demonstration in percentage

Note: question wording "There are different ways of being politically active. How often do you participate in the following political activities?" Response categories range from 1= never to 6=more than once a week. (China n=300, Germany n=300).

Patterns of participation protest among university students also show big differences between Germany and China. In General, German young people are more likely to take part in demonstration and strike than Chinese. By contrast, participation in legal demonstrations and strike are very rare in China. According to the data, only about one fourth (25.7%) of the German youth has never taken part in a legal demonstration (see Figure 6.2.12). On the contrary, Chinese youth is less inclined to demonstrate, even 84% of Chinese young people have never demonstrated. Besides, more than three fourth (76%) of students had never took part in strikes in Germany. In China, this percentage reaches even 88% (see Figure 6.2.13). These conclusions are in line with the previous experimental and theoretical results: spontaneous, single acts of political expression and communication are more accepted and welcomed by the young people than those of continuous involvement in political organizations and social movements (Spannring, et al., 2008).

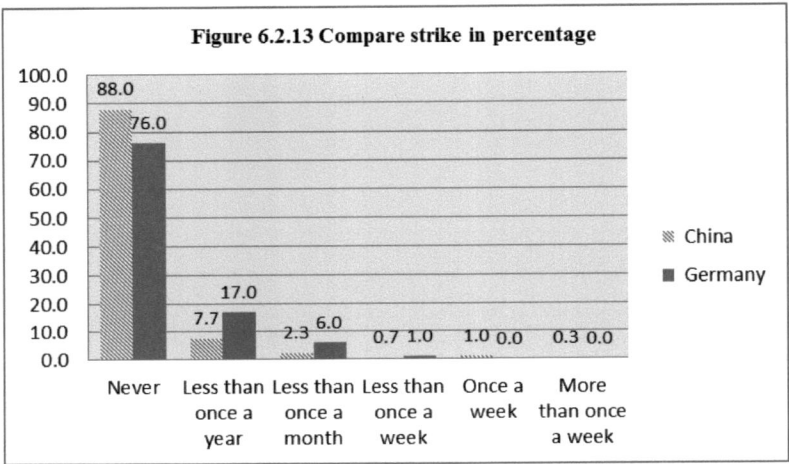

Note: question wording "There are different ways of being politically active. How often do you participate in the following political activities?" Response categories range from 1= never to 6=more than once a week. (China n=300, Germany n=300).

Illegal and violent forms of participation

After the study has investigated youth political participation within and outside the representative democratic system, the last big area of illegal and violent forms of participation should be examined in the following section. Illegal and violent modes of participation including writing graffiti on walls, participation in a political event where property is damaged, violent confrontation with the police or with the political opponent, occupation of buildings and blocking streets or railways are very rare in both countries. Indeed, none of these activities among Chinese youth reaches more than 20%. In Germany, illegal demonstrations are significantly accepted more frequently: 15.7% have at least once taken part in an illegal demonstration. 9.3% have taken part less than once a month and there are 2% that have taken part in such actions less than once a week. However, in China illegal demonstrations hardly attract young people.

In China, there is a rather small amount of young people who have ever participated in an illegal demonstration (8.7%). In terms of violent forms of participation, Germany also seems to have more university students tending to violent political participation: 22.7% ever experienced blocking street or railways. Besides, 20.3% ever had violent confrontation with an opponent. China with its 18% of young people that have ever participated in a political event where property was damaged, followed by 10.7% had ever wrote political message or graffiti on walls. For the rest of forms of violent political participation is negligible among Chinese youth: less than 10% of them had ever took in such kinds of participations (see Figure 6.2.14).

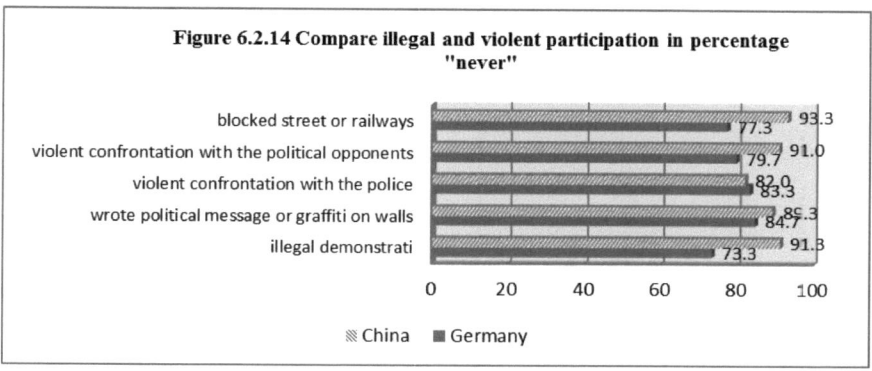

Figure 6.2.14 Compare illegal and violent participation in percentage "never"

Note: question wording "There are different ways of being politically active. How often do you partic.pate in the following political activities?" Response categories range from 1= never to 6=more than once a week. (China n=300, Germany n=300).

Political consumerism

By using the market as a venue to vent political and moral concerns, political consumerism is also known as "lifestyle politics" (Bennett, 1998). The politics of consumption seems to occupy an increasingly central place in the daily activities of ordinary citizens, becoming an essential element in young people's political consciousness recently.

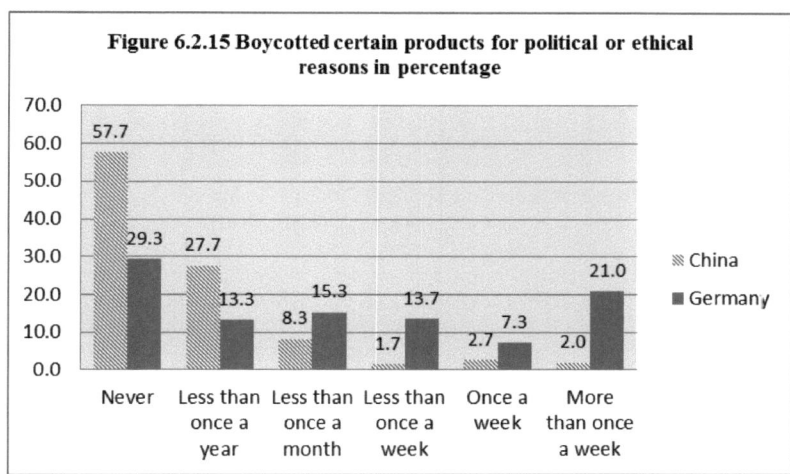

Figure 6.2.15 Boycotted certain products for political or ethical reasons in percentage

Note: question wording "There are different ways of being politically active. How often do you participate in the following political activities?" Response categories range from 1= never to 6=more than once a week. (China n=300, Germany n=300).

The data shown in figure 6.2.15, boycotting products is more widespread among young Germans than Chinese. In Germany, 70.7% of the young people said that that they have ever boycotted a product as means of political or moral expression. Even 21% of

German students had joined a boycott more than once a week. However, product boycott is less performed in China, where only 42.3% of all respondents have ever boycotted a product. In terms of the other dimension of political consumerism, the buying of products, the distribution is displayed as following: again, comparatively higher frequencies are also found for young Germans. About 81% of the Germans had ever bought certain products for political reasons. On the contrary, almost one third (34%) of young Chinese have ever bought a product for political reasons.

Thus it can be seen that significant differences are found between Germany and China. The overall frequency of political consumerism is higher among young Germans. By contrast, the young people of the China show the less general intention as well as intensity of active political consumption of certain products. However, it's worth mentioning that young people are more attracted by those activities than demonstration and strikes in both countries. This is in line with previous research that shows the younger generations prefer joining in looser and less hierarchical informal networks as well as various kinds of lifestyle-related, sporadic mobilization efforts (Eliasoph, 1998; Stolle, et al., 2005). Therefore, political consumption may become a more expedient way for young people to vent their dissatisfaction than demonstration or strike in the streets.

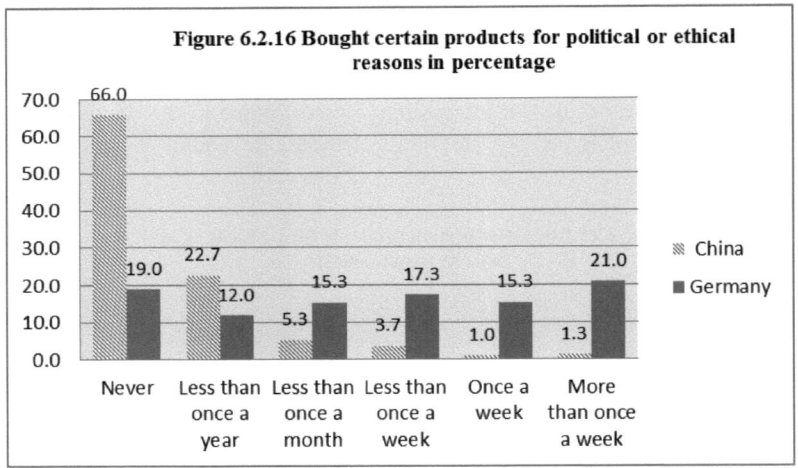

Note: question wording "There are different ways of being politically active. How often do you participate in the following political activities?" Response categories range from 1= never to 6=more than once a week. (China n=300, Germany n=300).

6.2.4 Compare effectiveness of different patterns of political participation

Another issue that should be taken into consideration is that the effectiveness of diverse participation among Chinese and German university students'. These measures aimed to uncover which of these types of political participation is effective for them. A comparison of two countries' profiles yields the following result: young people in Germany have a stronger belief in the effectiveness of working in a political party (60%) and voting in election (59.0%). They also have an outstanding share of young people who believe in obtaining attention form the media (40.0%). Compared to youth in

Germany, Chinese students put more trust in the effectiveness of getting attention from the media (35.0%), working in a political party (34.3%) and connecting with officials or government through social media directly (13.0%). However, it's worth mentioning that illegal and violent protest forms are deemed as the least effective by both German and Chinese students, due to only a minority of youth who believe in this an effective way to influence decisions (Figure 6.2.17).

All in all, young Germans tend to assign effectiveness to various forms of political participation more than the youth in China (e.g. work in voluntary organizations, work in a political party, signing petitions). Both "working in a political party" and "voting in election" is considered more effective than working to get media attention by Germans. However, most of Chinese youth consider media attention is the most effective way to influence decisions in society. And young Chinese people assign a surprisingly high influence to the social media (13.0%). These may be due to the differences with the policies and institutions of the two countries. In the one-party system society such as China, the traditional and untraditional forms of political participation do not let people with the feeling that they are able to change some top political and decision-making process. This is also verified what Shirky suggested the media have played a key role in shaping citizens' perceptions and policy agendas (Shirky, 2011).

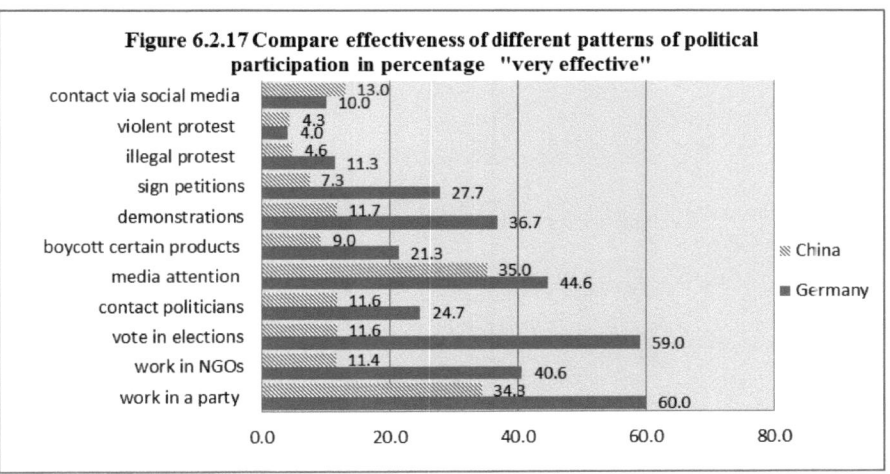

Figure 6.2.17 Compare effectiveness of different patterns of political participation in percentage "very effective"

Note: question wording "Here are many opinions on how one can effectively influence political decisions in society. I will give you some of the ways that are used. Please tell me on a scale from 0 to 5 how effective you think it is: 0 means "not at all effective" and 5 means "very effective" " (China n=300, Germany n=300).

In addition, previous studies have also suggested that social media remove barriers to collective action and empower citizens to connect with each other, influence and monitor the work of policy-makers by offering a low-cost and, in some cases, more personal and compelling ways of raising funds, delivering a wealth of political information and recruiting supporters from a broad range of backgrounds (Clarke, 2010). In addition, some stated that, by enabling people to connect across long distances, new information and communication technologies, including social media, have been instrumental in the growth of transnational political movements (Carty, 2010). Given the sometimes surprising power of social media, the follow section attempts to examine whether these political influence of social media has been recognized by young people in Germany and China.

The participants were asked the question of how much do they agree with the statement that "by using the social media, it will become easier for people like you to influence government and parliament (or National People's Congress)?" According to the data, approximately 45.7% of German samples fully believed that social media empower them to impact on government and parliament, only 16.4% hold a negative view of the use of social media are able to influence ideas in society. At the same time, 28.0% of Chinese respondents argued that they have confidence in that social media would affect government and the National People's Congress' decision making. Only a few numbers of them (16%) do not think social media has such effect on politics. Moreover, more half of the German study samples stated that they partly believe that social media is an effective way to influence decisions in society. Nearly 38.4% of Chinese sample were dubious about the statement (see Figure 6.2.18). These results above show that despite the proliferation of social media has become an important source of information, political knowledge as well as election turnout, many young people still don't believe that it is possible for them to influence on politics with the help of this media.

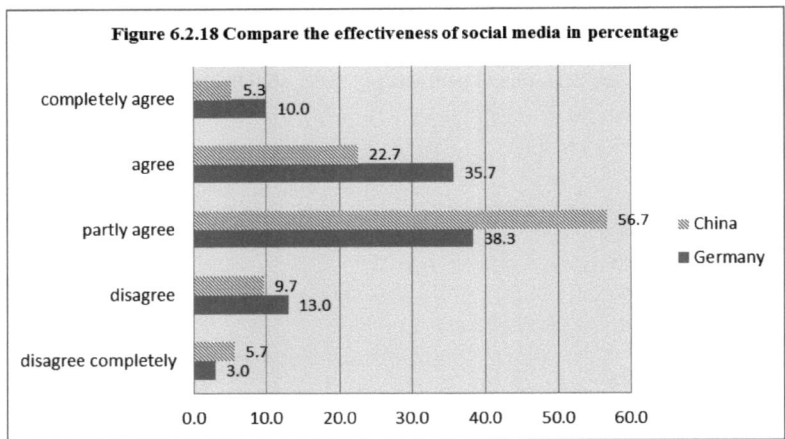

Note: question wording "By using the social media, it will become easier for people like you to influence government and parliament. Mark to what degree you agree with this statement?" Response categories range from 1= disagree completely to 5=completely agree. (China n=300, Germany n=300).

6.2.5 Barriers to use Internet for political participation

The Internet has brought specific changes and opportunities in the political communication field due to the characteristics of this medium, while it also throws up certain barriers for people to access political information as well as engage in political activity online. In the survey, the respondents were asked a question about the obstacles they face while they want to use Internet websites to involve in participation. In Germany the biggest two problems facing young people when surfing the Internet were: fees for the service of some websites (37.3%), followed by the low speed to view and download files (34.7%). While the main top two problems with accessing the Internet websites among Chinese were: 50.0% of users stated the reason for not accessing was the political regulation on Internet, 35% said that other problems block them to use Internet for participation (see Figure 6.2.19).

In addition, students were asked an open question about other problems they faced that become obstacles to their political participation while surfing the Internet. 18.8% Germans said they faced problems such as false information online and unwanted advertisement websites. By contrast, about 14.4% of Chinese stated these two reasons affect their online political participation. However, a plurality of 30.9% of Chinese students indicated that the reason lies in the lack of interest and confidence in network political participation in the political environment in China.

Through the comparison and analysis of data, there are some differences between Germany and Chinese youth in terms of barriers of online political participation. For Germany young people, financial considerations of getting online and lacking of information are the most obvious barriers. However, political regulations as well as traditional political culture are the primary obstacles for Chinese young people to effective adoption of the Internet to obtain political information and get involved in politics.

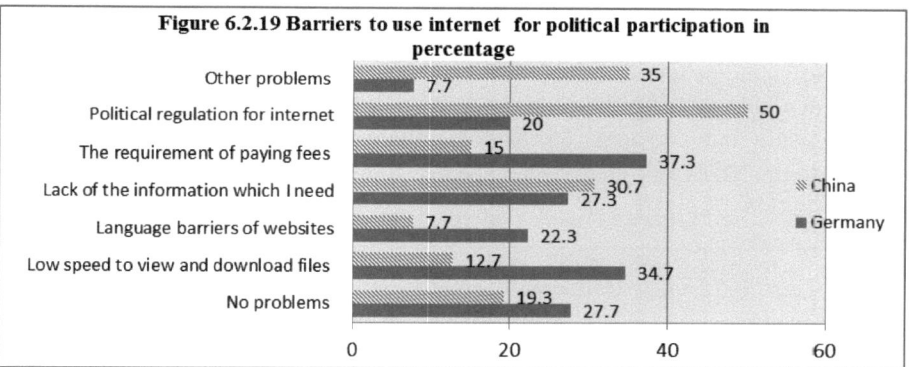

Figure 6.2.19 Barriers to use internet for political participation in percentage

Note: question wording "Which of the following factors do you think have become obstacles to your participation when you use Internet?" Responses recoded as follows: (0=no choose, 1=choose). (China n=300, Germany n=300).

6.2.6 Conclusion

The comparative studies surveys show some of the differences that exist between the two countries and the two political systems. First, although the issue of citizen participation has gradually gained importance since the end of the 1970s, the level and level of young citizens' political participation in the Chinese context were still lower than Germans. It can be explained by the reasons of the differences in membership induction, in organizational style, and in institutional constraint. Secondly, various forms of participation such as political consumerism that might improve the quality of democracy in China including participation through buy or boycott certain productions. It is clearly than the party-state's constraints at the macro-level on the civic associations are not translated into constraints on the activities of individual members in pursuing their interest. Thirdly, some illegal and violence modes of political participation are had a fairly limited role in China, because of "any political efforts outside of the control of the party-state to influence government policy making is strictly prohibited" (Guo, 2007). Compared with this, Germans has shown a greater degree of tolerance toward seemingly more destructive activities such as demonstrations or blocking traffic in which ordinary citizens vent their individual grievances.

6.3 Compare political factors related to political participation

In this section, we examine other political factors related with individual's political participation in Germany and China: including political efficacy, political knowledge as well as political trust.

6.3.1 Political efficacy

Political efficacy has an internal dimensions referring to the confidence of the citizen in her or his own political knowledge and competence to understand politics and to act politically, whereas an external dimensions constitutes the individual's belief about the responsiveness of the political system to their claims (Balch, 1974; Converse, 1972). Generally, comparisons between the two countries show higher levels of internal efficacy among German students but lower levels of external efficacy in China (Table 6.5). In Germany, the item 'Sometimes politics and government seem so complicated that a person like me can't really understand what's going on' receives the highest number of young people who support this view (67.4% strongly agree/ agree). Rank number two goes to 'I feel like I have a pretty good understanding of the important political issues in our society': 60.4% of German young people agree with this idea. However, only 32.0% of Chinese young people agree with the statement.

Table 6.5 Compare internal efficacy in percentage

Items	China(N=300)		Germany(N=300)	
	Strongly agree	Agree	Strong agree	Agree
People like me are generally well qualified to participate in the political activities and decision making of our country.	17.3	40	20.7	46.7
Sometimes politics and government seem so complicated that a person like me can't really understand what's going on.	16.7	31.3	11.7	33
I feel like I have a pretty good understanding of the important political issues in our society.	6.7	25.3	14.3	45.7
Today's problems are so difficult I feel I could not know enough to come up with any ideas that might solve them.	6.3	25.3	15.7	32
I feel like I could do as good a job in politics as most of the politicians we elect.	4.7	15.3	7	21.7

Note: question wording "To what extent do you agree or disagree with the following statements?" Response categories range from 1=strongly disagree to 6= strongly agree.

Furthermore, the differences in external efficacy were also found in China and Germany. It can be observed that more than half of the young population in Germany (59.0%) agrees with the statement "Politicians are supposed to be people's servants, but too many of them try to be masters." Similarly, this item is also agreed by most of Chinese youth (57.0% strongly agree/ agree) (Figure 6.3.1). Besides, the statements "I don't think public officials care much about what people like me think about politics." "Those we elect to public office lose touch with the people pretty quickly." tend to polarize the entire German young population: supporters and opponents of these two statements hold a similar share, with almost half of young people answering "agree or strongly agree". In general, the lowers level of internal political efficacy and slightly higher level of external political efficacy in China indicates that young people are still feeling of powerlessness in confront with politics, although government try to be accountable for citizens. By contrast, Germany has a long democratic tradition so that its citizens are more confident in themselves that they can understand politics and have competence to participation in political discussion.

Figure 6.3.1 Compare external political efficacy in percentage

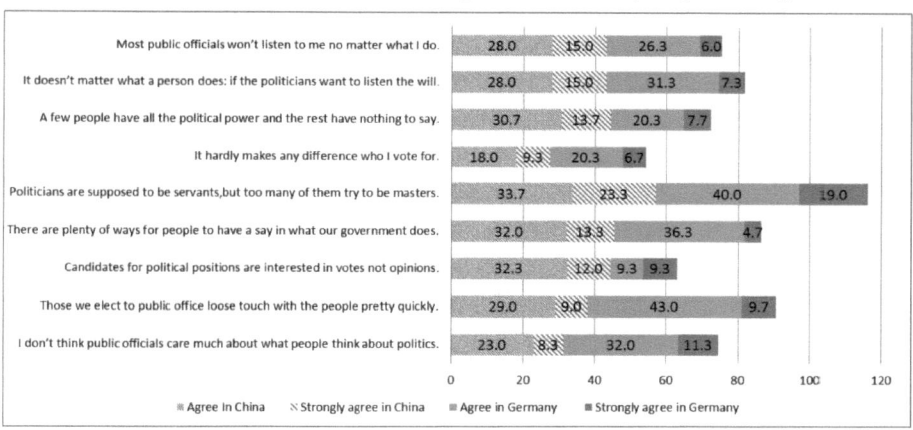

Note: question wording "To what extent they agreed or disagreed with the following statements?" Response categories range from 1= strongly disagree to 5= strongly agree (Light colour represents agree, deep colour represents strongly agree). (China n=300, Germany n=300).

6.3.2 Political knowledge

Previous literature has showed that an integral part of getting at individual's deeper understanding of politics is by being able to tap the connections one makes between the factual bits of political information (Thomson, 2007). Herein, the study applied two open-end questions to explore factual knowledge, and a knowledge-battery consisting of nine items to examine structure knowledge. The data indicates a high percentage of the answers were correct among Germany and Chines students, nearly 97% correctly reported that Angela Merkel is the current prime minister of Germany in 2013. Also, 98.3% of Chinese students filled correctly about the name prime minister of China is Xi Jinping at this time of 2013 (see Figure 6.3.2).

In addition to this, the respondents were asked a question about "what do you think, approximately how many members of Federal Parliament are there in your country?" This issue focus on individual's internal level of political knowledge and checks their ability to know the specific numbers number of parliament or federal parliament in their country. Their responses were coded as 1= correct, and 0 = incorrect (2987 in China's

National People's Congress parliament at present, and 598 members in Germany's federal parliament). The results show that about 10.7% of the Germans gave right answer to this question, whereas only 5.3% do so in China. So, Germans and Chinese are both seriously lack of internal political knowledge and understanding has been demonstrated by this survey. On average, there seems to be a better factual knowledge among Germany young people about politics than Chinese.

In order to test university students' level of structure political knowledge, the study applied a battery of political knowledge questions, which in combination with knowledge about public figures, institutional fact and foreign affairs. Items 1 to 3 are statements about the public figure. Most of respondents know their countries' current Prime Minister (item 1). In this case the Chinese respondents perform better (96.7%) than Germany's (85.3%). And almost all respondents gave the right answer about the political membership of the prime minister in their countries, with the highest rate of 99.7% respectively. This is not the case when it comes to answering about the deputy of the Federal Chancellor in Germany or the vice premiers of the state council in China (item 2): young people in Germany (80.3%) do better, whereas only 24.7% of the young people in China made a correctly recognize the vice premier.

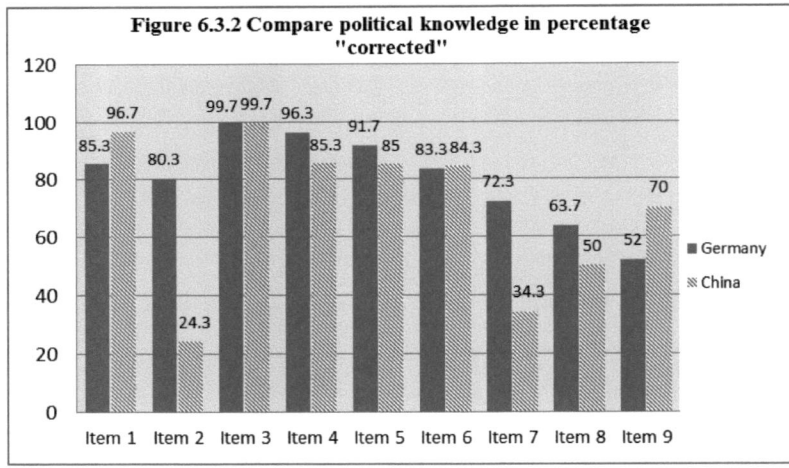

Note: question wording "Now look at the following statements about politics. For each statement, please tell me if you think it is true or false?" Responses recoded as follows: (0= incorrect, 1=correct). Tables indicate the frequency of correct answers as a percentage of all respondents. (China n=300, Germany n=300).

Item 1: "The current minister of the interior (or prime minister) is (Name)."

Item 2: "(Name) is now the deputy of the Federal Chancellor (or vice premiers of the state council)."

Item 3: "(Name of Prime Minister) is the member of (the name of party)."

Item 4: "Germany (or China) has the number of federal states or (province) now."

Item 5: "In Germany (or China), national election (or elections for the national leaders) must be held every 3 years".

Item 6: "In Germany (or China), the Federal president (or the president) is elected by the Federal Convention (or National People's Congress)."

Item 7: "There are currently 25 member states of the European Union."

Item 8: "Obama is the president of the U.S. since 8 years."

Item 9: "Every state of the U.S is represented by two senators".

Moreover, items 4 to 6 are statements about the national political system. The results indicate that both Chinese and German university students were highly able to recognize the institutional fact about their countries. Especially when Germany students are asking about whether Germany has 16 federal states after Reunification, 96.5% gave a correct answer. Similarly, 85.3% of Chinese students answered correctly about whether China has a total of 23 provinces at present. The answers to item 5: "In (country), whether elections for the national leaders must be held every 3 years?" also is well known 91.7 % in Germany and 85.0 %in China. In addition, in order to gauges the factual political knowledge through individual's ability to memorize some international political events, the university student's in both countries were asked three questions about knowledge about foreign affair items 6 to 9. The results indicate that both Chinese and German university students had relatively lowers level knowledge about international politics issue compared with their national knowledge (see Figure 6.3.2).

On average, there are significant differences on the structural political knowledge participation between China and Germany. This can be seen from the differences in the mean of right answers, shown in the Table 6.4. For example, in terms of knowledge about public figures, German students gave more correct answers (M=.88, SD=.187) than Chinese students (M=.74, SD=.152). Not only so: German students' levels of institutional and international political knowledge are both higher than Chinese. Thus there seems to be a better structural political knowledge among German young people. Besides, both Germany and China students' focus far more on the national political information happened in their counties than international political news. It is worth noting that only 34% of Chinese young people paid attention on the European political issues (see Figure 6.3.2).

6.3.3 Political trust

To better understand the role of political trust, the following section is dedicated to analysis the different trust rate in different types of political institutions between Germany and China. According to the data, people in China trust their government and political parties more than people in Germany. For Germans, more than one fourth (25.3%) of young people express very trust in their people's court, followed by 19.7% very trusting their police. Besides, more than half of Germans (57.7%) shows they have somewhat trust in people's court. Political parties are by far less popular among the German youth: they enjoy only a little bit over a third of the trust shown into this democratic institutions (36%). However, China's central government as well as political party are both the best trusted political institutions amongst young Chinese, nearly 47.7% of Chinese shows very trust in their central government or political parties, and 34.7% shows somewhat trust respectively (see Figure 6.3.3).

In general, the data indicates different trustworthiness of political institution in Germany and China. Interestingly, young Chinese seem to have more trust into political parties and government than Germans, which is partly explained by the fact that because authorities in China still have a tightly controlled unauthorized political expression, Chinese respondents may not dare to vent their true political views for reasons of personal safety. Moreover, from the viewpoint of political culture, this should be expected due to "democratic culture requires that citizens hold a certain amount of distrust of political authority" (Shi, 2001).

Figure 6.3.3 Compare political trust in percentage

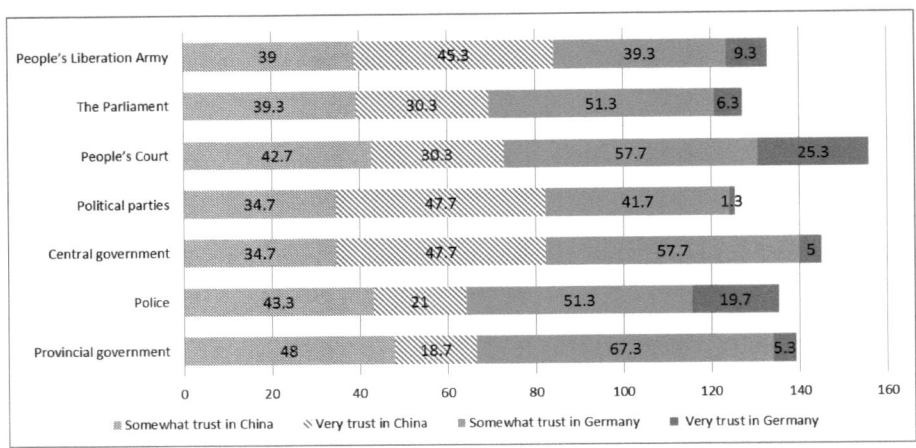

Note: question wording "In the following there are some names of different bodies such as the government and the European Commission. Please indicate how much you trust each of them from "trust not at all" and to "very trust" Response categories range from 1= trust not at all to 4= very trust. (Light colour represents somewhat trust, deep colour represents very trust). (China n=300, Germany n=300).

6.3.4 Conclusion

This study builds upon previous research in an attempt to clarify our understanding of the dimensions of these three significant political variables in the dynamics of young people's political behaviors in Germany and China. It has become apparent, however, that the level of political knowledge and political efficacy among Chinese university students is less than satisfactory. The findings of the study should ease the concerns of cyber-optimist who firmly believed that Internet would have a positive effect on the efficacy, knowledge, and participation. As we consider that Chinese students spend slightly longer on social media per day compared with German students, it seems that those young people tend to use social media to share jokes, images, videos and other types of online activities in isolation of related politics. In fact, social media allow young men and women to use in different ways they couldn't in the past. Therefore, social media is not seen as monolithic, different forms of social media as well as distinct types of use may lead to different impact on individual's political individual's political knowledge, efficacy, and participation.

6.4 Hypothesis testing

In this section, the study tested several hypotheses based on the data above, and explored the relations in these important political variables.

6.4.1 Social media use and political participation

This study attempts to disentangle the concept of political participation, which has been conceptualized and operationalized with three dimensions including political engagement, participation within the representative democratic system and political outside the representative democratic system. So, the measurement of the concept of political participation in the current study consists of four steps: (see Table 6.6)

Firstly, in order to gauge the index of political engagement (questions 1, 2, 3, 14 and 15, see appendix), the questions were recorded into new variables that have the same scale (rescaled onto the same range), as follows: (0=not at all interested or no; 1= interested or yes). The index which is based on a battery of items attached to the question including political interest, follow politics in the media and political discussion. On average, the results show that the Germans' level of political engagement (M=0.946, SD=0.750) is higher than Chinese's (M=0.859, SD=0.147).

Secondly, the study employed a number of questions to measure the second dimension of political participation: participation within the representative democratic system (questions 8, 9, 12, 13 and 20, recoded as 1=yes; 0=no). Our measure of this dimension taps whether respondents during the past year have participated in elections, became a member of a political party, became a member in the traditional organization or joined any political activities at school. The indicators of each question have been summed to a simple additive index standardized to range from 0 to 1. The results suggest that there are big differences between the two groups in terms of participation in election. Germans are more willing to participate in election than Chinese. However, Chinese students performed better in participation in university and becoming membership in a party, on average they have higher level of participation with the representative democratic system (M=0.329, SD=0.253) than Germans (M=0.312, SD=0.138).

Thirdly, the third dimension or the index of political participation was generated by adding of all questions of political outside the representative democratic system (questions 9, 13, see appendix) into a general index after recoding all the variable on the same scale (0=no; 1=yes). The results indicate that the political participation outside the representative democratic system among German's (M=0.390, SD=0.172) is higher than among Chinese's (M=0.190, SD=0.217).

Finally, a single index that combines all the above three indexes or dimensions into one measure of 'political participation' was created. The scale ranges between 0 and 10 including all above three variables. The results indicate that the level of political participation for German students was higher than level of political participation for Chinese students with Mean values of 1.647 (SD=0.288 among Germans) and 1.377 (SD=0.431 among Chinese) respectively. Therefore, the results confirmed the study hypothesis that "There are significant differences between German university student's and Chinese in the level of political participation".

One point worth considering is that how to deal with the problem of weighting and its function in statistical analysis in this study. Due to the previous studies did not mention the statistical method of how to handle this problem of weight in terms of the three dimensions of political participation mentioned above. Based on the broad definition of political participation in this research, each index of dimension has equal importance. Meanwhile, in order to ensure that the study is able to get the valid measurement of political participation without ignoring the appropriate weights of any dimensions of political participation, the author constructed the general index of political participation by using simple mathematical method like follows. The study firstly multiplied the index of political engagement by ×1, the index of participation within the representative democratic system by× 1, and the index of participation outside the representative democratic system by×1. Then, the study added up each participatory dimension to get a general index of political participation. The results in these analyses are summarized in Table 6.6.

Table 6.6 The measurement of political participation

Three dimensions	Germany(N=300)		China(N=300)	
	Mean	SD	Mean	SD
Political engagement ×1	**0.946**	**0.75**	**0.859**	**0.147**
Political interest	0.967	0.802	0.95	0.156
Follow politics in the media	1	0	0.987	0.115
Political discussion	0.869	0.197	0.641	0.32
participation within the representative democratic system ×1	**0.312**	**0.138**	**0.329**	**0.253**
Participation in election	0.907	0.223	0.35	0.365
Partisanship	0.1	0.296	0.43	0.653
Member in the traditional organization	0.072	0.217	0.13	0.25
Participation at school	0.17	0.197	0.4	0.253
Political participation outside the representative system ×1	**0.39**	**0.172**	**0.19**	**0.217**
Membership in NGO	0.082	0.232	0.071	0.221
Political discourse	0.439	0.24	0.26	0.289
Illegal and violent forms of participation	0.177	0.256	0.096	0.246
Political Protest	0.492	0.326	0.14	0.304
Political consumerism	0.758	0.369	0.382	0.446
Political participation	**1.647**	**0.288**	**1.377**	**0.431**

Based on the measurement of political participation, the results of the t-test also revealed a highly significant differences (t = 9.024, Sig. < 0.001) between the two countries regarding the level of political participation (Table 6.7), and the differences were in favor of China with a mean value of 1.38 and a standard deviation of 0.431, comparing to a mean value of 1.65 and a standard deviation of 0.288 in Germany. And these results confirmed the hypothesis that there are statistically significant differences between young Chinese and German in their level of political participation.

Here are some of the reasons why there are such very great differences between Chinese and German students' political participation: First, people in China have relatively limited channels to access to political information and participate in politics. Meanwhile, traditional political culture has a great impact on Chinese citizens' practice of political participation. As a result, Chinese university students are unlikely to discuss politics with friends and actively participate in politics.

Table 6.7 Independent Samples Test

		Levene's Test for Equality of Variances		t-test for Equality of Means					95% Confidence Interval of the Difference	
		F	Sig.	t	df	Sig. (2-tailed)	Mean Difference	Std. Error Difference	Lower	Upper
Political participation	Equal variances assumed	37.556	0	9.024	598	0	0.2698	0.0299	0.21108	0.32852
	Equal variances not assumed			9.024	521.42	0	0.2698	0.0299	0.21107	0.32853

Second, in general, German students are more likely to participate in illegal and violent forms of political actions. However, these kinds of political activities are not allowed by Chinese government. By contrast, Chinese students are more prefer to participate in political actions that are beneficial to the general public, that are lower in conflict with other participants (such as following hard news), that can be achieved without too much difficulties, and that have a lower risk of suppression by the Chinese government (Zhang & Lin, 2014). That also explains why Chinese students' level of participation at university is higher than German students'. It's worth pointing out that people in China tend to express political concerns or influence the governmental decisions by lobbying government officials privately or via bribery or cronyism (Shi, 1997; Shyu, 2010). Although the students may contact or lobby with include student cadres, university leaders and government officials, such types of political participation are not common in the campus due to the limitation of financial resources and conditions.

Third, although social media help Chinese students to participate in politics online, such as by joining online discussion groups or virtual organizations in a safe way. In fact, the positive effects of social media platforms on civic-political participation among university students were found to exist only marginally (Zhang, 2010). The main reason for this is that opportunities for political participation are a necessary but "far from sufficient" condition for democracy (Norris, 2002, p. 2). By contrast, German students have more channels for them to express political concerns and engage in different modes of online and offline political participation.

In order to investigate the influence of the time spent on the social media on political participation, we will use a General Linear model. This permits us to measure the effect of the social media while simultaneously taking the demographic variables (gender, age, education, personal income, hometown) into account. In our first analysis, we investigate the influence of intensive social media use on political participation. We argue that more time spent online increases the frequency and likelihood of online communication, which might positively influence student's political participation in Germany and China.

Table 6.8 Tests of Between-Subjects Effects (In Germany)

Dependent Variable: Political participation

Source	Type III Sum of Squares	df	Mean Square	F	Sig.
Corrected Model	2.205[a]	20	0.11	1.366	0.138
	47.128	1	47.128	583.869	0
Gender	0.03	1	0.03	0.372	0.543
Age	0.147	2	0.073	0.908	0.404
Education	0.321	3	0.107	1.326	0.266
Personal income	0.387	6	0.064	0.799	0.572
Hometown	0.338	3	0.113	1.398	0.244
Time spend per day	0.663	5	0.133	1.642	0.149
Error	22.52	279	0.081		
Total	838.566	300			
Corrected Total	24.725	299			

a. R Squared = .089 (Adjusted R Squared = .024)

However, if we look at Table 6.8, we notice that spending time on social media has no significant influence on German young people's demographic (including gender, age, education, personal income as well as come from) and political participation. Univariate analyses were then performed to test for the linear relationships between time spend per day on social media and political participation, but no linear function was found. Therefore, how much time students spend online does not influence their levels of political participation.

Table 6.9 Tests of Between-Subjects Effects (In China)

Dependent Variable: Political participation

Source	Type III Sum of Squares	df	Mean Square	F	Sig.
Corrected Model	4.447[a]	20	0.222	1.216	0.24
	67.344	1	67.344	368.376	0
Gender	0.99	1	0.99	5.414	0.021
Age	0.078	2	0.039	0.213	0.808
Education	1.69	3	0.563	3.081	0.028
Personal income	0.498	6	0.083	0.454	0.842
Hometown	0.529	3	0.176	0.965	0.41
Time spend per day	0.681	5	0.136	0.745	0.59
Error	51.005	279	0.183		
Total	624.505	300			
Corrected Total	55.452	299			

a. R Squared = .080 (Adjusted R Squared = .014)

As shown in Table 6.9 and Table 6.10, the study also finds that spending time on social media per day has no significant influence on Chinese students' political participation. Therefore, **H1： The frequency of social media use will correlate positively with their political participation.** But we find that both gender and students' educational level have a positive influence on political participation. Furthermore, men are more likely than women to take part in political participation in China (t=2.327, p<0.05), thus **H9 was confirmed in Chinese context**.

Table 6.10 Parameter Estimates

Dependent Variable: Political participation

Parameter	B	Std. Error	t	Sig.	95% Confidence Interval	
					Lower Bound	Upper Bound
Intercept	1.132	0.245	4.62	0	0.649	1.614
[Gender=0]	0.123	0.053	2.327	0.021	0.019	0.226
[Gender=1]	0[a]	.	.	.	.	.
[Age=1]	-0.069	0.108	-0.634	0.526	-0.282	0.144
[Age=2]	-0.041	0.098	-0.418	0.676	-0.233	0.151
[Age=3]	0[a]	.	.	.	.	.
[Education=1]	0.188	0.146	1.282	0.201	-0.1	0.475
[Education=2]	0.117	0.116	1.003	0.317	-0.112	0.346
[Education=3]	0.263	0.109	2.402	0.017	0.047	0.478
[Education=4]	0[a]	.	.	.	.	.
[Personal income=1]	-0.01	0.206	-0.049	0.961	-0.416	0.396
[Personal income=2]	-0.044	0.208	-0.212	0.832	-0.454	0.365
[Personal income=3]	0.042	0.208	0.202	0.84	-0.367	0.45
[Personal income=4]	-0.041	0.222	-0.185	0.853	-0.479	0.397
[Personal income=5]	-0.157	0.236	-0.663	0.508	-0.622	0.309
[Personal income=6]	-0.22	0.365	-0.602	0.548	-0.938	0.499
[Personal income =7]	0[a]	.	.	.	.	.
[Hometown=1]	0.002	0.07	0.032	0.975	-0.136	0.14
[Hometown=2]	-0.032	0.105	-0.303	0.762	-0.238	0.174
[Hometown=3]	0.089	0.064	1.394	0.164	-0.037	0.215
[Hometown=4]	0[a]	.	.	.	.	.
[Time spend per day =1]	0.006	0.102	0.063	0.95	-0.195	0.208
[Time spend per day=2]	0.102	0.09	1.134	0.258	-0.075	0.279
[Time spend per day=3]	0.104	0.089	1.179	0.239	-0.07	0.279
[Time spend per day=4]	0.001	0.093	0.014	0.989	-0.181	0.184
[Time spend per day=5]	0.058	0.109	0.531	0.596	-0.156	0.271
[Time spend per day =6]	0[a]	.	.	.	.	.

a. This parameter is set to zero because it is redundant. Female=1,male=0

However, men and women did not differ in their political participation in Germany. A big reason for the difference in terms of gender gaps in politics in Germany and China is that western democracies have made great strides in eradicating gender gaps in politics in the recent past. As a result, German women's overall position has improved significantly compared to the early 20th century (Glatte & de Vries, 2015). By contrast, China still lags far behind many other western countries which have made even greater progress in terms of facilitating women's representation in powerful political bodies and participation in politics (Guo & Zheng, 2008).

6.4.2 Political variables and political participation

Correlations were used to test the relationship between the dependent variable (political participation) and the independent variables, which were the three related political variables including political knowledge, political trust and political efficacy. Pearson correlations in Table 6.11 showed that there were significant correlations between the political participation and two of the political variables at the .005 level. Among the three factors, the findings show that political knowledge had the strongest correlation ($r=.133$) with political participation. The second strongest correlation ($r=.120$) with the political participation was political efficacy. In summary, Germany students' political participation had significant relationships with political knowledge and political efficacy. Thus, the hypothesis H4 and H5 was supported. Table 6.11 shows the correlation results.

Table 6.11 Pearson Correlations (In Germany)

		Political participation	Political knowledge	Political trust	Political efficacy
Political participation	Pearson Correlation	1	.133*	-0.085	.120*
	Sig. (2-tailed)		0.021	0.141	0.037
	N	300	300	300	300
Political knowledge	Pearson Correlation	.133*	1	0.064	-0.008
	Sig. (2-tailed)	0.021		0.27	0.887
	N	300	300	300	300
Political trust	Pearson Correlation	-0.085	0.064	1	-.357**
	Sig. (2-tailed)	0.141	0.27		0
	N	300	300	300	300
Political efficacy	Pearson Correlation	.120*	-0.008	-.357**	1
	Sig. (2-tailed)	0.037	0.887	0	
	N	300	300	300	300

*. Correlation is significant at the 0.05 level (2-tailed).
**. Correlation is significant at the 0.01 level (2-tailed).

Table 6.12 Pearson Correlations (In China)

		Political participation	Political knowledge	Political trust	Political efficacy
Political participation	Pearson Correlation	1	0.087	.115*	-0.061
	Sig. (2-tailed)		0.134	0.047	0.294
	N	300	300	300	300
Political knowledge	Pearson Correlation	0.087	1	0.109	-0.015
	Sig. (2-tailed)	0.134		0.058	0.801
	N	300	300	300	300
Political trust	Pearson Correlation	.115*	0.109	1	-.256**
	Sig. (2-tailed)	0.047	0.058		0
	N	300	300	300	300
Political efficacy	Pearson Correlation	-0.061	-0.015	-.256**	1
	Sig. (2-tailed)	0.294	0.801	0	
	N	300	300	300	300

*. Correlation is significant at the 0.05 level (2-tailed).
**. Correlation is significant at the 0.01 level (2-tailed).

In the same line, only political trust, as shown below in table 6.12, are strongly related with the variable of political participation ($r=.133$, $p<0.05$) in China. Therefore, only

H6: Students' political trust is positively correlated with their political participation was supported in a Chinese setting. The fundamental cause lies in that the CCP now strives to control the ideology of university students and conducted a program of "patriotic education" to maintain their authority in the university in China (Zhao, 1998). As a result, political trust among Chinese university students was higher than German students and it is affect their political participation in a positive way. By contrast, German students' political trust is not positively correlated with their political participation.

6.4.3 Social media news use and traditional media news use

Although our study above suggests no significant relationship between more social media use and more political participation, it is still possible that specific forms of online activities (such as joining groups on social networking sites, following the news, and reading news contributions) can positively influence individuals' level of political participation. First, we will test the bivariate relations between specific forms of social media use and the level of political participation in China and Germany separately (see Table 6.13). After that, we will run ordinary least squares regressions for each item of social media use separately (see Table 6.14 and Table 6.15). The reason for this is that we need to control these variables (age, gender, education, income and hometown) and related political variables in our analysis. In addition, we will use Correlations to find out the relationship between media news use and political participation for each country separately (see Table 6.15) .We argued that social media political news use is more related with political participation than traditional media news use.

As displayed in Table 6.13, "Following the political news," "Express opinions explicitly on government and politics," and "Organize political activities" are positively related to political participation of Germany students. The correlations between political participation and these three activities are, .230 (p < .001), .319 (p < .001) and .391 (p < .001).Young Germans who follow the news on the social media or express their opinions or organization political activities are more likely to participate politically. However, "obtain information for study" is negatively associated with German students' political participation. Perhaps the reason lies in that most of German university students use social media for recreational and entertainment needs.

For Chinese university students, "Following the political news", "Join groups on a social networking sites", "Express opinions explicitly on government and politics" and "Organize political activities" also increase levels of political participation. Surprisingly, "To discover new music, books and other entertainment," and "Obtain information for study" are positively associated with Chinese students' political participation. So a possible explanation can be that Chinese people who get information for study from the social media as well as obtain amusement can obtain a lot of social media use skills, which are helpful in boosting their level of political participation. Another possible reason is that "the line between entertainment, lifestyle issues and political issues is not clear-cut" for Chinese netizens, so when they use social media to post or comment about their everyday life, lifestyles and amusement issues always touched upon governmental policies and practices (Marolt & Herold, 2014, p. 147). These results above suggest that social media activities are significantly associated with levels of political involvement in Germany and China.

Table 6.13 Bivariate relation between social media use and political participation

Social media use	Germany	China
	r	r
Browse or update social networking profile	-0.032	0.111
Find information about friends	-0.05	0.047
Obtain information for study	-.196**	.138*
Following the political news	.230**	.148*
Keep in touch with friends/ family/ acquaintances	-0.089	0.088
Reader new contributions	0.014	0.111
Join groups on a social networking site	0.074	.141*
To discover new music, books and other entertainment	0.037	.161**
Express opinions explicitly on government and politics	.319**	.250**
Organize political activities	.391**	.237**

*. Correlation is significant at the 0.05 level (2-tailed).
**. Correlation is significant at the 0.01 level (2-tailed).

However, we did not control for a number of influential factors in Table 6.13, so we need to expand our analysis. Considering the effect of socioeconomic status on social media access and use, it is important to control these variables (age, gender, education, income and hometown) in our analysis. In addition, earlier studies have indicated that previous studies indicated that political attitudinal variables (political trust, political efficacy, and political knowledge) they were related to political participation (Grönlund & Setälä, 2007; Quintelier & Vissers, 2008). Therefore, in the following models, both demographic variables and political attitudinal variables were used as controls in the follow regression analyses.

In order to gain further insight into the relationship between social media use and political participation, Ordinary Least Squares Regression analyses were performed. Results of the regression analyses show that even when controlling for these attitudinal variables, certain social media activities remain significant predictors of political participation in Germany and China (see Table 6.14 and Table 6.15). Especially some online activities such as "Following the political news," "Express opinions explicitly on government and politics," and "Organize political activities" are clearly and significantly associated with political participation.

After that, by using multivariate linear regression analysis, the results indicate that there is still significantly positive correlation between "Organize political activities" and political participation among university students in Germany and China. Thus, results of the regression analyses indicate some specific social media activities especially for "Organize political activities" on the social media have an effect on the propensity to participate in public life. Therefore, **H2 was support.**

Table 6.14 Multivariate model for social media use and political participation in Germany

	Model 1	Model 2	Model 3	Model 4	Model 5	Model 6	Model 7	Model 8	Model 9	Model 10	Model 11
Control variables											
Age	0.073	0.075	0.009	0.083	0.067	0.085	0.088	0.084	0.072	0.1 2	-0.01
Gender	0.006	0.003	0.029	-0.028	0.008	-0.003	-0.001	0.002	-0.018	0.C1	0.039
Education	0.074	0.071	0.065	0.08	0.072	0.077	0.063	0.076	0.081	0.068	0.079
Personal income	0.056	0.055	0.045	0.051	0.054	0.057	0.057	0.058	0.033	0.098	0.004
Hometown	-0.068	-0.068	-0.084	-0.042	-0.07	-0.072	-0.059	-0.069	-0.058	-0.C39	-0.057
Political attitude											
Political efficacy	0.09	0.088	0.1	0.066	0.089	0.078	0.078	0.08	0.055	0.067	0.078
Political knowledge	.128*	.128*	.128*	0.11	.127*	.130*	.129*	.132*	.114*	.113*	0.091
Political trust	-0.048	-0.049	-0.04	-0.048	-0.043	-0.067	-0.051	-0.048	-0.071	-0.33	-0.011
Social media use											
Browse or update social networking profile	-0.019										-0.05
Find information about friends		-0.008									-0.009
Obtain information for study			-.167*								-.217 *
Following political news				.225***							0.134
Keep in touch with friends					-0.042						-0.091
Reader new contributions						0.067					0.05
Join groups on social networking site							0.069				-0.024
To discover new music, books and other entertainment								0.062			-0.036
Express opinions on politics									.308***		0.121
Organize political activities										.38P**	.317***
R²	0.064	0.064	0.085	0.113	0.066	0.068	0.069	0.068	0.157	0.205	0.278

Note: The dependent variable is political participation.

*** p < .001; ** p < .01; * p < .05.

Based on above analysis, the study expands our analysis to test the relationship between traditional media political news use and social media political news use in terms of students' political participation. Earlier studies have indicated that online news delivery systems will serve as a supplement or substitute for traditional news media, with some researchers suggesting the possibility of replacement among younger cohorts citizens (Althaus & Tewksbury, 2000). Therefore, in the following models, we test the relationship of traditional political news use; social media political news use and political participation in Germany and China (see Table 6.16). The standardized structural coefficients are displayed in Table 6.15. In Germany, traditional media news use was positively and significantly related to political participation (r=.402, p<0.01). Besides, social media use for political news also positively and significantly correlates with political participation (r=.230, p<0.01). These results confirm than more people used traditional and social media for political news, the more they engaged in political activities. Similarly, in China, informational use of traditional use for news (r=.222, p < 0.01) and social media news use (r=.148, p < 0.05) had a significant and positive association with political participation. However, social media news is not more associated with political participation than traditional media in both countries. **Thus, H3 are not supported.** Part of the reason may be that while social media had become an important medium for students to gather and discuss civil and political issues, students also faced problems such as false information online and unwanted advertisement websites.

Table 6.15 Multivariate model for social media use and political participation in China

	Model 1	Model 2	Model 3	Model 4	Model 5	Model 6	Model 7	Model 8	Model 9	Model 10	Model 11
Control variables											
Age	0.093	0.087	0.09	0.076	0.082	0.071	0.08	0.097	0.08	0.1	0.096
Gender	-0.096	-0.106	-0.103	-0.081	-.119*	-0.105	-0.082	-0.093	-0.058	-0.073	-0.067
Education	0.016	0.025	0.015	0.027	0.037	0.038	0.036	0.037	0.023	0.006	0.021
Personal income	-0.004	-0.009	-0.007	-0.011	-0.026	-0.007	-0.02	-0.006	-0.004	-0.008	-0.003
Hometown	0.025	0.027	0.039	0.028	0.046	0.032	0.018	0.033	0.047	0.013	0.055
Political attitude											
Political efficacy	-0.047	-0.04	-0.037	-0.04	-0.042	-0.043	-0.035	-0.038	-0.056	-0.05	-0.057
Political knowledge	0.082	0.059	0.069	0.061	0.071	0.049	0.066	0.078	0.059	0.069	0.087
Political trust	0.097	0.099	0.095	0.092	0.103	0.097	0.098	0.087	0.085	0.09	0.077
Social media use											
Browse or update social networking profile	.132*										0.054
Find information about friends		0.061									-0.066
Obtain information for study			.146*								0.062
Following political news				.123*							0.011
Keep in touch with friends					.129*						0.057
Reader new contributions						0.106					0.037
Join groups on social networking site							.127*				-0.053
To discover new music, books and other entertainment								.179*			0.064
Express opinions on politics									.239***		0.106
Organize political activities										.231***	.145*
R²	0.058	0.045	0.062	0.055	0.056	0.052	0.056	0.071	0.095	0.093	0.125

Note: The dependent variable is political participation.

*** p < .001; ** p < .01; * p < .05.

In addition, German student's political participation is more closely related to social media use than Chinese student's participation (see Table 6.16). **Therefore, H8 are also not supported.** The reasons can be attributed to the following factors: Firstly, potential for social media to affect students' political behaviors in China is constrained by conditions online and offline.

In China, although social media opened up new spheres for students to expression in several different modes, network information is under severe control and censorship. Even the Chinese government employed large group of Internet administrators to remove online posts or comments that "represent, reinforce, or spur social mobilization" (King, Pan, & Roberts, 2012, p. 326) on social media. Secondly, "the CCP maintains the Communist ideology through state-led patriotic campaigns as well as the nationwide education system and state-controlled media" (Zhao, 1998).

Table 6.16 Correlations

		Germany			China		
		Political participation	Traditional media news use	Social media news use	Political participation	Traditional media news use	Social media news use
Political participation	Pearson Correlation	1	.402**	.230**	1	.222**	.148*
	Sig. (2-tailed)		0	0		0	0.01
	N	300	300	300	300	300	300
Traditional media news use	Pearson Correlation	.402**	1	.350**	.222**	1	.599**
	Sig. (2-tailed)	0		0	0		0
	N	300	300	300	300	300	300
Social media news use	Pearson Correlation	.230**	.350**	1	.148*	.599**	1
	Sig. (2-tailed)	0	0		0.01	0	
	N	300	300	300	300	300	300

**. Correlation is significant at the 0.01 level (2-tailed).

*. Correlation is significant at the 0.05 level (2-tailed).

6.4.4 Summary of hypothesis testing in Germany and China

To sum up, this study suggests that young people who spend more time online do not participate in politics more frequently. However, social media political news use is related with political participation even control demographic variables. In addition, three political variables (political knowledge, and political trust and efficacy) are not all related to political participation. Due to the low level of political knowledge and political efficacy among Chinese students, there are no relationships these two political variables and political participation.

Moreover, although news consumption via social media for young people is a relatively new channel, the traditional news media is not likely to be supplemented or substituted by social media. Traditional news media still have important role in boosting the level of citizens' political participation by attracting large audience, especially when the appearance of network newspapers, electronic newspapers, television and other new generation media. Furthermore, the study finds the same relationship between political participation and gender difference as in the previous analysis: men are more likely to be involvement in the political activities in China. In conclusion, in Germany the four hypotheses, H2, H4, H5 and H7, were supported. Five hypotheses, H1, H3, H6, H8 and H9 were rejected. By contrast, H2, H6, H7, H9 were accepted in China. Table 6.17 summarizes all the results of hypothesis testing (Table 6.17).

Table 6.17 Summary of hypothesis testing in Germany and China

Hypotheses	Germany	China
H1: The frequency of social media use will correlate positively with political participation.	Not supported	Not supported
H2: Social media use for political news will correlate positively with their political participation.	Supported	Supported
H3: Use of social media for political news correlates more strongly with political participation than traditional media.	Not supported	Not supported
H4: Students' political knowledge is positively correlated with their political participation.	Supported	Not supported
H5: Students' political efficacy is positively correlated with their political participation.	Supported	Not supported
H6: Students' political trust is positively correlated with their political participation.	Not supported	Supported
H7: There are significant differences between German university student's and Chinese in the level of political participation.	Supported	Supported
H8: Chinese student's political participation is more closely related to social media use than German student's participation.	Not supported	Not supported
H9: Men are more likely to participate in politics than women.	Not Supported	Supported

Chapter 7 Conclusion in light of theory and hypothesis

7.1 Conclusion

The impact of the social media on the political sphere has been the topic of much debate in recent years. This study examines the relationship between the use of social media as well as traditional media and their political participation among university students in Germany and China. The focus is on university students due to they represent the next generation of adult voters who will have a large influence on the shape and form of the future democratization process. The analysis began with a hypothesis of the frequency of social media use could influence in political participation behaviors that was drawn from the work of previous studies. With the data, the research cannot confirm the hypothesis that young people who spend more time on social media in front of the computer are more frequently participate in politics. Then, this study particularly tackled the relationships between specific types of social media use (Reading new contributions, following the news, and joining groups on a social networking site) and various forms of political participation for the young people in Germany and China.

The empirical study found that certain social media activities are positively linked to levels of political participation. This research is consistent with empirical studies that have found that the amount of time spent online is less important than the certain patterns of online activities that young people engage in (Quintelier & Vissers, 2008). General Linear regression analysis supported hypothesis 2 granting an important role of social media use for political news in exerted a significant and positive impact on Germany and Chinese student' involvement in political actions. The more young people used social media for political news, the more they engaged in political activities.

Moreover, consistent with previous studies involving Western democracies that political efficacy and political knowledge, both of which play a powerful role in promoting Germany students' level of participation in political activity in the study. However, the study failed to find a relationship between the trustworthiness of politics and political participation among Germans. One explanation for these findings is "that politicians and political parties being in competition with each other, trying to maximize votes and shifting opinions in the course of political negotiations and consensus building appear more inconsistent and disloyal to their principle" (Spannring, *et al.*, 2008, p. 46).

Unlike Germany, political knowledge and political efficacy are not related to Chinese students' political participation behaviors. The reason is that low level of political knowledge background in understanding of political affairs as well as they fell powerless of themselves toward politics in such a one-party communist stat in China. It's worth mentioning that political trust among Chinese university students was higher and it is affect their political participation in a positive way. These results indicate that different political variables influence on individuals' participation in politics in different way, which extends our understanding of how these political variables related with political behaviors in accordance to different stages of democratic development and particular political system in Germany and China.

In addition to the contribution of social media use for news, the current study also taps the effects of traditional media news use on individuals' political behaviors. The relationship of traditional media political news use and political participation was significant for both the Germany and Chinese samples with the Chinese sample showing a slightly stronger relationship. Meanwhile, the study found traditional media news use is more associated with participatory behavior of youth than social media news use in both countries. Despite the fact that social media is developing swiftly in all over the world, social media do not substitute or replace traditional media in the political communication area. Results are more in line with the argue that "They coexist, integrating issues from the periphery of the political system or serving as a springboard for the democratic deliberation of content that is produced within the media subsystem" (Gil De Zúñiga, *et al.*, 2009).

Additionally, the results confirm that hypothesis that "There are significant differences between German university student's and Chinese in the level of political participation". The t-test shows that there is a highly significant difference between the two countries. Besides, there are other evidences of participation differences to support the statements. By focusing on the three dimensions in particular, namely political engagement, participation within the representative democratic system, and participation outside the representative democratic system, the study affirms that some differences exists in different aspects of political behaviors among Germans and Chinese. These difference can be explained partly by German university student's who have more exposure to Internet news in general were more involved in politics than Chinese university student's. Moreover, the political environment, media system as well as the related political regulations and laws are important components in university students' participation in the political life in their own country.

Finally, like many studies on the gender difference in political participation, our preliminary investigations have also found a gender gap in China. In China, the independent T- test shows there is significant difference between males and females. In Germany, there was no difference between the means and no gap between male and female related to their level of political participation. When asking their frequency of follow political news in the social media and traditional media, Chinese young men use social media more often than women. However, young Germany women and men stated no such gender difference in terms of social media news consumption.

Besides, our preliminary investigations have found a persistent gender difference in several main facets of political participation, with Chinese male respondents scoring higher on traditional media news use, political knowledge, political interest, political efficacy, and political discussion on the average level. Therefore, the hypothesis that "Men are more likely to participate in politics than women" is only supported in the Chinese context. This finding is consistent with other studies of gender differences in political participation (Tong, 2003). As China developed economically, many Chinese women have succeeded in a wide range of areas, they are still lagging far behind politically. At least in the political sphere, the women are discriminated against, and prejudice against the small number of female politicians and officials is widespread in China society (Howell, 2006).

At the same time, basic socio-economic factors were in directly controlled for in the research, variables concerning a person's demographic background such as age, level of education, personal income as well as come from. The sample respondents were approximately aged 18 to 31, and the education level was high education including undergraduate, postgraduate and doctorate students. General linear regress shows that, for Chinese citizens, when socio-demographic variables are considered, having higher personal income and with higher education are more likely to join in participation. However, the analysis of General linear regress suggests that, in Germany wealth and education play a more limited role in explaining political participation than in China. Such differences are to some extent expected as these reflect the different stages of technology adoption of particular societies and political system in the two countries. For example, China is a rapidly developing area of the world with respect to a range of technologies. ICTs were still very new at this time of the study, and most Chinese educational settings had only started to use computers in the middle of the 1990s (Li & Kirkup, 2007). Therefore, Chinese students had less experience and skill of the Internet, were less likely own private computers, or have good Internet access in their living accommodation, compared to their Germany counterparts.

Overall, our findings shed a positive light on the ongoing debate regarding the democratic potential of the social media in a different socio-political context. Besides the traditional resources and factors, some forms of social media use play a significant role in fostering political participation among young people in Europe and possibly also other Asian societies. Moreover, the study provide an important step forward by empirically demonstrating that the differences levels of Germany's and Chinese students' democratic engagement from a broader definition of political participation. The article demonstrates the limitations of previous research designs that are heavily focused on only the established online and institutional ways of participation and media use, passing over the wide-ranging and diverging patterns of participation among students. Only research takes into account broader political participation, including conventional, unconventional and other new forms of youth democratic engagement, so can one get a better understanding the challenges and changes political participation in the current study.

At last, the conclusions from this study have also important implications for the development of the social media and other information and communication technologies in the different political and media system, and should be studied in further depth. As the Internet rapidly becomes an important part of lives among young generations in all over the world, it is of great importance for governments, political parties, organizations, and universities to better understand the mechanisms of interaction of online media use and real political life.

7.2 Some limitations of the current study

All in all, these findings help to shed some light with respect to the effects of social media use for news in the democratic process. Nevertheless, there are some limitations of the current study in evidence, with one of the most noticeable being the nature of our data. Firstly, the samples were taken from student populations from two universities which may not be representative of young people in general. Therefore, we must stress that these results in the study cannot be generalized to all young people. More representative samples of the student population and the general population may offer further evidence of the relationships between different variables.

Secondly, this study depends on cross-sectional data and strictly speaking, the causal direction of the relations among the variables should be interpreted with caution, particularly with respect to the relationship between media news consumption and political participation. It may very well be that specific media information use for news drives on the intrinsic motivation of people to be politically active. This potentially reverse, or reciprocal causation, or maybe even reinforcing process of media news use is possible. Previous research employing panel data have indicated that an asymmetrical reciprocal model may be in order. For instance, Rojas has found that participating in politics might make one more likely to discuss about politics in the future, but the association between talking about politics at this time and participating in the future is much stronger (Rojas, 2008). Thus, more complicated measures of both cross-sectional and overtime analysis of panel data take into account to address these issues empirically.

Thirdly, although questionnaire survey is a very useful tool regarding our sample (young people) and the subject of this research (social media use), the survey may have led to a somewhat skewed distribution of our sample. Consequently, we are unable to make comparisons with youth that are rarely or hardly use the Internet and might be active in politics. Therefore, we envision these tasks as appealing lines of research for future studies in the political communication field.

Finally, our analysis only provides brief snapshots of political participation in Germany and China at this time and we are therefore unable to examine how, or indeed if, changes to political participation have happened over time. Along with the popularization of the network and the extensive usage of the news resources, whether social media news consumption can affect young people's degree and type of political participation, which is a phenomenon worthy of worrying about and researching.

Despite the current study has its limitations, this article still makes a modest but somewhat important contribution to comparative political communication research. The contribution of this emerging venue for information to participatory behaviors is now established. Given the growing popularity and penetration of social media, and the way they are embraced by today's society, these relatively immature relationships between media use and political participation beg further study. After all, communication through social media may indeed contribute to not only the proliferation of a networked society but also it may promote a more democratic world.

7.3 Suggestions for future research

Some of the findings will require further investigations, in particular further study should use larger number of participants in different geographical areas, conducted for a longer period in multiple waves survey panels to prove the causality relationship between media use and political participation, and considers other groups of population not only young people.

Moreover, future research is necessary to refine comparative measures of different types of media use and to examine the impact of this participation on a wider range of individual political attitudes and behaviors than those analyzed here, as well as taking into account increasing fluidity between the offline and online participation domains. In order to uncover address these causality quandaries and issues, additional comparative methods and longitudinal surveys must be developed and expanded in the near future.

In addition, although the focus of this study is to examine the effects of social media use on political attitudes and behavior, future research should pay more attention in their research to various forms of new media channels such as specific web sites, blogs, Facebook and other types of social networking sites to delineate their differential effects on political attitudes and behaviors as the Internet has been reckoned as a powerful tool for enhancing citizen democratic participation in daily life.

Finally, the key role of social media and other information and communication technologies in political transformation and democracy should be studied in further depth. It is not to be neglected that the increasing complexity of the media environment means that people in the developing countries also have more choices and options than in the past. Thus, scholars and professionals need to provide additional support for the notion that online news consumption matters for political engagement in the non-western context.

REFERENCES

Agran, M., Arden, K. K., & MacLean, W. (2014). Voting participation for people with intellectual and developmental disabilities.

Albrecht, A., & Verboord, M. (2010). Political trust and the role of social networking sites: an empirical study of German party youth organisations' Facebook and Twitter use and its influence on young citizens.

Alexa. (2015). World map of social networks. *http://vincos.it/world-map-of-social-networks/* Retrieved June 16, 2015

Allen, C. S. (1999). *Transformation of the German political party system: Institutional crisis or democratic renewal?* (Vol. 2): Berghahn Books.

Almond, G. A. (1974). *Comparative politics today*: Pearson Education India.

Althaus, S. L., & Tewksbury, D. (2000). Patterns of Internet and traditional news media use in a networked community. *Political Communication, 17*(1), 21-45.

Amnå, E., & Ekman, J. (2014). Standby citizens: diverse faces of political passivity. *European Political Science Review, 6*(02), 261-281.

Anduiza, E., Jensen, M. J., & Jorba, L. (2012). Digital media and political engagement worldwide : A comparative study: Cambridge University Press.

Anna Horvath, G. P. (2013). *Political participation and EU citizenship: Perceptions and behaviours of young people.*

Asher, H. B., Richardson, B. M., & Weisberg, H. F. (1984). *Political participation / an ISSC workbook in comparative analysis.* Frankfurt ; New York: Campus-Verlag.

Avery, J. M. (2009). Videomalaise or virtuous circle? The influence of the news media on political trust. *The International Journal of Press/Politics, 14*(4), 410-433.

Auškalnienė, L. (2012). Assessing participation online: youth and their involvement in social media. Informacijos Mokslai/Information Sciences, 59.

Baek, Y. M. (2015). Political mobilization through social network sites: The mobilizing power of political messages received from SNS friends. *Computers in Human Behavior, 44*, 12-19.

Bakker, T. P., & de Vreese, C. H. (2011). Good news for the future? Young people, Internet use, and political participation. *Communication Research, 38*(4), 451-470.

Balch, G. I. (1974). Multiple indicators in survey research: The concept "sense of political efficacy". *Political Methodology*, 1-43.

Balkin, J. M. (2004). Digital speech and democratic culture: A theory of freedom of expression for the information society. *NyuL rev., 79*, 1.

Bandurski, D. (2012). Obama victory tops Chinese social media *http://cmp.hku.hk/2012/11/07/28618/* Retrieved June 11, 2012

Barberá, P. (2014). How social media reduces mass political polarization. Evidence from Germany, Spain, and the US. *Job market paper, New York University.*

Barboza, D. (2008). Olympics are ratings Bonanza for Chinese TV. *http://www.nytimes.com/2008/08/22/sports/olympics/22cctv.html?_r=0* Retrieved September 3, 2012

Barnes, S. B. (2006). A privacy paradox: Social networking in the United States. *First Monday, 11*(9), 11-15.

Bartl, A. (2003). *Electoral systems in Australia and Germany-a comparative study*: GRIN Verlag.

Baskin, J. S. (2011). *Histories of social media* (1. ed. ed.). San Jose, Calif.: SNCR Press.

Bauman, Z. (2001). *The individualized society*: Polity Press Cambridge.

Baumann, S. (2012). *Development and current characteristics of social media in China*: GRIN Verlag.

Baumgartner, J. C., & Morris, J. S. (2009). MyFaceTube politics: Social networking web sites and political engagement of young adults. *Social Science Computer Review.*

Bay, B. (2012). Participatory media *characteristics of participatory media* Retrieved January 31, 2013

Beach, S. (2004). China: New Journalism, New Threats.

http://cpj.org/reports/2004/08/china-8-04.php Retrieved August 27, 2013

Beauregard, K. (2014). Gender, political participation and electoral systems: A cross - national analysis. *European Journal of Political Research.*

Bennett, W. L. (1998). The uncivic culture: Communication, identity, and the rise of lifestyle politics. *PS: Political Science & Politics, 31*(04), 741-761.

Bennett, W. L., & Iyengar, S. (2008). A new era of minimal effects? The changing foundations of political communication. *Journal of Communication, 58*(4), 707-731.

Best, S. J., & Krueger, B. S. (2005). Analyzing the representativeness of Internet political participation. *Political Behavior, 27*(2), 183-216.

Bimber, B., & Copeland, L. (2013). Digital media and traditional political participation over time in the US. *Journal of Information Technology & Politics*(just-accepted).

Blumler, J. G., Ewbank, A., Cayrol, R., Geerts, C., & Thoveron, G. (1978). A three - national analysis of voters' attitudes to election communication. *European Journal of Political Research, 6*(2), 127-156.

Bohua, H. E. X. (2013). The development of China's Internet in the New Century *http://vu.chineseembassy.org/eng/xwdt/t1035445.htm* Retrieved September 10, 2013

Brady, H. E., Verba, S., & Schlozman, K. L. (1995). Beyond SES: A resource model of political participation. *American Political Science Review*, 271-294.

Brants, K. (1998). Who's afraid of infotainment? *European Journal of Communication, 13*(3), 315-335.

Brunty, J. L., & Helenek, K. (2012). *Social Media Investigation for Law Enforcement*: Newnes, 2012.

Cai, Y. (2011). Why a western-style multi-party system would not be suitable for *China. http://english.qstheory.cn/selections/201109/t20110924_112471.htm*

Retrieved August 3, 2011

Calenda, D., & Meijer, A. (2009). Young people, the Internet and political participation: findings of a web survey in Italy, Spain and The Netherlands. *Information, Communication & Society, 12*(6), 879-898.

Campbell, A., & Valen, H. (1961). Party identification in Norway and the United States. *Public Opinion Quarterly, 25*(4), 505-525.

Carpini, M. X. D. (2000). Gen. com: Youth, civic engagement, and the new information environment. *Political Communication, 17*(4), 341-349.

Carty, V. (2010). New information communication technologies and grassroots mobilization. *Information, Communication & Society, 13*(2), 155-173.

Castells, M. (2009). *Communication power*: Oxford University Press.

Chan, M., Wu, X., Hao, Y., Xi, R., & Jin, T. (2012). Microblogging, online expression, and political efficacy among young Chinese citizens: the moderating role of information and entertainment needs in the use of Weibo. *Cyberpsychology, Behavior, and Social Networking, 15*(7), 345-349.

Chang, H. (2011). Civil political participation political participation report: China has undergone four stages. *http://politics.people.com.cn/GB/30178/15005962.html* Retrieved September 12, 2013

Chapman, C. (2009). The history and evolution of social media *http://www.webdesignerdepot.com/2009/10/the-history-and-evolution-of-social-media/* Retrieved September 12, 2012

Chen, G. M. (2011). Tweet this: A uses and gratifications perspective on how active Twitter use gratifies a need to connect with others. *Computers in Human Behavior, 27*(2), 755-762.

Chen, J., & Zhong, Y. (2002). Why do people vote in semicompetitive elections in China? *Journal of Politics, 64*(1), 178-197.

Chen, S. (2004). The gradual reform of the electoral system in China. Social Science in China -English edition, 25(1), 95-101.

Chen, Z., Rau, P.-L. P., Frank, B., Ignazio, F., Zhou, J., Sajed, S., *et al.* (2013). How to make friends in social network service? A comparison between Chinese and German *cross-cultural design. Cultural Differences in Everyday Life* (pp. 373-382): Springer.

Cheng, J. Y., Zheng, Y., & Chan, C. K.-c. (2012). *China: A new stage of development for an emerging superpower*: City University of HK Press.

Cheng, Y., Liang, J., & Leung, L. (2014). Social network service use on mobile devices: An examination of gratifications, civic attitudes and civic engagement in China. *New Media & Society*, 1461444814521362.

Cheung, C. M., Chiu, P.-Y., & Lee, M. K. (2011). Online social networks: Why do students use facebook? *Computers in Human Behavior, 27*(4), 1337-1343.

Cheuvront, M. (2009). The social media revolution isn't coming. *http://www.lifewithoutpants.com/social-media-revolution/* Retrieved March 26, 2015

China, I. (2011). Demographic profiles of China's top social networking sites *http://www.chinaInternetwatch.com/1312/social-networking-sites-demographics/#ixzz2C R2x60PU* Retrieved March 26, 2015

China.org. (2005). The system of multi-party cooperation and political consultation. *http://english.mofcom.gov.cn/aarticle/topic/bizchina/politicsandsociety/200510/20051000 615915.html* Retrieved April 18, 2013

China.org.cn. (2001). Mass Media *http://www.china.org.cn/english/features/Brief/193358.htm* Retrieved September 12, 2013

China.org.cn. (2007). *White paper on China's political party system.* *http://www.china.org.cn/english/news/231852.htm* Retrieved September 15, 2013

Chiu, L. (2013). How China's National People's Congress is Elected *The NPC is one part of a series of representative elections* Retrieved May 7, 2013

Christmann, S., Melcher, J., Hagenhoff, S., Stock Gissendanner, S., & Krumbein, W. (2010). Web 2.0-Technologien in Meinungsbildungsprozessen von politischen Parteien. *i-com, 9*(3), 21-27.

Chu, G. C. (1988). In search of an Asian perspective of communication theory. *Communication theory: The Asian perspective*, 204-210.

Chu, G. C., & Ju, Y. (1993). Family relations. *The Great Wall in ruins: Communication and cultural change in China*, 63-85.

Cinalli, M., & Füglister, K. (2008). Networks and political contention over unemployment: a comparison of Britain, Germany, and Switzerland. *Mobilization: An International Quarterly, 13*(3), 259-276.

Chiu, C., Ip, C., & Silverman, A. (2012). Mckinsey: Understanding social media in China. *http://businesswatch.21cbh.com/index.php?m=content&c=index&a=show&catid=13&id =212023*, 2013 Retrieved May 7, 2013

Citrin, J. (1974). Comment: the political relevance of trust in government. American Political Science Review, 68(03), 973-988

Clarke, A. (2010). Social Media 4. Political uses and implications for representative democracy. *Background Paper*(2010-10).

CNNIC. (2013). *Statistical Report on Internet Development in China.*

Comscore. (2012). Analytics for a digital world. *http://www.comscore.com/* Retrieved 2013 16 January

Conge, P. J. (1988). The concept of political participation: Toward a definition: JSTOR.

Conradt, D. P., & Langenbacher, E. (2013). *The German Polity*: Rowman & Littlefield.

Consulting, M. F. (2013). TV in China. *http://www.m-f-consulting.com/en/* Retrieved Sepetember 3, 2013

Converse, P. E. (1972). Change in the American electorate. *The human meaning of social change*, 263-337.

Coutaz, G. Digital Revolution? The increasing impact of Internet on China politics. *Journal of Contemporary Eastern Asia, 11*(2), 13-25.

Craig, S. C., & Maggiotto, M. A. (1982). Measuring political efficacy. *Political Methodology*, 85-109.

Crampton, T. (2012a). Infographic: China's social media evolution. *http://www.thomascrampton.com/china/china-social-media-evolution/* Retrieved January 1, 2013

Crampton, T. (2012b). Social media in China: The same, but different. *http://www.thomascrampton.com/china/social-media-china-business-review/* Retrieved January 1st, 2013

Cwalina, W., Falkowski, A., & Kaid, L. L. (2000). Role of advertising in forming the image of politicians: Comparative analysis of Poland, France, and Germany. *Media Psychology, 2*(2), 119-146.

Czernich, N. (2012). Broadband Internet and political participation: Evidence for Germany. *Kyklos, 65*(1), 31-52.

Dahlgren, P. (2006). Doing citizenship The cultural origins of civic agency in the public sphere. *European journal of cultural studies, 9*(3), 267-286.

Dahlgren, P. (2009). *Media and political engagement: Citizens, communication and democracy*: Cambridge University Press.

Dahlgren, P. (2011). Young citizens and political participation online media and civic cultures. *Taiwan Journal of Democracy, 7*(2), 11-25.

Dahlgren, P., & Alvares, C. (2013). Political participation in an age Mediatisation. *Javnost-The Public, 20*(2).

Dalton, R. J. (1985). Political Parties and Political Representation Party Supporters and Party Elites in Nine Nations. *Comparative Political Studies, 18*(3), 267-299.

Dalton, R. J. (2008). Citizenship norms and the expansion of political participation. *Political Studies, 56*(1), 76-98.

Dalton, R. J. (2009). Particiation in politics. Retrieved October 29, 2013

Davis, E. L. (2009). *Encyclopedia of contemporary Chinese culture*: Taylor & Francis.

De Vreese, C. H., & Boomgaarden, H. (2006). News, political knowledge and participation: The differential effects of news media exposure on political knowledge and participation. *Acta Politica, 41*(4), 317.

De Zúñiga, H. G. (2009). Blogs, journalism and political participation . *Journalism and Citizenship: New agendas in communication, Z. Papacharissi, Ed., Routledge: New York*, 108-123.

De Zúñiga, H. G., Puig-I-Abril, E., & Rojas, H. (2009). Weblogs, traditional sources online and political participation: an assessment of how the Internet is changing the political environment. *New Media & Society, 11*(4), 553-574.

Delisle, J. (2010). What's happened to democracy in China? : Election law and political reform *Election with chinese* Retrieved May 13, 2013

Delli Carpini, M. X. (2000). Youth, civic engagement, and the new information environment. *Political Communication, 17*(4), 341-349.

Demetriou, K. N. (2012). *Democracy in transition: Political participation in the European Union*: Springer.

Derichs, C. (2014). *Die politischen systeme Ostasiens: eine Einführung*: Springer-Verlag.

Detsch, R. (2012). Social Media – The Che Guevara of the 21st Century *http://www.goethe.de/wis/med/idm/tre/en7989345.htm* Retrieved January 18, 2013

Detterbeck, K., & Renzsch, W. (2003). Multi-level electoral competition: the German case. *European Urban and Regional Studies, 10*(3), 257-269.

Di Gennaro, C., & Dutton, W. (2006). The Internet and the public: Online and offline political participation in the United Kingdom. *Parliamentary Affairs, 59*(2), 299-313.

Diepstraten, I. (2007). Participation in transition: motivation of young adults in Europe for learning and working. *Análise Social*(184), 932-940.

Dimitrova, D. V., Shehata, A., Strömbäck, J., & Nord, L. W. (2011). The effects of digital media on political knowledge and participation in election campaigns: Evidence from panel data. *Communication Research*.

Dugan, L. (2012). Twitter to surpass 500 million registered users on wednesday. *http://www.mediabistro.com/alltwitter/500-million-registered-users_b18842* Retrieved December 13, 2012

Duignan, B. (2013). *Political parties, interest groups, and elections*: Britannica Educational Publishing.

Dunne, Á., Lawlor, M.-A., & Rowley, J. (2010). Young people's use of online social networking sites–a uses and gratifications perspective. *Journal of Research in Interactive Marketing, 4*(1), 46-58.

Dutton, W. H. (2008). The fifth estate: Democratic social accountability through the emerging network of networks. *Social Science Research Networks. Available at: ssrn. com/abstract.*

Economist.com. (2013). Like the sun, newspaper circulation rises in the east and falls in the west. *http://www.economist.com/blogs/graphicdetail/2013/06/daily-chart-1* Retrieved August 27, 2013

Economist Intelligence Unit. (2012). The democracy index 2011. *http://www.eiu.com/public/thankyou_download.aspx?activity=download&campaignid=De mocracyIndex2011* Retrieved August 29, 2013

Effing, R., van Hillegersberg, J., & Huibers, T. (2011). Social media and political participation: are facebook, twitter and YouTube democratizing our political systems? *Electronic Participation*, 25-35.

Egeler, R. (2010). Representative electoral statistics of the 2009 Bundestag Election. *Public Choice* Retrieved October 29, 2013

Eimeren, B. v. (2015). Nachrichtenrezeption im Internet. *Befunde aus der ARD/ZDF-Onlinestudie 2014 http://www.media-perspektiven.de/publikationen/fachzeitschrift/2015/artikel/nachrichtenr ezeption-im-Internet/* Retrieved July 24, 2015

Eldersveld, S. J., & Shen, M. (2001). Support for economic and political change in the China countryside: An empirical study of cadres and villagers in four counties, *1990-1996*: Lexington Books.

Eliasoph, N. (1998). *Avoiding politics: How Americans produce apathy in everyday life*: Cambridge University Press.

Elizabeth C. Economy. (2011). China: The new virtual political system. *http://www.cfr.org/china/china-new-virtual-political-system/p24805* Retrieved April 15, 2013

eMarketer. (2012). German consumers highly connected and social. *http://www.emarketer.com/Article/German-Consumers-Highly-Connected-Social/100906 9* Retrieved July 24, 2013

eMarketer. (2015a). Number of social network users in Germany from 2012 to 2018 (in millions). *http://www.statista.com/statistics/260716/number-of-social-network-users-in-germany/* Retrieved Aprl 12, 2015

eMarketer. (2015b). Number of social network users worldwide from 2010 to 2018 (in millions). *http://www.statista.com/statistics/278414/number-of-worldwide-social-network-users/* Retrieved Aprl 20, 2015

Emmer, M., Wolling, J., & Vowe, G. (2012). Changing political communication in Germany: Findings from a longitudinal study on the influence of the Internet on political information, discussion and the participation of citizens. *Communication-European journal of communication research, 37*(3), 233-252.

Emruli, S., & Baca, M. (2011). Internet and political communication-Macedonian case. *arXiv preprint arXiv:1109.2417.*

Endeshaw, A. (2004). Internet regulation in China: The never-ending cat and mouse game. Information and Communications Technology Law, 13(1), 41–57. doi:10.1080/1360083042000190634

Epstein, Z. (2013). Why low-end phones are so important: Mobile user base grows to 1.17 billion in China. *http://bgr.com/2013/06/26/china-mobile-phone-user-base-may-2013/* Retrieved September 10, 2013

Esarey, A., & Qiang, X. (2011). Digital communication and political change in China. *International Journal of Communication, 5*, 298-C319.

Esche, J. v. d., & Hennig-Thurau, T. (2012). German social media report 2012 /2013.

Esser, F., & Hanitzsch, T. (2012). *Handbook of Comparative Communication Research*: Taylor & Francis.

Evangelista, B. (2012). Two-thirds use social networking for political, civic activities *http://pewInternet.org/Media-Mentions/2012/Two-thirds-use-social-networking-for-political-civic-activities.aspx* Retrieved September 10, 2012

Fan, Q. (2005). Regulatory factors influencing Internet access in Australia and China: a comparative analysis. *Telecommunications Policy, 29*(2), 191-203.

Farrell, D. M., & Wortmann, M. (1987). Party Strategies in the electoral market: Political marketing in West Germany, Britain and Ireland. *European Journal of Political Research, 15*(3), 297-318.

Feezell, J. T., Conroy, M., & Guerrero, M. (2009). *Facebook is... fostering political engagement: A study of online social networking groups and offline participation.* Paper presented at the APSA 2009 Toronto Meeting Paper *http://papers. ssrn. com/sol3/papers. cfm.*

Feldmann-Wojtachnia, E., Gretschel, A., Helmisaari, V., Kiilakoski, T., Matthies, A.-L., Meinhold-Henschel, S., *et al.* (2010). Youth participation in Finland and in Germany. *Status analysis and data based recommendations, Helsinki/München.*

Fellow, G. A. (2012). Facebook: One Billion and Counting. *http://online.wsj.com/article/SB10000872396390443635404578036164027386112.html#* Retrieved December 13, 2012

Feng, L. (2013). Reform of the electoral system of the People's Congresses in China- A case study of disctrict People's Congress election. Retrieved May 4th, 2013

Fenton, N., & Barassi, V. (2011). Alternative media and social networking sites: The politics of individuation and political participation. *The Communication Review, 14*(3), 179-196.

Ferketich, S. (1990). Internal consistency estimates of reliability. *Research in nursing & health, 13*(6), 437-440.

Forbrig, J. (2005). Introduction: democratic politics, legitimacy and youth participation. *Revisiting youth political participation, 7.*

Francisco, S. (2013). TV and radio broadcasting in China industry research report *http://www.prweb.com/releases/china/tv-radio-broadcasting/prweb11032182.htm* Retrieved August 30, 2013

Freeden, M., & Vincent, A. (2013). *Comparative Political Thought: Theorizing Practices*: Routledge.

Fu, K.-w. (2013). Impact of IT - Beijing and Hong Kong young people's social media use and online/offline political participation: a comparative study

Gabriel, O. W., Keil, S. I., & Kerrouche, E. (2012). Political participation in france and germany: ECPR Press Colchester.

Gaiser, W., De Rijke, J., & Spannring, R. (2010). Youth and political participation—empirical results for Germany within a European context. *Young, 18*(4), 427-450.

Gang, D. (2013). On the participation in politics of the youth in contemporary Chinese cities. Retrieved November 14, 2013

Geck, C. (2007). The generation Z connection: Teaching information literacy to the newest net generation. *Toward a 21st-Century School Library Media Program*, 235.

Gerhards, J., & Schäfer, M. S. (2010). Is the Internet a better public sphere? Comparing old and new media in the USA and Germany. *New Media & Society, 12*(1), 143-160.

German TV Market Report 2009. (2009). International Television Expert Group.

Gershtenson, J., & Plane, D. L. (2007). Trust in Government: 2006 American National Election Studies Pilot Report. Ann Arbor, MI: University of Michigan, Center for Political Studies.

Gibson, R., Römmele, A., & Ward, S. (2003). German parties and Internet campaigning in the 2002 federal election. *German Politics, 12*(1), 79-108.

Gibson, R. K., & Ward, S. J. (1998). UK Political Parties and the Internet "Politics as Usual" in the New Media? *The Harvard International Journal of Press/Politics, 3*(3), 14-38.

Giddens, A. (1991). Modernity and Self-Identity; Selfand Society in the Late. *Modern Age.*

Gidengil, E. (2004). *Citizens* (Vol. 3): UBC Press.

Gil de Zúñiga, H. (2012). Social media use for news and individuals' social capital, civic engagement and political participation. *Journal of Computer - Mediated Communication, 17*(3), 319-336.

Gil de Zúñiga, H., Molyneux, L., & Zheng, P. (2014). Social media, political expression, and political participation: Panel analysis of lagged and concurrent relationships. *Journal of Communication, 64*(4), 612-634.

Glaeßner, G.-J. (2011). The party system of the 'old'Federal Republic. *20 Years Since the Fall of the Berlin Wall: Transitions, State Break-Up and Democratic Politics in Central Europe and Germany*, 203.

Glaessner, G.-J. (2005). *German Democracy : From Post-World War II to the Present Day*: Berg Publishers.

Glatte, S., & de Vries, C. E. (2015) Gender norms and gender gaps in political participation in Unified Germany.

Goble, B. G. (2012). The history of social network. *http://www.digitaltrends.com/features/the-history-of-social-networking/* Retrieved August 12, 2012

Goldkorn, J., & Danwei. (2013). China's newspaper industry. Retrieved August 29, 2013

Goodman, D. (2002). *Deng Xiaoping and the Chinese Revolution: A Political Biography*: Routledge.

Goren, P. (2005). Party identification and core political values. *American Journal of Political Science, 49*(4), 881-896.

Gosnell, H. F. (1930). *Why Europe Votes* (Vol. 19): "The" University of Chicago Press.

Grönlund, K. (2007). Knowing and not knowing: The Internet and political information. *Scandinavian Political Studies, 30*(3), 397-418.

Grönlund, K., & Setälä, M. (2007). Political trust, satisfaction and voter turnout. *Comparative European Politics, 5*(4), 400-422.

Greuling, K., & Kilian, T. (2013). Motives for active participation in political blogs: A qualitative and quantitative analysis of eight German blogs. *Social Science Computer Review*, 0894439313508611.

Groebel, J. (2013). Media-a multi-faceted system *The press-a wide range of newspaper* Retrieved September 13, 2013

Guo, G. (2005). Party recruitment of college students in China. *Journal of Contemporary China, 14*(43), 371-393.

Guo, G. (2007). Organizational involvement and political participation in China. *Comparative Political Studies, 40*(4), 457-482.

Guo, L. (2007). Surveying Internet usage and its impact in seven Chinese cities. *Beijing: Center for Social Develop.*

Guo, Q. (2011). Internet and Political Participation in China. *Masaryk UJL & Tech., 5*, 83.

Guo, X. (2003). *State and society in China's democratic transition: Confucianism, Leninism, and economic development*: Routledge.

Guo, X., & Zheng, Y. (2008). Women's political participation in China. *Briefing Series*(34).

Gurevitch, M., Coleman, S., & Blumler, J. G. (2009). Political communication—old and new media relationships. *The ANNALS of the American Academy of Political and Social Science, 625*(1), 164-181.

Hallin, D. C. (2004). *Comparing media systems: Three models of media and politics*: Cambridge University Press.

Hallin, D. C., & Mancini, P. (2004). *Comparing media systems: Three models of media and politics*: Cambridge University Press.

Hamrin, C. L., & Zhao, S. (1995). *Decision making in Deng's China: perspectives from insiders*: ME Sharpe.

Harp, D., Bachmann, I., & Guo, L. (2012). The Whole Online World is Watching: Profiling Social Networking Sites and Activists in China, Latin America and the United States. *International Journal of Communication, 6*, 24.

Hayes, B. C., & Bean, C. S. (1993). Political efficacy: a comparative study of the United States, West Germany, Great Britain and Australia. *European Journal of Political Research, 23*(3), 261-280.

Hays, J. (2012). Chinese newspapers and magazines and their battle against corruption and censorship *Chinese newspapers and magazines* Retrieved August 28, 2013

He, Z. (2009). Political communication in dual discourse universes. *Political communication in Asia*, 43.

Heberer, T., & Derichs, C. (2008). Einführung in die politischen Systeme Ostasiens: VR China, Hongkong, Japan, Nordkorea, Südkorea, Taiwan: Springer-Verlag.

Helms, L. (1996). Executive leadership in parliamentary democracies: The British prime minister and the German chancellor compared. *German Politics, 5*(1), 101-120.

Hemphill, L., Otterbacher, J., & Shapiro, M. (2013). *What's congress doing on twitter?* Paper presented at the Proceedings of the 2013 conference on Computer supported cooperative work.

Hetherington, M. J. (2005). Why trust matters. Princeton, NJ: Princeton University.

Hill, K. A., & Hughes, J. E. (1999). *Cyberpolitics: Citizen activism in the age of the Internet*: Rowman & Littlefield Publishers, Inc.

Himelboim, I., Lariscy, R. W., Tinkham, S. F., & Sweetser, K. D. (2012). Social media and online political communication: The role of interpersonal informational trust and openness. *Journal of Broadcasting & Electronic Media, 56*(1), 92-115.

Hoffman, L. H., & Thomson, T. L. (2009). The effect of television viewing on adolescents' civic participation: Political efficacy as a mediating mechanism. *Journal of Broadcasting & Electronic Media, 53*(1), 3-21.

Holt, K., Shehata, A., Strömbäck, J., & Ljungberg, E. (2013). Age and the effects of news media attention and social media use on political interest and participation: Do social media function as leveller? *European Journal of Communication, 28*(1), 19-34.

Holtz-Bacha, C. (2004). Political communication research abroad: Europe. *Handbook of political communication research*, 463.

Holtz - Bacha, C., Kaid, L. L., & Johnston, A. (1994). Political television advertising in western democracies: A comparison of campaign broadcasts in the United States, Germany, and France. *Political Communication, 11*(1), 67-80.

Hong, J. (1998). *The internationalization of television in China: The evolution of ideology, society, and media since the reform*: Greenwood Publishing Group.

Hong, J. (2013). The role of media in China's democratization Retrieved August 20, 2013

Howard, P. N., & Parks, M. R. (2012). Social media and political change: Capacity, constraint, and consequence. Journal of Communication, 62(2), 359-362.

Howell, J. (2006). Women's political participation in China: in whose interests elections? *Journal of Contemporary China, 15*(49), 603-619.

Howse, H. (1960). The use of radio in China. *The China Quarterly*(2), 59-68.

Hsieh, Y. P., & Li, M.-H. (2013). Online political participation, civic talk, and media multiplexity: how Taiwanese citizens express political opinions on the Web. *Information, Communication & Society* (ahead-of-print), 1-19.

Hu, X. (2012). *The contemporary college students' political psychology analysis in China*. Southwest University.

Hu, Y., Fang, K., Liu, Y., Ha, I., Zhang, Y., Wang, M., et al. (2012). *Mapping Digital Media:China*.

Huckfeldt, R. R. (1995). *Citizens, politics and social communication: Information and influence in an election campaign*: Cambridge University Press.

Hyun, K. D. (2012). Americanization of web-based political communication? A comparative analysis of political blogospheres in the United States, the United Kingdom, and Germany. *Journalism & Mass Communication Quarterly, 89*(3), 397-413.

Hyun, K. D., & Kim, J. (2015). Differential and interactive influences on political participation by different types of news activities and political conversation through social media. *Computers in Human Behavior, 45*, 328-334.

IDEA, I. (2011). Voter turnout data for Germany.
http://www.idea.int/vt/countryview.cfm?CountryCode=DE Retrieved March 20, 2012

Inglehart, R. (1997). *Modernization and postmodernization: Cultural, economic, and political change in 43 societies* (Vol. 19): Cambridge Univ Press.

InternetWorldStats. (2014). Internet stats and Facebook usage in Europe 2014 mid-year statistics. *http://www.internetworldstats.com/stats4.htm* Retrieved March 17, 2015

Ishiyama, J. T. (2011). *Comparative Politics : Principles of Democracy and Democratization*: Wiley.

Jacobs, J. B. (1991). Elections in China. *The Australian Journal of Chinese Affairs*(25), 171-199.

Java, A., Song, X., Finin, T., & Tseng, B. (2007). *Why we twitter: understanding microblogging usage and communities.* Paper presented at the Proceedings of the 9th WebKDD and 1st SNA-KDD 2007 workshop on Web mining and social network analysis.

Jay, B. (2013). The Internet and the sociopolitical development of Nation-States. *The Proceedings of GREAT Day.*

Jensen, M. J., & Anduiza, E. (2012). Online political participation in the United States and Spain. *Digital Media and Political Engagement Worldwide. A Comparative Study*, 80-101.

Jin, F. (2003). The director of the state administration talk about the main task of the development of broadcast in 2003. Retrieved September 5, 2013

Johnsson-Smaragdi, U., d'Haenens, L., Krotz, F., & Hasebrink, U. (1998). Patterns of old and new media use among young people in Flanders, Germany and Sweden. *European Journal of Communication, 13*(4), 479-501.

Jungherr, A., & Jürgens, P. (2010). The political click: political participation through e-petitions in Germany. *Policy & Internet, 2*(4).

Kaid, L. L. (1999). Comparing and contrasting the styles and effects of political advertising in European democracies. *Television and politics in evolving European democracies*, 219-236.

Kaid, L. L. (2002). Political advertising and information seeking: Comparing exposure via traditional and Internet channels. *Journal of Advertising, 31*(1), 27-35.

Kaid, L. L. (2004). *Handbook of political communication research.* Mahwah, N.J. [u.a.]: Lawrence Erlbaum.

Kalvani, M. (2010). A Comparative analysis: German and Italian media in the twenty-first century

Kaplan, A. M., & Haenlein, M. (2010). Users of the world, unite! The challenges and opportunities of Social Media. *Business horizons, 53*(1), 59-68.

Keller, A. (2013). *Of enclaves and Internet: How social media affects political participation in authoritarian states.* The Ohio State University.

Kenski, K., & Stroud, N. J. (2006). Connections between Internet use and political efficacy, knowledge, and participation. *Journal of Broadcasting & Electronic Media, 50*(2), 173-192.

Kestilä-Kekkonen, E. (2009). Anti-party sentiment among young adults Evidence from fourteen West European countries. *Young, 17*(2), 145-165.

Kim, M., & Park, H. W. (2012). Measuring Twitter-based political participation and deliberation in the South Korean context by using social network and Triple Helix indicators. *Scientometrics, 90*(1), 121-140.

King G, Pan J and Roberts M (2012) How censorship in China allows government criticism but silences collective expression. Working paper. Available at: *http://gking.harvard.edu/publications/how-censorship-china-allows-government-criticism-silences-collectiveexpression/*

Klandermans, B. (1984). Mobilization and participation: Social-psychological expansisons of resource mobilization theory. *American sociological review*, 583-600.

Kleinsteuber, H. J., & Thomass, B. (2007). The German Media Landscape. *European media governance national and regional dimensions.*

Klingemann, H.-D., & Wessels, B. (1999). *Political consequences of Germany's mixed-member system: Personalization at the grass-roots?* : WZB Discussion Paper.

Klinger, U., & Svensson, J. (2014). The emergence of network media logic in political communication: A theoretical approach. *New Media & Society*, 1461444814522952.

Koçak, N. G., Kaya, S., & Erol, E. (2013). Social media from the perspective of diffusion of innovation approach.

Koopmans, R. (1996). New social movements and changes in political participation in Western Europe. *West European Politics, 19*(1), 28-50.

Koopmans, R., & Zimmermann, A. C. (2003). *Internet: A new potential for European political communication?* : Veröffentlichungsreihe der Arbeitsgruppe Politische Öffentlichkeit und Mobilisierung des Wissenschaftszentrums Berlin für Sozialforschung.

Kruikemeier, S., van Noort, G., Vliegenthart, R., & de Vreese, C. H. (2013). Unraveling the effects of active and passive forms of political Internet use: Does it affect citizens' political involvement? *New Media & Society*.

Kweon, S. H., & Kim, W. G. (2010). Political communication and participation trend in the social media: Focus on the O1-S-O2-R model application. *Journal of Media and Communication Studies, 2*(8), 176-190.

Lacharite, J. (2002). Electronic decentralisation in China: A critical analysis of Internet filtering policies in the People's Republic of China. Australian Journal of Political Science, 37(2), 333–346. doi:10.1080/10361140220148188

Lambert, R. D., Curtis, J. E., Brown, S. D., & Kay, B. J. (1986). Effects of identification with governing parties on feelings of political efficacy and trust. *Canadian Journal of Political Science, 19*(4), 705-728.

Lardinois, F. (2009). Social media in Germany: 5 years behind - still lots to learn. *http://readwrite.com/2009/07/08/social_media_in_germany_5_years_behind_-_still_lot_t o_learn* Retrieved February 11, 2013

Lariscy, R. W., Tinkham, S. F., & Sweetser, K. D. (2011). Kids these days: examining differences in political uses and gratifications, Internet political participation, political information efficacy, and cynicism on the basis of age. *American behavioral scientist, 55*(6), 749-764.

Larson, K. G. (2004). *The Internet and political participation the effect of Internet use on voter turnout* Georgetown University.

Lawrence, S., & Martin, M. F. (2012). Understanding China's political system: Congressional Research Service.

Lee, C. S., & Ma, L. (2012). News sharing in social media: The effect of gratifications and prior experience. *Computers in Human Behavior, 28*(2), 331-339.

Lee, P. S. n. (1994). Mass communication and national development in China: Media roles reconsidered. *Journal of Communication, 44*(3), 22-37.

Leggewie, C. (2013). Politics and contemporary history in Germany -background. *political culture in Germany*, 2013

Lei, Y.-W. (2011). The political consequences of the rise of the Internet: Political beliefs and practices of Chinese netizens. *Political Communication, 28*(3), 291-322.

Letki, N. (2003). *Explaining political participation in East-Central Europe: social capital, democracy and the communist past*: Centre for the Study of Public Policy, University of Strathclyde.

Leung, K., & Van de Vijver, F. (1996). Cross-cultural research methodology. *The psychology research handbook: A guide for graduate students and research assistants*, 351-358.

Lewis-Beck, M. S. (1986). Comparative economic voting: Britain, France, Germany, Italy. *American Journal of Political Science, 30*(2), 315-346.

Li, J. (2011). Social media In China: Tigers in a cage. *http://www.holmesreport.com/opinion-info/10724/Social-Media-In-China-Tigers-In-A-Ca ge.aspx* Retrieved January 6, 2013

Li, J. (2012). *The current higher vocational students' political participation research* Hebei Normal University.

Li, L. (2011). *Social network sites comparison between the United States and china: case study on facebook and renren network.* Paper presented at the Business Management and Electronic Information (BMEI), 2011 International Conference on.

Li, N., & Kirkup, G. (2007). Gender and cultural differences in Internet use: A study of China and the UK. *Computers & Education, 48*(2), 301-317.

Li, P. (2013). China radio, film and television development report (2013).

Li, X. (1991). The Chinese television system and television news. China Quarterly, 126, 340-355.

Li, X., & He, S. (2007). More political participation for Chinese citizens. *http://www.china.org.cn/english/China/239494.htm* Retrieved May 24, 2013

Lilleker, D., & Jackson, N. (2011). *Political campaigning, elections and the Internet : comparing the US, UK, France and Germany*: Taylor & Francis.

Lilleker, D., & Vedel, T. (2013). The Internet in campaigns and elections.

Lin, F. (2008). *Turning gray: Transition of political communication in China, 1978--2008*: ProQuest.

Liu, H. (2006). *China's newspaper industry development strategy*: Shanghai People's Publication.

Loader, B. D. (2007). Young citizens in the digital age : Political engagement, young people and new media Available from *http://slub.eblib.com/patron/FullRecord.as px?p=35627*

Loader, B. D., & Mercea, D. (2012). *Social media and democracy : Innovations in participatory politics*: Taylor & Francis.

Lu, G. (2012). The rise of social media in China. *http://www.bestfreeonline.net/* Retrieved April 7, 2012

Lu, X. (2002). Chinese political communication: Roots in tradition and impacts on contemporary Chinese thought and culture. *Intercultural Communication Studies, 6*(1), 97-116.

Lusoli, W. (2005). A second-order medium? The Internet as a source of electoral information in 25 European countries. *information Polity, 10*(3), 247-265.

Lye, L. F., & Hofmeister, W. (2010). *Political parties, party systems and democratization in East Asia*: World Scientific Publishing Company.

MacKinnon, R. (2008). Flatter world and thicker walls? Blogs, censorship and civic discourse in China. *Public Choice, 134*(1), 31-46.

MacKuen, M., & Rabinowitz, G. (2003). *Electoral democracy*: University of Michigan Press.

Mangold, W. G., & Faulds, D. J. (2009). Social media: The new hybrid element of the promotion mix. *Business horizons, 52*(4), 357-365.

Margetts, H., John, P., Escher, T., & Reissfelder, S. (2009). Experiments for web science: examining the effect of the Internet on collective action. *Proceedings of the WebSci, 9*, 18-20.

Marien, S., Hooghe, M., & Quintelier, E. (2010). Inequalities in non-institutionalised forms of political participation: A multi-level analysis of 25 countries. *Political Studies, 58*(1), 187-213.

Marolt, P., & Herold, D. K. (2014). *China online: Locating society in online spaces*: Routledge.

Marta Cantijoch, L. J. a. J. S. M. (2008). *Exposure to political Information in new and old Media: which Impact on political participation?* Paper presented at the 2008 Annual Meeting of the American Political Science Association.

Martin, A. (2012). Young people and politics : political engagement in the Anglo-American democracies Available from *http://slub.eblib.com/patron/FullRecord.aspx?p=981665*

McCormick, B. L. (1998). Political change in China and Vietnam: Coping with the consequences of economic reform. *The China Journal*(40), 121-143.

McGoveran, C. (2013). Evaluating the uses and realizing the benefits of social media use in politics.

McKinsey. (2012). China's advanced social media environment – without Facebook, Twitter, or YouTube *http://www.mediabuzz.com.sg/asian-emarketing/may-2012/1566-chinas-advanced-social-media-environment-without-facebook-twitter-or-youtube* Retrieved January 11, 2013

McNair, B. (2011). *An Introduction to political communication*: Taylor & Francis.

McNaughton, M. (2012). 77% of German Internet users access social media via Mobile.*http://therealtimereport.com/2012/03/29/77-of-german-Internet-users-access-soci al-media-via-mobile/* Retrieved January 16, 2013

Mei, Y. (2012). Chinese social networks you need to watch. *http://mashable.com/2012/07/02/china-social-networks/* Retrieved January 3, 2013

Mi, X. (2013). Top 10 new media trends in China. *China.org.cn* Retrieved September 10, 2013

Miller, W. E. (1991). Party identification, realignment, and party voting: Back to the basics. *The American Political Science Review*, 557-568.

Millward, S. (2012). China's forgotten 3rd Twitter clone hits 260 million users. *http://www.techinasia.com/netease-weibo-260-million-users-numbers/* Retrieved January 1, 2013

Mobilfunk, I. (2012). The development of digital mobile communications in Germany.

http://www.izmf.de/en/development-digital-mobile-communications-germany
Retrieved August 5, 2013

Mohanty, M. (1993). The state and the socialist market economy: The eighth National People's Congress. *China Report, 29*(3), 319-325.

Mou, Y., Atkin, D., Fu, H., Lin, C. A., & Lau, T. (2013). The influence of online forum and SNS use on online political discussion in China: Assessing "Spirals of Trust". Telematics and Informatics, 30(4), 359-369.

Muniglia, V., Cuconato, M., Loncle, P., & Walther, A. (2013). The analysis of youth participation in contemporary literature: a European perspective. *Youth Participation in Europe: Beyond Discourses, Practices and Realities, 1.*

Muntinga, D. G., Moorman, M., & Smit, E. G. (2011). Introducing COBRAs. *International Journal of Advertising, 30*(1), 13-46.

Naisbitt, J., & Naisbitt, D. (2010). *China's megatrends: The 8 pillars of a new society*: HarperCollins.

News, B. (2012). How China is ruled: Communist Party.
http://www.bbc.co.uk/news/world-asia-pacific-13904437 Retrieved April 19, 2013

Newton, K. (1999). Mass media effects: mobilization or media malaise? *British Journal of Political Science, 29*(04), 577-599.

Nie, N. H., Powell, G. B., & Prewitt, K. (1969). Social structure and political participation: developmental relationships, Part I. *The American Political Science Review, 63*(2), 361-378.

Nielsen. (2012). How Chinese netizens use China social media.
http://www.resonancechina.com/2012/10/17/how-chinese-netizens-use-china-social-media/ Retrieved January 6, 2013

Norris, P. (1999). Who surfs. *New technology, old voters and virtual democracy. In democracy. com: Governance in a Networked World, ed. Elaine Ciulla Kamarck and Jr. Joseph S. Nye. Hollis, NH:: Hollis Publishing.*

Norris, P. (2000). *A virtuous circle: Political communications in postindustrial societies*: Cambridge University Pres.

Norris, P. (2002). *Democratic phoenix: Reinventing political activism*: Cambridge University Press.

Norris, P. (2003a). *Digital divide: Civic engagement, information poverty, and the Internet worldwide* (Vol. 40): Taylor & Francis.

Norris, P. (2003b). *Tuned out voters? Media impact on campaign learning.* Paper presented at the Politeia Conference.

Norris, P. (2003c). Young people and political activism: From the politics of loyalties to the politics of choice. *Ponencia presentada en el Simposium "Young People and Democratic Institutions: From Disillusionment to Participation". Consejo de Europa, Estrasburgo. Disponible en Internet. URL: http://ksghome. harvard. edu/~ pnorris.*

Noyes, D. (2013). The top 20 valuable Facebook statistics
http://zephoria.com/social-media/top-15-valuable-facebook-statistics/ Retrieved January 7, 2014

Nunnally, J. C. (1978). Psychometric theory (2) McGraw-Hill. *New York.*

Olesen, A. (2012). China undergoes people's social media revolution.
http://www.3news.co.nz/china-undergoes-peoples-social-media-revolution/tabid/417/artic leid/276663/default.aspx#ixzz2edzo Retrieved December 15, 2012

Önder, Ö., & Gümüşkaya, H. (2011). Architectural platform: a social network site for architects. *Procedia Computer Science, 3,* 469-473.

Orum, A. M. (1974). On participation in political protest movements. *The Journal of Applied Behavioral Science, 10*(2), 181-207.

Otto, A. (2012). *Success of political communication on social networking sites*: GRIN Verlag.

Pan, Z., Jing, G., Liu, Y., Yan, W., & Zheng, J. (2012). Digital divide and Internet use in China: can the Internet facilitate citizenship engagement?

Panagopoulos, C., Druckman, J., Kifer, M., Parkin, M., Pirch, K., Gueorguieva, V., *et al.* (2009). Politicking online : the transformation of election campaign aommunications Available from *http://slub.eblib.com/patron/FullRecord.aspx?p=1016474*

Papacharissi, Z. (2009). The virtual geographies of social networks: a comparative analysis of Facebook, LinkedIn and ASmallWorld. *New Media & Society, 11*(1-2), 199-220.

Park, N., Kee, K. F., & Valenzuela, S. (2009). Being immersed in social networking environment: Facebook groups, uses and gratifications, and social outcomes. *Cyberpsychology & Behavior, 12*(6), 729-733.

Patton, D. F. (2013). The Left Party at Six: The PDS–WASG Merger in Comparative Perspective. *German Politics*(ahead-of-print), 1-16.

Pavie, X. (2011). Strategic Analysis of the Internationalization of the Social Network Facebook.

Pfetsch, B. (2001). Political communication culture in the United States and Germany. *The Harvard International Journal of Press/Politics, 6*(1), 46-67.

Pfetsch, B., & Esser, F. (2004). Comparing political communication. *Comparing political communication: Theories, cases, and challenges*, 3.

Picot, G. (2013). Party Systems and Social Policy: A historical comparison of Italy and Germany. *West European Politics*(ahead-of-print), 1-21.

Quick, A. C. (2003). *World Press Encyclopedia: AM* (Vol. 1): Gale.

Quintelier, E., & Vissers, S. (2008). The effect of Internet use on political participation an analysis of survey results for 16-year-olds in Belgium. *Social Science Computer Review, 26*(4), 411-427.

Raacke, J., & Bonds-Raacke, J. (2008). MySpace and Facebook: Applying the uses and gratifications theory to exploring friend-networking sites. *Cyberpsychology & Behavior, 11*(2), 169-174.

Rainie, L., & Smith, A. (2012). Social networking sites and politics. *Washington, DC: Pew Internet & American Life Project. Retrieved June, 12, 2012.*

Redmond, B. F. (2013). Reinforcement Theory. *Overview of Reinforcement Theory* Retrieved November 212013

Riaz, S. (2013). Effects of new media technologies on political communication. *Journal of Political Studies, 1*(2), 161-173.

Riordan, T. (2003). Technology & Media: Patents; Idea for Online Networking Brings Two Entrepreneurs Together. *The New York Times.*

Roberts, G. K. (2006). German electoral politics Available from *http://slub.eblib.com/patron/FullRecord.aspx?p=1069518*

Robertson, S. P., Semaan, B., Douglas, S., & Maruyama, M. (2013). *Mixed media: interactions of social and traditional media in political decision making.* Paper presented at the System Sciences (HICSS), 2013 46th Hawaii International Conference on.

Rogers, E. M. (2010). *Diffusion of innovations*: Simon and Schuster.

Rogers, E. M. (1995). Diffusion of innovation theory: New York: Free Press.

Rojas, H. (2008). Strategy versus understanding how orientations toward political conversation influence political engagement. *Communication Research, 35*(4), 452-480.

Rong, C. (2009). *Newspaper coverage of environmental probems in China:an analysis of the Chinese newspapers.*

Saalfeld, T. (2002). The German party system: Continuity and change. *German Politics, 11*(3), 99-130.

Saleh, A. (2005). *Uses and effects of new media on political communication in the United States of America, Germany and Egypt*: Tectum-Verlag.

Salisbury, R. H. (1975). Research on political participation. *American Journal of Political Science*, 323-341.

Schoenhals, M. (1999). Political movements, change and stability: The Chinese Communist Party in power. *The China Quarterly, 159*(1), 595-605.

Schroeder, J. (2012). Chinese social media 101 *http://blog.hootsuite.com/chinese-social-media-101/* Retrieved January 2, 2013

Scotton, J. F., & Hachten, W. A. (2010). New media for a new China Available from *http://slub.eblib.com/patron/FullRecord.aspx?p=514418*

Semetko, H. A. (1996). Political balance on Television campaigns in the United States, Britain, and

Germany. *The Harvard International Journal of Press/Politics, 1*(1), 51-71.

Shah, D. V. (1998). Civic engagement, interpersonal trust, and television use: An individual-level assessment of social capital. *Political Psychology, 19*(3), 469-496.

Shan, C. (2013). *The sources young people trust: The credibility ratings of sources of national political news in China.*

Shi, T. (2001). Cultural values and political trust: a comparison of the People's Republic of China and Taiwan. *Comparative Politics*, 401-419.

Shirk, S. L. (2010). *Changing media, changing China*: Oxford University Press.

Shirky, C. (2011). The political power of social media: Technology, the public sphere, and political change. *Foreign Affairs*, 28-41.

Shyu, H. (2009). Psychological resources of political participation: Comparing Hong Kong, Taiwan, and Mainland China. Journal of International Cooperation Studies, 17(2), 25-47.

Simon, R. J., & Gueorguieva, V. (2008). Voting and elections the world over Available from *http://slub.eblib.com/patron/FullRecord.aspx?p=466943*

Skoric, M. M., & Poor, N. (2013). Youth engagement in Singapore: The interplay of social and traditional media. *Journal of Broadcasting & Electronic Media, 57*(2), 187-204.

Sloam, J. (2011). Rejuvenating politics? Youth, citizenship and politics in the United States and Europe. *Youth, Citizenship and Politics in the United States and Europe.*

Smith, M. A. (1999). *Communities in cyberspace*: Routledge.

Snobmonkey. (2013). Social media in China *http://blog.snobmonkey.com/2013/10/08/social-media-in-china/* Retrieved January 2, 2014

Solsten, E. (1999). *Germany: a country study*: DIANE Publishing.

Spannring, R., Ogris, G., & Gaiser, W. (2008). *Youth and political participation in Europe: results of the comparative study EUYOPART*: Barbara Budrich.

Spannring, R., Wallace, C., & Datler, G. (2008). What leads young people to identify with Europe? An exploration of the impact of exposure to Europe and political engagement on European identity among young Europeans. *Perspectives on European Politics and Society, 9*(4), 480-498.

Sparks, C. (2008). Media systems in transition: Poland, Russia, China. *Chinese Journal of Communication, 1*(1), 7-24.

Stats, I. w. (2013). Top 50 countries with the highest Internet percentration rate *Germany* Retrieved November 11, 2013

Stieglitz, S., Brockmann, T., & Xuan, L. D. (2012). Usage of social media for political communication.

Stieglitz, S., & Dang-Xuan, L. (2013). Social media and political communication: a social media analytics framework. *Social Network Analysis and Mining, 3*(4), 1277-1291.

Stockton, H. (2001). Political parties, party systems, and democracy in East Asia lessons from Latin America. *Comparative Political Studies, 34*(1), 94-119.

Stolle, D., Hooghe, M., & Micheletti, M. (2005). Politics in the supermarket: political consumerism as a form of political participation. *International Political Science Review, 26*(3). 245-269.

Strömbäck, J., & Dimitrova, D. V. (2006). Political and media systems matter a comparison of election news coverage in Sweden and the United States. *The Harvard International Journal of Press/Politics, 11*(4), 131-147.

Sullivan, J. (2012). A tale of two microblogs in China. *Media, Culture & Society, 34*(6), 773-783.

Sullivan, J. (2013). China's Weibo: Is faster different? *New Media & Society.*

Swanson, D. L. (2000). The homologous evolution of political communication and civic engagement: Good news, bad news, and no news. Political Communication, 17(4), 409–414. doi:10.1080/10584600050179031

Tai, Z. (2015). Networked Resistance: Digital populism, online activism, and mass dissent in China. Popular Communication, 13(2), 120-131.

Tang, W., & Iyengar, S. (2011). The emerging media system in China: Implications for regime change. *Political Communication, 28*(3), 263-267.

Tang, W., & Iyengar, S. (2013). *Political communication China media*: Routledge.

Taubman, G. (1998). A not-so world wide web: the Internet, China, and the challenges to nondemocratic rule. *Political Communication, 15*(2), 255-272.

Taylor, V., & Whittier, N. (1992). Collective identity in social movement communities: Lesbian feminist mobilization. *Social perspectives in lesbian and gay studies (New York: Routledge, 1998)*, 349-365.

Thomass, H. J. K. B. (2013). Media Landscapes Germany. Retrieved September 13, 2013

Thomson, T. L. (2007). *Examining dimensions of political discussion and political knowledge.* The Ohio State University.

Tolbert, C. J., & McNeal, R. S. (2003). Unraveling the effects of the Internet on political participation? *Political Research Quarterly, 56*(2), 175-185.

Tong, J. (2003). The gender gap in political culture and participation in China. *Communist and Post-Communist Studies, 36*(2), 131-150.

Tumasjan, A., Sprenger, T. O., Sandner, P. G., & Welpe, I. M. (2010). Predicting Elections with Twitter: What 140 Characters Reveal about Political Sentiment. *ICWSM, 10*, 178-185.

V. Shah, N. K., R. Lance Holbert, Dhavan. (2001). "Connecting" and "disconnecting" with civic life: Patterns of Internet use and the production of social capital. *Political Communication, 18*(2), 141-162.

Vaccari, C., Valeriani, A., Barberá, P., Bonneau, R., Jost, J. T., Nagler, J., *et al.* (2015). Political Expression and Action on Social Media: Exploring the Relationship Between Lower ‐ and Higher ‐ Threshold Political Activities Among Twitter Users in Italy. *Journal of Computer ‐ Mediated Communication.*

Valenzuela, S., Kim, Y., & de Zúñiga, H. G. (2012). Social networks that matter: Exploring the role of political discussion for online political participation. *International Journal of Public Opinion Research, 24*(2), 163-184.

Valenzuela, S., Park, N., & Kee, K. F. (2009). Is There Social Capital in a Social Network Site?: Facebook Use and College Students' Life Satisfaction, Trust, and Participation1. *Journal of Computer ‐ Mediated Communication, 14*(4), 875-901.

Van de Donk, W. (2004). *Cyberprotest: New media, citizens and social movements*: Routledge.

Van Deth, J. W., Montero, J. R., & Westholm, A. (2007). *Citizenship and involvement in European democracies: A comparative analysis*: Routledge.

Verba, N., & Norman, N. (1978). Kim, Participation and Political Equality. *Verba, Schlozman, and Brady, Voice and Equality.*

Verba, S., & Almond, G. (1963). The civic culture. *Political Attitudes and Democracy in Five Nations, Princeton.*

Verba, S., & Nie, N. H. (1972). Participation in America: Social equality and political democracy. *New York.*

Verba, S., Schlozman, K. L., & Brady, H. E. (1995). *Voice and equality: Civic voluntarism in American politics*: Harvard University Press.

Vergeer, M., Hermans, L., & Cunha, C. (2013). Web campaigning in the 2009 European Parliament elections: A cross-national comparative analysis. *New Media & Society, 15*(1), 128-148.

Vissers, S., & Stolle, D. (2014). Spill-over effects between Facebook and on/offline political participation? Evidence from a two-wave panel study. *Journal of Information Technology & Politics, 11*(3), 259-275.

Wallraff, B. (2000). What global language. *The Atlantic Monthly, 286*(5), 52-66.

Watson, J.(2013). Gen why? Don't write off missing youth vote
http://www.smh.com.au/federal-politics/political-opinion/gen-why-dont-write-off-missing-youth-vote-20131010-2vb7m.html Retrieved November 1, 2013

Wan, J., & Yuce, A. (2007). Listing regulations in China and their effect on the performance of IPOs and SOEs. *Research in International Business and Finance, 21*(3), 366-378.

Wang, C. (2003). *One China, many paths*: Verso Books.

Wang, H. (2013). On the warning mechanism of online public opinion in the university campus. China Newspaper Industry, 6, 33–35. Accession number: 1671-0029(2013)03(B)-0033-03. [In Chinese]

Ward, J., & de Vreese, C. (2011). Political consumerism, young citizens and the Internet. *Media, Culture & Society, 33*(3), 399-413.

Ward, J. R. (2009). *Youth, citizenship and online political communication.*

Warf, B. (2013). Global Internet Censorship *Global Geographies of the Internet* (pp. 45-75): Springer.

Wasko, J. (2009). *A companion to television*: Wiley. com.

Wee, W. (2011). The social media landscape in China
http://www.techinasia.com/social-media-landscape-in-china/ Retrieved January 1, 2013

Wei, R. (2013). Mobile media: Coming of age with a big splash. *Mobile Media & Communication, 1*(1), 50-56.

Willnat, L., & Aw, A. (2009). *Political communication in Asia*: Routledge.

Wines, M. (2012). China expands program requiring real-name registration online.
http://www.nytimes.com/2012/01/19/world/asia/china-expands-program-requiring-real-n ame-registration-online.html?ref=internetcensorship&_r=0 Retrieved January 11, 2013

Wong, J., & Li, J. (1998). *China After the Ninth National People's Congress: Meeting Cross-century Challenges*: World Scientific Publishing Company.

Woodly, D. (2008). New competencies in democratic communication? Blogs, agenda setting and political participation. *Public Choice, 134*(1-2), 109-123.

Xenos, M., & Moy, P. (2007). Direct and differential effects of the Internet on political and civic engagement. *Journal of Communication, 57*(4), 704-718.

Xi, Y. (2013). *Analysis of the status quo and the reasons for students' political participation in the period of the social transformation.* Paper presented at the Intelligent System Design and Engineering Applications (ISDEA), 2013 Third International Conference on.

Xie, B. (2008). Civic engagement among older Chinese Internet users. *Journal of Applied Gerontology, 27*(4), 424-445.

Xie, B., & Jaeger, P. T. (2008). Older adults and political participation on the Internet: A cross-cultural comparison of the USA and China. *Journal of cross-cultural gerontology, 23*(1), 1-15.

Yang, G. (2003). The Internet and civil society in China: A preliminary assessment. *Journal of Contemporary China, 12*(36), 453-475.

Yang, G. (2009). *The power of the Internet in China: Citizen activism online*: Columbia University Press New York, NY.

You, J. (2013). "Big Brother, We Are Watching on You"-Weibo and the bottom-up surveillance in China.

Yu, J. (2010). Protest or not?: Comparing protest participation between China and western democratic countries. Paper presented at the Asia Barometer study 2011.

Yuen, L. (2013). Communist party membership Is still the ultimate resume booster.
http://www.theatlantic.com/china/archive/2013/05/communist-party-membership-is-still-t he-ultimate-resume-booster/276347/2/ Retrieved December 26, 2014

Zang, X. (2011). *Understanding Chinese society*: Routledge.

Yu, Z. (2002). Enhancing and Developing the Political Party System of China with "Three Representatives" as the Guideline. *Journal of The Central Institute of Socialism, 1*, 000.

Zeh, R., & Holtz-Bacha, C. (2015). Internet, social media use and political participation in the 2013 parliamentary election in Germany. *Political Parties in the Digital Age: The Impact of New Technologies in Politics*, 43.

Zeng, B. (2014). Women's political participation in China: Improved or Not? *Journal of International Women's Studies, 15*(1).

Zerfaß, A., Van Ruler, B., Rogojinaru, A., Vercic, D., & Hamrefors, S. (2007). European communication monitor 2007. *Trends in Communication Management and Public Relations–Results and Implications, Leipzig [www. communicationmonitor. eu].*

Zhang, Q., & Chan, J. L. (2013). New development: Fiscal transparency in China—government policy and the role of social media. *Public Money & Management, 33*(1), 71-75.

Zhang, W. (2012). The effects of political news use, political discussion and authoritarian orientation on political participation: evidences from Singapore and Taiwan. *Asian Journal of Communication, 22*(5), 474-492.

Zhang, W., Johnson, T. J., Seltzer, T., & Bichard, S. L. (2010). The revolution will be networked the influence of social networking sites on political attitudes and behavior. *Social Science Computer Review, 28*(1), 75-92.

Zhang, X. (2010). The impact of online social networking on university students' civic participation: A case of two universities in Southern China. In G. Zhang (Ed.), Communication in e-society: Innovation, collaboration, and responsibility (pp. 95–115). Shanghai, China: Shanghai People's Press.

Zhang, X., & Lin, W.-Y. (2014). Political Participation in an Unlikely Place: How Individuals Engage in Politics through Social Networking Sites in China. *International Journal of Communication (19328036), 8*.

Zhang, Y., & Leung, L. (2014). A review of social networking service (SNS) research in communication journals from 2006 to 2011. *New Media & Society*, 1461444813520477.

Zhao, D. (2000). State-society relations and the discourses and activities of the 1989 Beijing student movement. American Journal of Sociology, 105(6), 1592–1632. Retrieved from *http://www.jstor.org/stable/10.1086/210467*

Zhao, S. S. (1998). A state-led nationalism: The patriotic education campaign in post-Tiananmen China. Communist and Post-Communist Studies, 31(3), 287–302. doi:10.1016/S0967-067X(98)00009-9

Zhao, Y. (2008). *How does commercialisation and globalisation of media in China affect China's political structure?* Paper presented at the The growth of media in China.

Zhao, Y. (2012). Understanding China's media system in a world historical context. *Comparing media systems beyond the western world*, 143-173.

Zheng, H. (2013). When Huntington meets China: analysis of chinese people's desire for political participation.

Zheng, Y. (2009). *The Chinese Communist Party as organizational emperor: culture, reproduction, and transformation* (Vol. 12): Routledge.

Zheng, Y. (2011). Young people and SNS political communication in China: Participatory practices in alternative community-oriented spaces. Communications & Convergence Review 2011, 3(2), 144-155.

Zheng, Y., & Wu, G. (2005). Information technology, public space, and collective action in China. *Comparative Political Studies, 38*(5), 507-536.

Zhou, C. (2011). Statement by H.E. Mr. ZHOU Changkui, Head of the Chinese Delegation to United Nations High-level Meeting on Youth *http://www.china-un.org/eng/chinaandun/socialhr/t842920.htm* Retrieved September 11, 2012

Zhou, X. (2009). The political blogosphere in China: A content analysis of the blogs regarding the dismissal of Shanghai leader Chen Liangyu. *New Media & Society, 11*(6), 1003-1022.

Zhou, Z. (2013). Liberal rights and political culture : Envisioning democracy in China Available from *http://slub.eblib.com/patron/FullRecord.aspx?p=1474919*

Zhu, W. (2013). Infographics: Trends in online, digital, social usage in China.

Ziccardi, G. (2013). Digital resistance, digital liberties and digital transparency *resistance, liberation technology and human rights in the digital age* (pp. 27-71): Springer.

Zittel, T., & Fuchs, D. (2006). *Participatory democracy and political participation: can participatory engineering bring citizens back in?* : Taylor & Francis.

Appendix: Questionnaire

Comparing German and Chinese Student´s Social Media Use with a Focus on Political Participation

Dear reader: I am a PhD student in the institute of media and Communication at the Technische Universität Dresden. Currently, I am conducting a comparative study on young people's use of social media in Germany and China. If you are a college student, I would like you to participate in my study. Your answers will be treated anonymously and will be used only for the purely scientific purposes of the project. Thank you very much!

1. How interested are you in politics?

    ○ Very interested ○ Somewhat interested ○ Not very interested ○ Not at all interested

2. How often do you follow politics in the news on television, on the radio, in the newspapers?

    ○ Everyday ○ Several times a week ○ Once or twice a week ○ Less often ○ Never

3. People's political interest sometimes varies across different regions of politics. Are you personally very interested, somewhat interested, not very interested or not at all interested in......?

	Very interested	Somewhat interested	Not very interested	Not at all interested
Local politics	○	○	○	○
National politics	○	○	○	○
European politics	○	○	○	○
Asian politics	○	○	○	○
International politics	○	○	○	○

4. If you want information about a recent happed political event, how important are the following media to you? Please rank by giving number 1 to the most important, number 2 to the second most important, and so on).

    _____Television _____Radio _____Newspaper _____Facebook/Renren _____Blog _____Twitter/Weibo
    _____YouTube _____News websites
    _____Others und namely_____

5. How often do you use social networks (Facebook/Renren, Blog, Twitter/Weibo......) for the following activities?

How often do you use social networks......	Daily	3-6 times a week	1-2 times a week	Less often	Never
Browse or update your social networking profile	□	□	□	□	□
Find information about friends	□	□	□	□	□
Obtain information for study	□	□	□	□	□
Follow political in the news	□	□	□	□	□
Keep in touch with friends/ family/ acquaintances	□	□	□	□	□
Reader new contributions	□	□	□	□	□
Join groups on a social networking sites	□	□	□	□	□
To discover new music, books, films and other entertainment	□	□	□	□	□
Express opinions explicitly on government and politics	□	□	□	□	□
Organize political activities					

6. On the average, how many minutes every day do you spend on online social network sites, such as Facebook/Renren, Blog, or Twitter/ Weibo?

    ○ Less than 10 minutes ○ 10–30 minutes ○ 31–60 minutes ○ 1–2 hours ○ 2–3 hours
    ○ More than 3 hours

7. In comparison to traditional media, do you prefer social media over traditional media in the following aspects?

Do you prefer social media over traditional media...	Prefer social media	Both equally	Prefer traditional media
Speed in delivering and obtaining news	○	○	○
Interactiveness	○	○	○
Entertainment function	○	○	○
Amount of political information	○	○	○
More easily and freely to express political opinions	○	○	○
More chance to take part in politics	○	○	○
Others, namely	○ _____	○ _____	○ _____

8. Did you vote in the last general elections/village election in 2013?

    ○ Yes ○ No

9. There are different ways of being politically active. How often do you participate in the following political activities?

How often have you......	More than once a week	Once a week	Less than once a week	Less than once a month	Less than once a year	Never
voted in elections	○	○	○	○	○	○
cast an invalid vote	○	○	○	○	○	○
not voted out of protest	○	○	○	○	○	○
contacted a politician	○	○	○	○	○	○
attended a public meeting dealing with political or social issues	○	○	○	○	○	○
signed a petition	○	○	○	○	○	○
collected signatures	○	○	○	○	○	○
held a political speech	○	○	○	○	○	○
distributed leaflets with political content	○	○	○	○	○	○
boycotted certain products for political ethical or environmental reasons	○	○	○	○	○	○
bought certain products for political ethical or environmental reasons	○	○	○	○	○	○
wrote political message or graffiti on walls	○	○	○	○	○	○
worn a badge with a political message	○	○	○	○	○	○
participated in a legal demonstration	○	○	○	○	○	○
participated in an illegal demonstration	○	○	○	○	○	○
participated in a strike	○	○	○	○	○	○
donated money to support the work of political group or organization	○	○	○	○	○	○
contributed to a political discussion on the Internet	○	○	○	○	○	○
wrote an article, e.g. in a students' newspaper, organization journals or the Internet	○	○	○	○	○	○
wrote or forwarded a letter/an email with a political content	○	○	○	○	○	○
participated in a political event where property was damaged	○	○	○	○	○	○
participated in apolitical event where there was a violent confrontation with the police	○	○	○	○	○	○
participated in a political event where there was a violent confrontation with the political opponents	○	○	○	○	○	○
occupied houses, school/university buildings factories or government offices	○	○	○	○	○	○
blocked street or railways	○	○	○	○	○	○

10. With the spread of computers, how often do you participate in the following online activities?

How often do you......	Daily	Once a week	2-3 times a month	Once a month	Less than once a month.	Never
visit websites with political content not present by government (online news, blogs,......)	□	□	□	□	□	□
visit websites of government and public administration	□	□	□	□	□	□
sign online petitions	□	□	□	□	□	□
edit a blog or website to display political information	□	□	□	□	□	□
like fan pages of parties, politicians, political organizations/ institutions	□	□	□	□	□	□
participate in online political discussion	□	□	□	□	□	□
forward political messages or news stories via email or social media	□	□	□	□	□	□
comment on political articles /blogs/tweets/posts	□	□	□	□	□	□
start a political group/page online or on a social networking site	□	□	□	□	□	□
contact political public officials online via email or social networking sites	□	□	□	□	□	□
participate in online poll	□	□	□	□	□	□

11. Which of the following factors do you think have become obstacles to your participation when you use Internet? (Multiple responses possible)

□ No problems □ Low speed to view and download files □ Language barriers of websites □ Lack of the information which I need □ The requirement of some websites to pay fees □ Political regulation for Internet □ Other problems, namely _____

12. And have you ever done any of the following at school?

	Yes	No
have been a member of a student council	○	○
had a function as a speaker for the class	○	○
attended a students' meeting	○	○
taken an active role in such a meeting	○	○
participated in a protest movement at school	○	○
organized a political event at school	○	○
joined a political group online though social media	○	○

13. In the follow there is a list of organizations. Please indicate for each organization if you are a member. Also, please indicate if during the last 12 months, you participated in an activity arranged by this organization or if you have done voluntary work for this organization (Multiple responses possible).

Please indicate for each organization if you......	Member	Participated in any activity	Done voluntary work	None applies
Youth association or organization	□	□	□	□
Youth organization of a political party	□	□	□	□
Religious or Church organization, including religious youth organization	□	□	□	□
Trade Union, including youth organization of a trade union	□	□	□	□
Political party	□	□	□	□
Environmental organization	□	□	□	□
Animal rights or animal protection	□	□	□	□
Peace organization	□	□	□	□
Human rights or Humanitarian Aid organization	□	□	□	□
Charity or social-welfare organization	□	□	□	□
Professional organization, e.g. farmers' organization, business or employee's organization	□	□	□	□
Consumer association	□	□	□	□
Culture, music, dance or theatre group	□	□	□	□
Immigrant's organization	□	□	□	□
Women's organization	□	□	□	□
Anti-globalization organization	□	□	□	□
Sport clubs	□	□	□	□

14. When you hold a strong opinion on a political issue, do you always, often, sometimes, rarely or never try to persuade your friends, relatives or fellow workers to share your views?

○ Always ○ Often ○ Sometimes ○ Rarely ○ Never

15. How often do you discuss political issues when you get together with the following people:

	Daily	Once a week	2-3 times a month	Once a month	Less than once a month	Never
friends and family	○	○	○	○	○	○
co-workers and acquaintances	○	○	○	○	○	○
strangers	○	○	○	○	○	○
people who agree with me	○	○	○	○	○	○
people who disagree with me	○	○	○	○	○	○
people who are more knowledgeable about politics	○	○	○	○	○	○
people who are less knowledgeable about politics	○	○	○	○	○	○
people outside my family who do not share my ethnicity, socio-economic status, or gender	○	○	○	○	○	○
people who back up their arguments with evidence	○	○	○	○	○	○
people who are unreasonable and illogical when stating their point of view	○	○	○	○	○	○
people who propose alternatives or policies for problem solving	○	○	○	○	○	○

16. To what extent do you agree or disagree with the following statements:

	Strongly disagree	Disagree	Neither agree nor disagree	Agree	Strongly agree
Sometimes politics and government seem so complicated that a person like me can't really understand what's going on.	○	○	○	○	○
People like me are generally well qualified to participate in the political activities and decision making of our country.	○	○	○	○	○
I feel like I have a pretty good understanding of the important political issues in our society.	○	○	○	○	○
Today's problems are so difficult I feel I could not know enough to come up with any ideas that might solve them.	○	○	○	○	○
I feel like I could do as good a job in politics as most of the politicians we elect.	○	○	○	○	○

17. To what extent they agreed or disagreed with the following statements:

	Strongly disagree	Disagree	Neither agree nor disagree	Agree	Strongly agree
I don't think public officials care much about what people like me think about politics.	○	○	○	○	○
Generally speaking, those we elect to public office lose touch with the people pretty quickly.	○	○	○	○	○
Candidates for political positions are interested in people's votes, but not in their opinions.	○	○	○	○	○
There are plenty of ways for people like me to have a say in what our government does.	○	○	○	○	○
Politicians are supposed to be servants of the people, but too many of them try to be our masters.	○	○	○	○	○
It hardly makes any difference who I vote for, because whoever gets elected does whatever he or she wants to do anyway.	○	○	○	○	○
In this country, a few people have all the political power and the rest of us have nothing to say.	○	○	○	○	○
It doesn't matter what a person does: if the politicians want to listen the will, and if they don't want to listen they won't.	○	○	○	○	○
Most public officials won't listen to me no matter what I do.	○	○	○	○	○

18. By using the social media, it will become easier for people like you to influence government and parliament. Mark to what degree you agree with this statement:

○ disagree completely ○ disagree ○ partly agree ○ agree ○ completely agree

19. Here are many opinions on how one can effectively influence political decisions in society. I will give you some of the ways that are used. Please tell me on a scale from 0 to 5 how effective you think it is: 0 means "not at all effective" and 5 means "very effective".

	0 Not at all effective	1	2	3	4	5 Very effective
work in a political party	○	○	○	○	○	○
work in voluntary organizations and associations	○	○	○	○	○	○
vote in elections	○	○	○	○	○	○
personally contact politicians	○	○	○	○	○	○
work to get attention from the media	○	○	○	○	○	○
boycott certain products	○	○	○	○	○	○
participate in public demonstrations	○	○	○	○	○	○
sign petitions	○	○	○	○	○	○
participate in illegal protest activities	○	○	○	○	○	○
participate in violent protest activities	○	○	○	○	○	○
connect with officials or government through social media directly	○	○	○	○	○	○

20. Are you a member or have you been a member of a political party?

○ Yes ○ No

21. Which political party do you identify with?

○ Conservatives (CDU/CSU) ○ The Social Democrats (SPD)
○ The Liberal Democrats (FDP) ○ The Greens(Bundnis 90/Die Grünen)
○ The Left Party (Die Linke) ○The Communist Party
○ Some other party ○ No political party

22. In the following there are some names of different bodies such as the government and the European Commission. Please indicate how much you trust each of them from "trust not at all" and to "very trust".

	Trust not at all	Not very trust	Somewhat trust	Very trust
Provincial government	○	○	○	○
Police	○	○	○	○
Central government	○	○	○	○
political parties	○	○	○	○
People's Court	○	○	○	○
the European Parliament/People's Congress	○	○	○	○
Army	○	○	○	○

23. Who is the current prime minister in your country? (blank-filling) _____

24. What do you think, approximately how many members of Federal Parliament/the National People's Congress are there in your country? (blank-filling)_____

25. Now look at the following statements about politics. For each statement, please tell me if you think it is true or false.

	TRUE	FALSE
The current minister of the interior (or prime minister) is (Name).	○	○
(Name) is now the deputy of the Federal Chancellor (or vice premiers of the state council).	○	○
(Name of Prime Minister) is the member of (the name of party).	○	○
Germany (or China) has the number of federal states or (province) now.	○	○
In Germany (or China), national election (or elections for the national leaders) must be held every 3 years.	○	○
In Germany (or China), the Federal president (or the president) is elected by the Federal Convention (or National People's Congress).	○	○
There are currently 25 member states of the European Union.	○	○
Obama is the president of the U.S. since 8 years.	○	○
Every state of the U.S is represented by two senators.	○	○

SOCIODEMOGRAPHICS

26. What is your gender?   ○ Female ○ Male

27. What is your nationality? (blank-filling)_____

28. Please indicate your age in years? (blank-filling)_____

29. What's your major? (blank-filling)_____

30. What is the highest level of education you achieved so far?
○Abitur oder Fachabitur/High school degree
○Bachelor-Abschluss/ College or bachelor degree
○ Mater-Abschulss or Diplom-Abschluss or Magister-Abschluss/Postgraduate degree
○ Promotion/Doctor's degree

31. What is your personal monthly net-income?
○below €130/ below 1000yuan ○€130–€399/1000–3000 yuan
○€400–€799/3001–6000 yuan ○€800–€1199/6001–9000 yuan
○€1200–€1499/9001–12000 yuan ○€1500–€ 1899/12001–15000 yuan
○above €1900/ above 15001 yuan

32. Which of the following do you think best describes the area where you come from?
□ A big city □ The suburbs or outskirts of a big city
□ A town or a small city □ A village or a farm

THANKS FOR YOUR COOPERATION!